The
Zoning Game
Revisited

Books from the Lincoln Institute of Land Policy / OG&H

Introduction to Computer Assisted Valuation
Edited by Arlo Woolery and Sharon Shea

Land Acquisition in Developing Countries: Policies and Procedures of the Public Sector
Michael G. Kitay

Second World Congress on Land Policy, 1983
Edited by Matthew Cullen and Sharon Woolery

Advanced Industrial Development: Restructuring, Relocation, and Renewal
Donald Hicks

Land Markets and Land Policy in a Metropolitan Area: A Case Study of Tokyo
Yuzuru Hanayama

The Zoning Game Revisited

Richard F. Babcock
Charles L. Siemon

A Lincoln Institute of Land Policy Book

Published by
Oelgeschlager, Gunn & Hain
in association with the
Lincoln Institute of Land Policy

Copyright © 1985 by Oelgeschlager, Gunn & Hain, Publishers, Inc. All rights reserved. No part of this publication may be reproduced or transmitted in any form or by any means, electronic or mechanical, including photocopying and recording, or by any information storage or retrieval system, without the prior written consent of the publisher.

International Standard Book Number: 0-89946-199-9

Library of Congress Catalog Card Number: 85-21659

Printed in the U.S.A.

Oelgeschlager, Gunn & Hain, Publishers, Inc.
131 Clarendon Street
Boston, MA 02116

Library of Congress Cataloging-in-Publication Data
Babcock, Richard F.
  The zoning game revisited.

  "Published in association with the Lincoln Institute of Land Policy."
  Bibliography: p.
  Includes index.
  1. Zoning law—United States. 2. Zoning—United States—Case studies. I. Siemon, Charles L. II. Lincoln Institute of Land Policy. III. Title.
KF5698.B27   1985   346.7304′5   85-21659
ISBN 0-89946-199-9   347.30645

Publication of a manuscript by the Lincoln Institute of Land Policy signifies that it is thought to be worthy of public consideration but does not imply endorsement of conclusions or recommendations. Views expressed in Lincoln Institute publications should be understood to be solely those of the authors and should not be attributed to the Lincoln Institute, its directors, officers, or staff members, or to the organization that supported research leading to any such publication.

To the late Arden Rathkopf, beloved friend, superb counselor, wonderful storyteller, and happy companion.

Contents

Foreword, *Sir Desmond Heap*   ix
Lincoln Institute Foreword, *Frank Schnidman*   xiii
Acknowledgments   xv
 1. The Zoning Game and Other Epic Tests   1
 2. Tuxedo, New York: How to Beat Big Money   11
 3. Palm Beach, Florida: The Rich vs. The Very Rich   37
 4. Grand Central Station: Beware the Establishment Aroused   59
 5. San Antonio: Politics Make Strange Bedfellows, or Everything You Ever Wanted to Know about Aquifers   77
 6. Sanibel Island: A Paradise Lost and Saved   95
 7. Sioux City, Iowa: Don't Tell Us Where to Build a Shopping Center   119
 8. The Pinelands: A Radical Experiment Works   135
 9. *Gautreaux:* Chicago's Tragedy   159
10. *Hernandez* v. *City of Lafayette:* Longfellow Replayed   183
11. *Mount Laurel II:* Après Nous le Déluge   207
12. Sea Ranch, California: The Devil's Due   235
13. The Game Goes On   255
Comments   267
Brief List of Books Cited   295
Index   297

Foreword

I am an Englishman. I believe that the British system of planning control over land development is based on government policy—the policy of our central government (National Parliament at Westminster) now in control of the nation's entire political administration. Once this fact is accepted, it follows that the *modus operandi* of this system—unlike the development control system in the United States—is bound, necessarily, to bypass the judiciary and the courts of law (since judges cannot interfere with government policy). The exception is, of course, if there has been some breach of the relevant legal statutes, rules, or regulations which operate and function in the day-to-day administration of the system, or some misinterpretation of these guidelines.

Furthermore, I add that the British system of planning control over land development is based on a principle from the Town and Country Planning Act of 1947. Under the Act, a man can continue using, *ad infinitum,* his own land for its *existing* use (subject to compensation if he is stopped), but he cannot *as of right* proceed to develop that land without first getting a grant of planning permission from a local government planning authority which has discretion to refuse the grant if it thinks fit. If this concept (astonishing and quasi-revolutionary when first promulgated in 1947) is also accepted, then the yawning gulf between the U.S. and British systems of planning and development control becomes unmistakably obvious.

It is because of these two fundamental differences between the U.S. and British systems of land development control that I have found the case studies as told in this book by my old friend, Richard Babcock, and his colleague, Charles Siemon, quite fascinating. They are stories of events that could not happen in Britain. That, let me hasten to add, does not prove that there is anything necessarily *right* with the British system of land use control. What it *does* prove is that the two systems are wildly different. Well, *chacun à son goût* and, "What do they know of England who only England know?"

As the authors are at pains to point out in their first chapter, this is not a book about planning and development *law* — about how to draft legal planning suits and motions, resolutions, and judgments. It is not really a book for lawyers at all, although they will get many a wry smile from it. Rather, it is a book for the general reader and especially the general reader who already has been (or will be) enmeshed in the intricacies of U.S. zoning control and land development. It is not a set (thank Heaven) of law reports. It is a "Tale of Several Cities" (and, at times, a very sad tale), and it is because this sort of tale could not (for the reasons given above) occur in my own country that I have found each and every one of the stories most compelling reading.

None of the stories takes us into the courtrooms where learned, and sometimes exasperating, legal battles are played out. On the contrary, they take us into the heart of all the side-play and shadow-boxing, all the chatter and jostling for position, all the attempts (sometimes devious) at probing the depths and strengths of an opponent's case before it ever gets into court at all. These stories expose the bargaining (some of it undignified) that goes on when those who have benefited from development control seek to ensure that no one else does the same. As the "sad story" of Sea Ranch, California, shows, human nature in operation is not always an edifying spectacle. "Sea Ranch" reminded me of the wry prayer of the English Dwellers in the Green Belt, the ring of protected countryside around the big towns:

> We thank Thee, Lord, that by Thy grace,
> Thou brought us to this lovely place—
> And now, dear Lord, we humbly pray
> Thou wilt all others keep away.

Human nature in Britain can be unedifying too!

After reading this book, one is left with an impression that I am bound to describe as bittersweet. Indeed, the authors themselves, in their last chapter, go so far as to declare, "Looking back we must still acknowledge that the process of land use control remains unfair" (p. 260), and "The system is patently in need of reform." (p. 264). I respectfully agree with all this. Perhaps this book, and the situations it exposes, will play a part in the complex process of achieving such reform.

" 'Tis a consummation devoutly to be wished," and, because of this, I wish this book all success and good fortune.

Desmond Heap

Sir Desmond Heap, LL.M., Hon. LL.D.
President, Law Society in England, 1972-1973
President, Royal Town Planning Institute, 1955-1956
Associate, Royal Institution of Chartered Surveyors
Honorary Fellow, American Bar Foundation

Lincoln Institute Foreword

The Lincoln Institute of Land Policy is an educational institute dedicated to the development and exchange of ideas and information pertaining to land policy and property taxation. It is a school offering opportunities for instruction and research. It welcomes government officials, working practitioners, and students to the pursuit of advanced studies.

The Lincoln Institute is also a center for linking the university and the practice of government; for bringing together scholars, professionals, and officials; and for blending the theory and practice of land policy.

We have the opportunity to work with many academics and practitioners during specific research projects. Some projects depend on detailed statistical analysis, or numerous case studies, seeking to discover a common theme or hypothesis. Other projects rely on the skill and experience of the researcher to discover findings or conclusions of merit. For the past three years, the Lincoln Institute has been engaged in a unique hybrid research project with Richard Babcock and Charles Siemon. These "oral troubadors," as Harvard Law School Professor Charles M. Haar described them during a peer-review session in June 1984, traveled the country interviewing the protagonists of many land use controversies, and were themselves embroiled in the heat of most of these struggles. They now bring us eleven fascinating stories from their experiences, illustrating, as always, that the human variable plays a key role in all land policy activity.

When the first draft came in, we gently coaxed them to add additional case studies, and when the final draft arrived, a rich fabric of fact and emotion was finished, and ready for any "student" of land policy. Yet, how could the authors make any sense out of seemingly diverse case examples? They did, and we leave it to the reader to discover how it was accomplished. We have a few suggestions, however. Richard Babcock's previous book, *The Zoning Game* (1966), should be read before this volume is attempted. Then, as each chapter of this book is finished, the reader should turn to the back of the book and review the Comments which are provided. These Comments will foster much debate on the meaning of the chapters and on the health of zoning and land use regulation. The manner in which the Comments enrich and augment the case studies makes this book an excellent tool for training land use professionals.

It has been pointed out many times during the review process, however, that the greatest enjoyment comes from reading the book straight through, and later going back to dissect the hidden meaning in these pages. Either way, *The Zoning Game Revisited* will do much to help the reader understand how zoning has evolved and how it is implemented.

Frank Schnidman
Senior Fellow
September 1985

Acknowledgments

We are indebted to the academics and practitioners who met with us in Cambridge, Massachusetts, on June 13-14, 1984, and gave us the benefits of their reviews of six draft chapters. In particular are we in debt to John Delaney, land use lawyer from Silver Spring, Maryland; Professor James Brown of George Washington University Law Center; George Lefcoe of the University of Southern California Law School; Malcolm Misuraca, of Santa Rosa, California; and Dennis J. Getman, General Counsel of Avatar Holdings, a developer from Coral Gables, Florida, who took the time to send us written observations after that session. We also must acknowledge the suggestions of our former partner, R. Marlin Smith. He made many useful corrections on the comments at the back of the book, and helped enormously in the *Palm Beach* and *Tuxedo* cases in which he participated. We would like as well to thank Wendy Larsen for her support of the project. She and Siemon started their own law firm shortly after we commenced work on the project, and her good humor and encouragement were vital.

We must also thank Carole Davis, the editor assigned to the book. Her editing was superb even though we had to veto most of her brave attempts to scuttle our conversational slang.

But most of all, we are beholden to Frank Schnidman of the Lincoln Institute of Land Policy in Cambridge, which supported this study. Frank encouraged us, organized the June 1984 conference, and generally and with great imagination pushed us along the road to publication.

R.F.B.
C.L.S.

1

The Zoning Game and Other Epic Tests

This is the story—or a series of stories—of eleven land use disputes. It is not a textbook, nor is it a casebook (although it could be so used); there are many of those and good ones, too. Rather, for the most part, this is an account of what transpired *outside* the courtroom. It is brazenly anecdotal, with no apologies. Few legal tangles are more anecdotal than land use conflicts; that is the name of the game.

It has always struck us that teaching land use law through the decisions of appellate courts presents a distorted view of reality. Perhaps that is why so many luminaries in land use law—such as Alfred Bettman, Edward Bassett, and Arden Rathkopf—were practitioners. The real-life conflicts among the players of the game may be one of the reasons for the continued popularity of *The Zoning Game* twenty years after its initial publication.

Many people have suggested that *The Zoning Game* be updated. Unfortunately, however, much of what was wrong with land use policy in 1966 is still wrong today. New zoning techniques flourish, but localisms, fiscal appetites, and xenophobia remain pervasive. For example, the exclusive single-family zone continues in good health despite dramatic demographic changes in the last thirty years. Similarly, the suburban architectural review board—the "Pretty Committee," as one North Carolina town officially labels it—has proliferated.

And yet, in fairness, we should note that there have been some changes since the sixties. First, there is an awareness in some jurisdictions that it is beyond time to review our state-enabling acts, those anachronisms which often are little changed since they were adopted in the 1920s. A few states have revised them to take back some of the power they granted municipalities. Most of these states are the "exotic" states—California, Florida, Maine, Oregon, Vermont, and Hawaii—infested with tourists or immigrants. Some of these experiences have been good news; others are not so happy. One of the hardly exotic jurisdictions is New Jersey, where, by legislative command—with a statutory and financial push from the federal government—a regional commission was created in 1979 to prepare a plan and write regulations to preempt the zoning power of local governments over 1 million acres of wild land roughly between Philadelphia and Atlantic City.

In fact, *The Zoning Game* anticipated many techniques that are now accepted by many jurisdictions. It challenged the "legislative" description of a city council's action of granting or denying a zoning change long before *Fasano* (p. 158); it suggested the need to consider damages as a form of relief before Justice William Brennan let loose with his blast in *San Diego* (pp. 168–171); it raised the antitrust implications of some practices well in advance of *Lafayette* (pp. 73–75); and it urged greater state participation (pp. 159–165) prior to Oregon's experiment. Perhaps the most notable challenge in that volume was the author's plea that the U.S. Supreme Court step in and provide a uniform rule of law (pp. 109–110). Considering that Court's record in land use in the last ten years, that plea now seems regrettable.

Perhaps the most serious flaw in *The Zoning Game* was that it sought to cover so much ground that it did not focus sufficiently on particular cases and the events surrounding them. *The Zoning Game Revisited* seeks to correct that omission.

The conflicts in this work cover eight states: California, Illinois, Louisiana, Florida, Iowa, New Jersey, New York, and Texas. We were involved in one fashion or another in all but three—The *Grand Central* case, *Mount Laurel II,* and the long, bitter battle over Sea Ranch in Sonoma County, California. All but one, the grand story of the Pinelands, involved litigation. These accounts focus more on what went on outside the courtroom than the litigation itself. We believe it important that lawyers, planners, and laymen understand the bargaining, haggling, and dealing that is part of the game; one rarely can uncover this "mishmash" by reading the appellate decisions or, indeed, most treatises.

The Pinelands tale is a remarkable victory over suspicious farmers, outraged local officials, and hungry developers. The regulations that the Pinelands Commission and its consultants drafted are tough. In the "preservation area," the center of the Pines (about 400,000 acres), practically no new use was permitted except blueberry and cranberry farming. Landowners in this area were granted development rights, so they could hope to sell to developers in the "growth areas," where the Commission wanted to encourage growth.

The astonishing fact is that in spite of the ferocious opposition, there has been no significant litigation. In our chapter on the Pinelands, we suggest that the reasons for this are the Pinelands Commission and its staff's tireless and service-oriented efforts, the state and federal commitment to the Pines, and the strength and thoroughness of the Comprehensive Management Plan. Perhaps another reason was because, as the *Trenton Times* put it, "The Pinelands Plan has had more public airings than Bing Crosby's White Christmas."

Less heartening are the accounts of Proposition 20 in California, the creation of the California Coastal Commission, and the experience of Sea Ranch—a proposed 5,200-acre residential development—under Proposition 20 as first adopted by initiative in 1972. Perhaps that was because Pinelands was created by the legislature, while the Coastal Commission was created by direct vote of the people. Sea Ranch, a development along the northern California coast, was under development when Proposition 20 was adopted. At that time, 1,700 lots had been sold and about 300 houses had been built. As a result of interminable negotiations between Sea Ranch and the regional commission and a half-dozen lawsuits by Sea Ranch (all unsuccessful), lot owners who bought in the late 1960s and early 1970s effectively were prevented from getting building permits for ten years. In the interval, building costs had skyrocketed, and many of those who bought lots earlier could no longer afford to build.

Perhaps our most disturbing investigation involved the studies of two cases—*Gautreaux* and *Mount Laurel II*. These cases raise an incredibly hard issue in a republic: the relationship between the judiciary and the legislature.

Gautreaux, started in 1966, is not over yet. It all began when the American Civil Liberties Union filed suit in federal court in Chicago on behalf of Dorothy Gautreaux (a resident of public housing) and others, alleging that Chicago's housing policies violated the U.S. Constitution because they segregated blacks into all-black areas. In 1969, the federal judge entered an order, finding this system to be unlawful. He then ordered that five public housing units had to be built in white areas for every one built in a black area. (A "black" area was defined as a census tract that was 25 percent or more black—called the "tipping point.")

We tell how Mayor Daley, his City Council, his Chicago Housing Authority (CHA), and his successors evaded this order for better than fifteen years even though threatened by contempt of court and the possibility of putting the CHA into receivership. In places, the tale has its amusing sides, but it is really a tragic story and one that poses the dilemma of what kind of court decree is enforceable against intransigent and shrewd opponents.

Everyone of us in the land use field knows the progression of decisions from Justice Hall's dissent in *Vickers* through *Mount Laurel I* and *Mount Laurel II*. The court order in *Mount Laurel II* set forth many guidelines, two of which were difficult for the municipalities to tolerate. First, it gave a "builder's remedy" to developers who challenged a zoning ordinance. This is unheard of in most states but it is not unknown. Second, the Court suggested that at least 20 percent of any development must be below-market housing (low income was up to 50 percent of the regional median income, and moderate income up to 80 percent).

Few outside New Jersey, however, know of the incredible account of what has happened since *Mount Laurel II*. It was as though a dozen tornadoes had slammed into New Jersey. The aftermath was panic in suburban municipal halls, scores of lawsuits, attempted legislative responses, and the Governor's call for a moratorium on the decision's implementation.

One bill finally passed the legislature and Governor Kean, as expected, conditionally vetoed it. (That is akin to a line veto.) As vetoed, it has passed the legislature and imposed a moratorium of one year on "builder's remedies." There are now about 150 lawsuits involving *Mount Laurel II* issues. *Mount Laurel II* is an exciting judicial experiment, but whether the experience since its order will encourage other jurisdictions to embrace the doctrine is dubious. The case certainly has become the "Lawyers and Planners Relief Act."

The most surprising story probably is that behind the *Grand Central* case. When the trial judge found that the New York City Landmark Ordinance was a "taking," he withheld any finding on the plaintiff's request for damages. Then the Municipal Art Society, a prestigious local organization, learned—quite by accident—that the New York City Corporation Counsel had recommended to Mayor Beame that the City accept Penn Central's offer to waive any claims for damages if the City would agree not to appeal. What followed was one of the most astonishing public relations campaigns ever seen in a land use case. Recommended form letters to the Mayor, and other pressure, led him to reverse the recommendation and order that an appeal be taken. There followed TV spots, a movie of cuts from old shows featuring Grand Central Station, weekly tours, and of course, tee-shirts. There was a whistlestop train to Washington, D.C. (by coincidence just two days before the oral arguments in the U.S. Supreme Court). And famous names offered their services seemingly without end: Jackie Onassis, Dick Cavett, Benny Goodman, and Joan Mondale, to mention only a few. New York City's most prestigious law firms volunteered their help, and the J. Walter Thompson Advertising Agency took on the publicity without charge. Bear in mind that most of this hullabaloo took place while the case was moving up through the courts. No one dared assert that this show influenced the successful outcome in the Appellate Division, the New York Court of Appeals, or the U.S. Supreme Court—but, if not, what was the purpose of this parade of stars?

Probably the two most "hysterical" cases (we use the word with care) were those involving Tuxedo, New York, and Lafayette, Louisiana. We represented the developers in Tuxedo; in Lafayette, we represented the City. Both cases are examples of the battle that often takes place in zoning disputes between neighbors and landowners and developers.

The Town of Tuxedo is about thirty-five miles north of LaGuardia Airport. The Harriman family once owned 8,000 acres in the Town but sold it in the late 1950s, plus 15,000 other acres in the surrounding area, to City Investing Company, a very large corporation listed on the New York Stock Exchange. City Investing created a subsidiary corporation, Sterling Forest Corporation, which proceeded with elaborate plans to develop light research and industrial and housing on its 8,000 acres. It had reasonably good success with the research and industrial and built three single-family subdivisions. Sterling Forest spent bundles on planning for all the acreage, but after ten or fifteen years the Corporation decided it should focus on smaller parcels. As a result, it entered into a joint venture with Urban Investment and Development Company, then a subsidiary of Aetna Life Insurance Co., to build 3,900 units on 1,500 acres. That is when the egg hit the fan. And its most mortal enemies came from those three single-family subdivisions. This case cannot be called classic because it is so extraordinary, but it is generally what happens when neighbors are pitted against a corporation prepared to spend a million dollars: the neighbors are victorious at the local level. We lost, and the property—all 8,000 acres—remains much as it has been.

The Louisiana case, *Hernandez* v. *City of Lafayette,* was a bit different but no less frantic. Lafayette is the big city in Cajun country, settled by immigrants from Acadia after they were brutally evicted by the British in 1755.

Layafette, known for its incredible food, is also the center of the oil industry in southern Louisiana. In the 1960s and 1970s, its growth was explosive, and unfortunately there was little planning to establish policies. This account can be described only as a vendetta between the Mayor of Lafayette, Kenneth Bowen, and Mr. and Mrs. James Hernandez. It seems the Hernandezes wanted their residential property rezoned so they could speculatively build a medical office project. They were stalled and hassled for three or four years. Finally, their attorney brought two suits, one in the state circuit court asking the court to find the ordinance unreasonable and invalid, the other in the federal district court seeking a million dollars damages. Eventually, the City won both cases.

One lesson was underscored in the protracted litigation—the importance of highly qualified expert witnesses and the corollary: that you prepare for trial with the probable necessity of an appeal. The zoning lawyer always faces the question of whether to rely on local experts or bring in the best from wherever they may come. The problem with out-of-town experts is illustrated by this excerpt from *The Zoning Game* in which a planner from Westchester County, New York, was testifying in a case in Michigan:

Q: Mr. Pomeroy, when did you first come to the City of Ann Arbor?

A: My first visit to the City of Ann Arbor was twenty years ago.

Q: How long did you stay that time?

A: Just passing through.

Q: I see. And when was the next time you came to Ann Arbor?

A: Last November.

Q: Is that the first time you have been in Ann Arbor—how long did you stay that time?

A: My testimony will indicate—

Q: [interposing] Just answer.

A: Two days.

Q: How much?

A. Two days.

Q: What days were those?

A: Saturday and Sunday, as my testimony stated.

Q: I see. And when was the next time you came to Ann Arbor?

A: As my testimony stated, last Sunday.

Q: So you have been in the City of Ann Arbor two days, and then you came just prior to this lawsuit; is that correct?[1]

There is of course a different problem with local experts—they may have appeared so often that their coinage may be debased. (After all, most zoning cases are bench trials before a judge; it is not, for example, the same as the orthopedic surgeon who is constantly called as a witness but always before a fresh jury.)

In the *Hernandez* case, we chose to bring in a planner from Reston,

---

[1]Richard F. Babcock, *The Zoning Game: Municipal Practices and Policies* (Madison: University of Wisconsin Press, 1966), p. 85.

Virginia, and a traffic expert from Evanston, Illinois. The state trial judge held for the Hernandezes. At one point during the direct examination of our traffic expert (perhaps traffic testimony is one of the dullest of sports), the judge fell asleep and fell off the bench! But we won in the higher Louisiana court; and the Fifth Circuit Court of Appeals finally had to concede that if the zoning was not unreasonable, then there was no cause of action for damages.

Perhaps there is another lesson for zoning lawyers, particularly those who may be called in to represent a municipality: by the time the zoning lawyer comes on the scene, most of the damage to the municipality's case has already been done by actions of city officials.

This lesson was clear in the case of San Antonio when the City was sued in a class action case for $1.5 billion damages because it imposed a total moratorium on all development. We were called in by Councilman—now Mayor—Henry Cisneros. What had led up to this suit was a remarkable twist in San Antonio politics. The City had for generations been run by Anglos—the local term for persons who were neither of Spanish descent nor black. Under pressure from the U.S. Department of Justice, the City had finally restructured its elections to the City Council by wards, and in 1972 five members (of the eleven) were elected from Spanish-speaking areas in central San Antonio.

This did not give them a majority, but another incident led to control by nonestablishment persons: the Edwards Underground Aquifer. Allegedly, the aquifer was in danger of pollution. Moreover, growth and development were sprawling toward the "Anglo" northwest—in the path of the recharge areas of the aquifer.

Ardent environmentalists were calling for a halt to this development, and two of them were also elected to the City Council. Together with the alderman of Spanish descent, they combined in what must be one of the oddest political alliances in modern U.S. history. The environmentalists wanted to prevent pollution of the aquifer; the Mexican-Americans wanted to stop spending public money for the infrastructure of Anglo development to the north and to redirect funds to the inner city. Hence the total ban and the lawsuit. Once again, when the lawyers were called in, it was a bit late. We told the City Council in a closed executive session that their moratorium ordinance was invalid and had to be rewritten. We thought it was an "executive session," but the next day the headline in the *San Antonio Light* heralded: "TOTAL AQUIFER BAN 'NO BUENO.'" We rewrote the moratorium and a new zoning ordinance to bring them both into conformity with due process, and the suit was eventually settled.

Two other cases involve an unlikely pair of cities: Palm Beach, Florida, and Sioux City, Iowa. In the former, we represented the owner of twenty-five acres abutting the Atlantic Ocean along Highway A-1A that winds through the posh precincts of the Town. In the latter, we represented the City when it was sued by a shopping center developer who alleged a conspiracy to prevent his proposed development from competing with an attempted $20 million revitalization of the central business district.

The moral of both these cases is the same: Never ignore the political climate when trying a zoning case. Palm Beach may be the only town in the United States that has a provision in its charter to disallow any municipal actions "except during the months of December, January, February, and March." In spite of this provision, the south end of the Town (below Sloan's Curve) had gradually been changing in character with high-rise condominiums moving northward. The Town Council wanted to stop this by substantially lowering the densities. (Our client's acreage was brought down from thirty units per acre to two.) So they hired a planning firm to carry out their wishes. And it did.

The task of the lawyers was to show that the Town's "plan" was a sham. This meant dissecting every aspect of this document—the statements about projected growth, traffic, sewer, water, air pollution, and effect of the new regulations on property values. We won in the trial court, were sent back by the Florida Appellate Court, and finally compromised by settling for twelve units per acre.

Sioux City, Iowa, was a more straightforward political battle that started in the courts but ended up at the polling booths. The City was one of the few Iowa cities that was trying to resurrect its decaying central business district. The City Council in 1973 supported this and adopted some unusual regulations to keep a shopping center developer out. Litigation followed. The developer exerted a great deal of pressure to have its way, including media ads that headlined: "Has the Twentieth Century Passed Sioux City By?" and "84% . . . *That* is a majority. From 4,256 petitions presented to Sioux City citizens, 84% gave approval to build a shopping mall. . . ." They were right. At an election, a new majority in favor of the mall was elected, the suit was dismissed, and the mall was built. It was plainly a defeat.

One other moral to this account: few residents really care about downtown. They move outward and enjoy the apparent luxury of a new shopping emporium. As Weaver and Babcock observed in *City Zoning: The Once and Future Frontier,* "[There is] an awareness that, especially in the central business district, zoning is a matter of indifference to the city residents who elect the city politicians."[2]

---

[2]Cliff Weaver and Richard Babcock, *City Zoning: The Once and Future Frontier* (Chicago: American Planning Association, 1979), p. 295.

And then there is the story of Sanibel Island, off the west coast of Florida, that beautiful haven known as the Seashell Capital of the World. The Island's inhabitants, fed up with the indifference of the County to development, incorporated and had to fight off a dozen or so lawsuits from developers for the next ten years. The chapter tells of the concentrated efforts of dedicated individuals to save a fragile environment.

Perhaps our readers may find other lessons. We simply have tried to tell the stories. Nothing in these pages will tell a practitioner how to draft a complaint, cross-examine a witness, or argue a case on appeal. What *The Zoning Game Revisited* should provide is an insight into what to expect in a land use contest—the frustration, the anger, and perhaps the laughs.[3]

---

[3]Comments on each chapter appear at the end of the book, to help provide additional insight into these land use controversies.

2

Tuxedo, New York: How to Beat Big Money

> *They don't tell Polish or elephant jokes, they tell Sterling jokes. An individual isn't classified by whether he's yellow or black, Christian or Jew, Communist or Capitalist, clean or dirty, ugly or beautiful, Democrat or Republican. You are a good guy or a bad guy depending on which stance you adopt in the Sterling issue.*
>
> Jennifer Clarke, *Middletown Record*
> January 10, 1978

How would you place your wager on a contest between these adversaries? On one side, there is a small town of 3,800 population with at least one-third moderate- to low-income descendants of Italian and Polish tradesmen and servants who immigrated in the nineteenth century. Also included in this group are a few hundred others scattered in three small subdivisions, including a famous former resort community, Tuxedo Park, full of enormous mansions and a tiny population of 700 clinging to a short, opulent past. The Town's annual budget is about $485,000, and its business district can only be described as anemic.

The opponent, City Investing Company—with $5.1 billion in assets ($7.5 billion in 1982) and revenues of $3.7 billion ($5.7 in 1982)—is listed on the New York Stock Exchange and operates across the United States and in seventeen foreign countries. Among its subsidiaries are Rheem Air Conditioning; UARCO; World Color Press; and General Development Corporation, Florida's largest developer of planned com-

---

Authors' note: Ross and Hardies, then our law firm, together with Arden Rathkopf, were attorneys for Sterling Forest Corporation.

munities. Indeed, City Investing is the fourth largest housing company in the United States.

The conflict was a fierce zoning dispute over Sterling One, a development proposal by City Investing Company on 1,500 acres of Sterling Forest and the Town of Tuxedo.

The outcome of the battle? If you assumed the corporation walked all over the Town you would be wrong. If you were told that this would be a bitter zoning struggle, and as a sophisticated observer of such fights, you wagered on the Town, you would be right.

This is the tale of the conflict, which was carried out from 1973 to 1980. The vivid details embrace myriad side duels and adventures, including arrests of Town Councilmen while in session; a Republican committee chairman who was caught trying to remove the American flag from the chambers; name calling by Town Council members ("evil little man," "the town clowns"); five lawsuits; and friendships — political and social — ending in reciprocal loathing. As one of the leaders wrote to the local paper: "It is, therefore, disillusioning to be the intended target of a 'stop-at-nothing' individual who is attempting a personal attack based on hatred and personal vendetta, which represents the last remaining taint of the ill-fated Sterling One fiasco."[1] Further, add to all this a "100-year flood" on a crucial election day, when key council members in the dispute stood for reelection, rumors that the polling booths were kept open beyond specified hours to accommodate the commuters from New York City, and the decision of the Town Supervisor (who lost by only nineteen votes) to go on a marriage retreat instead of campaigning the last weekend.

This case cannot be called classic because it is so extraordinary, but it is a paradigm of what happens when neighbors are pitted against a corporation prepared to spend a million dollars for expenses.

The neighbors are generally victorious at the local level.

Historical Background

The area at the center of this imbroglio is a magnificent collection of woods and rock known as Sterling Forest, situated about thirty-five miles north of LaGuardia Airport on the west side of the Hudson and abutting the New York Thruway. It is a place of spectacular beauty, heavy with American history. Forested with a very shallow topsoil, the underlying gneiss erupting from the ground lends an appearance of natural wilderness and makes the construction of houses a challenge.

The property was originally given by patent from Queen Anne to Eng-

---

[1] *Middletown Record,* October 28, 1981.

lish colonists in 1702. Later, it passed to the Fifth Earl of Sterling and then passed to his son, William Alexander, known to Americans as Lord Sterling. Lord Sterling chose to fight on the side of George Washington. It was here that the Sterling Furnace was established. Here too the Great Chain was built that was strung across the Hudson just below West Point to keep British ships from moving farther up the river. Smelting continued for more than a century, and in the meantime (in 1893) Mr. E. H. Harriman, father of former Governor Averell Harriman, bought most of the Forest.

There is one more bit of history. In 1885, Pierre Lorillard, the founder of the tobacco fortune, began to develop Tuxedo Park, around a gemlike lake in the Forest, as a hunting and fishing preserve for his friends. He brought in over 1,800 Italian and Slavic immigrants as servants and builders. Mr. Lorillard put in sewer, water, and roads and built seven "cottages," some with twenty rooms, around the lake. The story was described in a local paper:

> But the game preserve failed, and at the turn of the century Tuxedo Park . . . became a playground for the very rich. Elegant mansions, some of which employed up to 90 servants, were constructed and the Tuxedo Autumn Ball became a highlight of the New York social circuit.
> . . . The Great Depression changed the park's character again. Many of the magnificent mansions were torn down during the 1930s and '40s because of heavy taxes. The occupants moved into their carriage houses and many of the large estates were subdivided into smaller lots.[2]

In 1953, Tuxedo Park was incorporated as a village, which resulted in one municipal corporation being surrounded by a second municipal corporation, the Town of Tuxedo.[3]

One of the distinctive marks of the village still remains today: there is a gatehouse at the entrance to the village where police guard around-the-clock against unauthorized intruders into the 1,800-acre municipal corporation. This practice, not unheard of in exclusive subdivisions, is a rarity among incorporated municipalities and, as far as we know, it has not been challenged. The village has, of course, its own government separate from the Town of Tuxedo, and much of its charm and exclusivity remains in 1985. The village played an important role in the forthcoming conflict over development in the Town. Some of the most bitter opposition to Sterling One as well as the proposal's eventual strong

---

[2]Ibid., September 24, 1978.
[3]It should be noted that while Tuxedo was the originator of man's formal dress it was *not* the source of the 1930s big-band piece "Tuxedo Junction," although the railroad station in the hamlet carries a large sign with that name.

Twenty-four-hour guarded gate to Tuxedo Park. (Photo by Edward Hausner/NYT Pictures.)

supporter, then Councilman Neal Martineau, lived in Tuxedo Park Village.

Origins of the Dispute

City Investing Company bought the Forest in 1954 — about 23,000 acres divided among the Town of Tuxedo, the Town of Warwick, and some acreage in New Jersey — from Averell Harriman. The Chairman of the company, Robert Dowling, had a vision of a development to include both industry and housing. His plan was relatively successful in establishing industry; the housing he promoted was the principal cause of his successor's downfall twenty years later.

A City Investing subsidiary, Sterling Forest Corporation, aggressively promoted the Forest as an area for research and development. It managed to induce IBM, International Paper Co., Union Carbide, International Nickel, and Reichold Chemicals to locate facilities there, each on large tracts of land with the buildings professionally designed and placed to blend in with Forest. No new significant corporation facilities have come to the Forest since 1969.

In addition, Sterling Forest Corporation built a Conference Center adjacent to Sterling Lake with two dozen tastefully designed and furnished chalets in the surrounding woods. The corporation also designed and operated Sterling Forest Gardens, a fun and games park in a setting of floral munificence, as well as a ski facility nearby. Both the park and the ski facility closed during 1976. The ski center has since reopened.

Housing was quite another situation. The corporation laid out three subdivisions in the Forest in Tuxedo between 1960 and 1963: Clinton Woods, Laurel Ridge, and Maplebrook. Lots were sold and detached single-family homes were built and occupied mainly by commuters who rode the Erie Railway back and forth to New York City — stockbrokers, lawyers, and middle-level executives. It was from these enclaves of the newly arrived homeowners that the resistance to the Sterling One proposal would come, and from these residents emerged the mastermind of the earliest opposition, Jerry Fix. Also residing in this subdivision was Fred Maute, an opportunist who tried to use the popular side of the issue to make himself a public savior and launch his political career. Apparently no one in the corporation gave a serious thought to the consequences of almost 200 single-family detached residences on future development, but those developments were to be the rock on which the proposal eventually foundered and sank. Neal Martineau, a former councilman, describes the opponents' feelings:

> An issue like development brings forth the warriors in a community. And who are the warriors? The young, hot teenagers. They want to go fight, and kill. And every community has its share of teenagers. Some of them are 40 or 50 years old. They are still teenagers. These people bob to the surface to oppose us and among other things, they had themselves a hell of a good time. They feasted on you, on Sterling, on the new idea, and the more earnest you became, the more earnest the project appeared to be, the more self-righteous, the more they enjoyed giving you a good kick in the slats. So that's the sort of emotional side of it. The sort of psychological and behavioral side. I find that it is the most important part of it.

Nick Rossetti, right-hand man to Miles Shanahan, President of Sterling Forest Corporation, describes how he, on the other side, saw it:

> The opposition came from people who moved in after the three residential areas were built in the early sixties. The people who moved in really shut the door without allowing anything else to come in. I try to think objectively and I try to sit on the other side and ask how would I feel about it if I were one of those affected. I did, of course, live in the community for six years. I did have a feeling of what it was like to have all that beautiful land and have full and free use of it.

16 · *The Zoning Game Revisited*

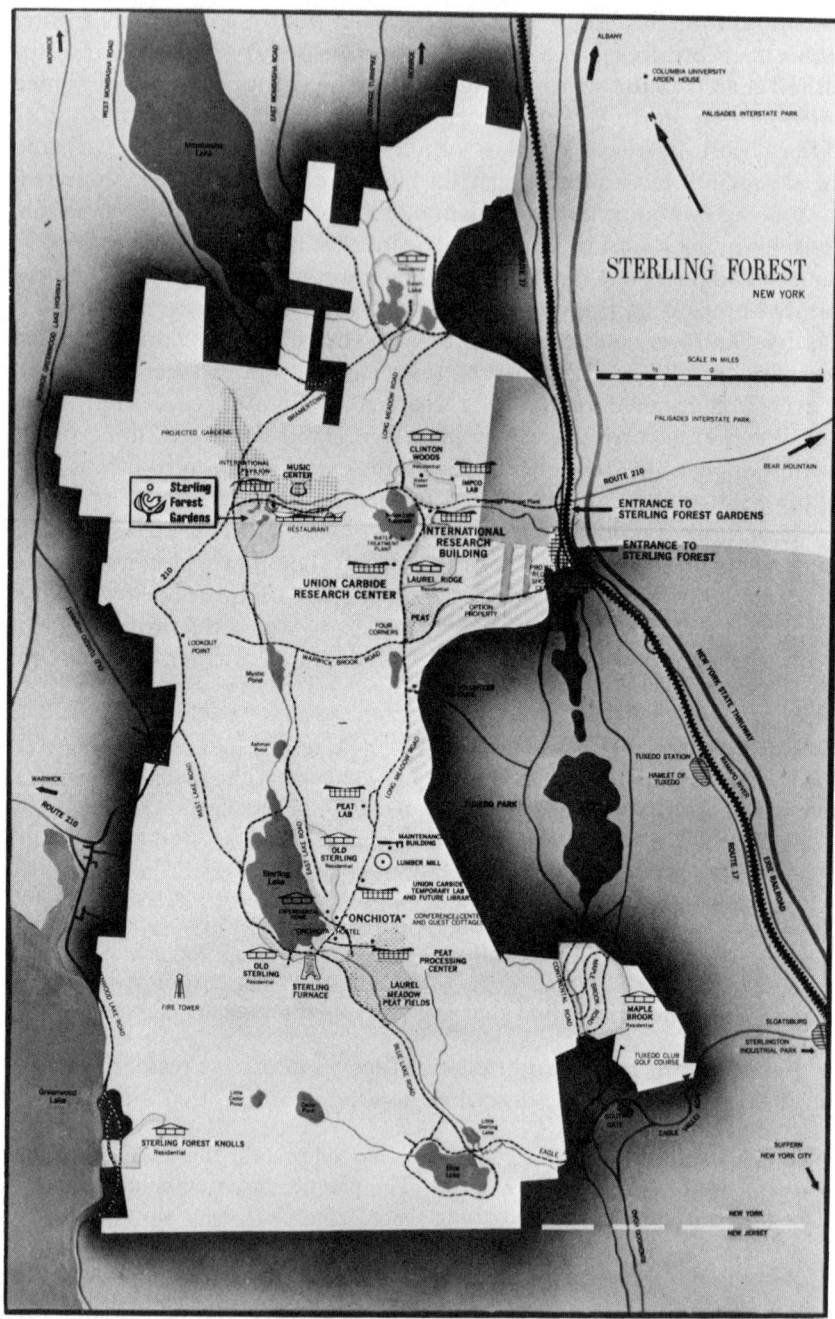

Map of Sterling Forest.

Aerial view of area proposed for Sterling Forest (delineated by superimposed map).

Soon after City Investing bought the acreage from Averell Harriman, Robert Dowling began hiring experts to study the 23,000 acres. Studies ranging from water-resource reports (Malcolm Pirnie, Inc.) to land use charts (Gimore Clarke and Michael Rapuano) and labor studies (Fantus Area Research, Inc., of New York) were upgraded and used as background for policy decisions. In 1965, Dean McClure joined the staff of Sterling Forest Corporation and used these various consultant reports to create permanent display charts for review in the corporate offices. These charts illustrated Sterling Forest and its relationship to the northeast seaboard and the New York region, as well as indicating existing and proposed development sites. Also included was a chart that illustrated proposed land use and circulation systems.

In 1963, Sterling Forest Corporation produced a colorful pictorial brochure entitled "Sterling Forest, New York." Photographs of the Sterling Forest Gardens, Ski Center, Conference Center, and Park were complemented by photographs of existing residential and industrial uses. These photographs were centered around a map showing a conceptual plan for all of Sterling Forest. This brochure was circulated as a foldout supplement to the 1963 City Investing Company Annual Report and was readily available as a free informational handout at all Sterling Forest facilities.

Then, in 1966, the firm of Peat, Marwick, Mitchell and Co. of Los Angeles, California, was commissioned by Sterling Forest Corporation to prepare a land inventory and assess the market potential of Sterling Forest. This report, finished in January 1967, pointed to the need for increased residential units in the early 1970s. People who worked in the Forest simply could not find housing in the vicinity. Based on this information, Sterling Forest Corporation began to gather the necessary technical information that would be required to undertake additional housing.

In 1969, Sterling Forest Corporation retained William L. Pereira Associates of Los Angeles, California, for the development of a master plan for Sterling Forest. In February 1970, Pereira formulated what, in its final form, was known as the "Sterling Forest Preliminary Master Plan."

Thereafter, professionals were called on to supplement this work. R. T. Schnadelbach of Philadelphia, landscape and ecological consultant, completed an intensive ecological study entitled "Site Feasibility Investigation." Gladstone Associates of Washington, D.C., economic consultants, completed three reports: "Sterling Forest New Community Preliminary Financial Feasibility Analysis"; "Sterling Forest Fiscal Impact on the Town of Tuxedo"; and "Sterling Forest Fiscal Impact Analysis" (final report draft). The findings of Schnadelbach and Gladstone were added to Pereira's findings and resulted in the document known as the "Sterling Forest Preapplication Proposal for a New Community." This study was submitted to the Office of New Communities Development, U.S. Department of Housing and Urban Development (HUD), and resulted in an invitation from HUD to submit a final application. Sterling Forest Corporation, however, decided not to submit an application at that time.

As a result of these studies, Sterling Forest Corporation became convinced that a master plan for the entire 23,000 acres was impractical. So Miles Shanahan, then President of Sterling Forest, began negotiations with Urban Investment and Development Co. (UIDC) of Chicago, a subsidiary of Aetna Life and Casualty Co., to find a specific area of the Forest to be the object of development.[4] It was UIDC that hired Ross and Hardies (our law firm), which in turn brought in Arden Rathkopf of Glen Cove, New York, to provide legal service.

From these negotiations came an agreement for a joint venture (to be known as Sterling One) for a development on 1,500 acres (of the 8,600 acres) in the Forest and in the Town of Tuxedo. The plan consisted of 3,900 units with the following range of housing types:

---

[4]Urban Investment is no small shakes. Developer of Park Forest, south of Chicago, the first newtown in the United States after World War II, UIDC was involved in housing and shopping centers across the country.

Detached single-family	5 to 8 percent
Attached single-family	40 to 55 percent
Garden apartments and multiple-family dwellings	55 to 65 percent

In 1977, Sterling One made the following statement:

> It is a major objective of the Joint Venture for Sterling One to provide housing for those families in the middle and moderate income groups who are, and can be expected to be, employed in the types of research and light industrial facilities which have been welcomed in Tuxedo (as evidenced by the 1972 Master Plan and the 1975 Ordinance, as amended, and in neighboring communities in the north and northeast section of the New York metropolitan region. [Emphasis in original.]
>
> It is expected that the range of housing prices will be from $32,000 to $80,000.

Approximately 850 of the 1,500 acres would be left as open space. Clustering of housing was the basic concept. This, of course, meant that the average density of 2.6 dwelling units per acre would be increased in the acreage selected for housing to as much as 15 units to the acre.

The joint venture group spared no funds to prepare the plan. Among the experts brought in to prepare reports on everything from vegetation to absorption of units in the markets were Llewelyn-Davies (planners), Schnadelbach-Braun (environmental impact), Raymond Keyes (consulting engineers—traffic), Malcolm Pirnie (water and sewer engineers), James D. Landauer Associates (real estate market), and S. J. Schulman (planning consultant). The plan was first submitted to the Planning Board of the Town of Tuxedo in 1975.

The Town Board's immediate reaction was to ask for a postponment of the application while it examined its zoning ordinance. Tuxedo had first adopted a zoning ordinance in 1966, and it was not designed to handle such a major development. The Town passed an ordinance placing a moratorium on all development pending a revision of the ordinance; then, it hired Emanuel and Associates, planners, of Nyack, New York, to draft a new ordinance.

The battle lines began to form.

Town Master Plan/New Ordinance

During the building moratorium, the Town Board worked closely with the Planning Board to create a new town master plan and zoning ordinance. The key figures on the Town Board at that time were Jerry Fix and John Gourlay, who led the rest of the Board easily. The rest of the Board were relatively uneducated men who were intimidated by the education and legal backgrounds of both these men.

It is important to remember also that both Fix and Gourlay lived in the newly created subdivisions of Sterling Forest, the source of the most intense and immediate opposition. The two men, in effect, were representing a small faction of the population, and the remaining Board members appeared too naive to understand the implications.

The hidden agenda, successfully manipulated by Jerry Fix with the help of a majority of the Planning Board, was to draft and pass a zoning ordinance which gave the appearance of legally permitting planned, mixed-style housing with even low-income housing, but which effectively gave the Planning and Town Boards wide discretionary powers for review of any development.

In this way, both Boards used the principle of killing a project by imposing countless reviews.

In fact, Jerry Fix and the rest of the Town Board did actually consider the Sterling One application during 1975. After much to-do and reviewing and passing of documents between Town and Planning Boards, it appeared as if the application would be approved. But at the last minute, on the night of the vote, Fix suddenly demanded that Sterling Lake be given to the Town in exchange for permit approval.

Thus the second strategy for the defeat of Sterling was brought into the open — the last-minute, impossible demand. Fix convinced weaker Board members to go along with his demand, particularly William Clarke, who caved in to much behind-the-scenes pressure from Fix and other fellow Republicans. In fact, he would do it again four years later — again demanding Sterling Lake.

Strategy and the New Board

Oddly enough, at the end of Fix's last term, he engineered three unexpected moves. First, the Town was declared a "Class A" town, which meant he had to resign from the Board, because he also served as Justice of the Peace.

A resident of Tuxedo Park, Neal Martineau, was handpicked by Fix and the other Republicans to run for the vacated seat in the 1976 elections. (At that time, if you were a Republican in Tuxedo, you were automatically elected.)

His second move was to get John Gourlay off the Board because Gourlay was a Democrat. Even though Gourlay had been his ally in the first defeats of Sterling One, Fix now decided he was no longer useful, and a Republican should take his place.

Fix went to court to have Gourlay removed on the grounds that he was also serving as Orange County Representative, and the law clearly stated he could not be both a town councilman and a county representative. At the last minute, Gourlay chose not to be a town councilman and vacated his seat. The Town Board then appointed Fred Maute to fill the vacated seat. The plan was to get Maute on the Board to accomplish what Fix wanted, and to try to keep him seated on the Board after the election. In the election of 1976, then, four Board positions were up for election, and Fix had maneuvered it so that a majority would continue to confound the Sterling application.

What actually happened took other unexpected turns.

Fred Maute ran for election for the seat he had recently been appointed to, but lost. Neal Martineau ran to fill Jerry Fix's last two years of a four-year term, and won. William Clarke was reelected, his seat uncontested. Ted Hoffman, a Democrat, long-time resident of the hamlet, and a local history teacher in the Tuxedo High School, ran against a weak incumbent Republican supervisor and won. Sam Venezia, another hamlet resident, ran uncontested and won. Although he was a Democrat, he was endorsed by the Republicans, largely because of behind-the-scenes lobbying by Katherine St. George, former Congresswoman and Republican Committee Chairwoman.

St. George felt she would influence Venezia easily because he was, among other things, a long-term employee of hers; in fact, he was her gardener. (She proved wrong later, and was not able to influence Venezia to defeat Sterling. It soon became evident that he favored Sterling.)

The first meeting of the new Board was a bit hysterical. Ted Hoffman, the new Town Supervisor, ran the meeting. He presided over newly elected Martineau, a Republican also making his debut that night; over Clarke, in his midterm; and over Venezia, making his debut, as a Democrat endorsed by Republicans.

Then Fred Maute entered and insisted that, because of his former appointment to the Board, he had a right to sit with the new Council as a holdover councilman, even though he had not won the recent election.

During the battle that Maute staged to be seated, Hoffman had him arrested. Martineau fought to have Maute seated. So did Albert Winslow, newly elected chairman of the Republican Committee, replacing Katherine St. George.

Then Winslow, in a gesture of misplaced patriotism, decided that Hoffman had no right to arrest Maute and, consequently, that the American flag had no reason to be flying over proceedings, which Winslow deemed to be "Gestapo" in character. Winslow took the American flag out of its holder in the back of the meeting room and proceeded to head out the door with it. Then Hoffman had Winslow arrested as well.

In the first of numerous lawsuits over Sterling One, Fred Maute took his case to be seated as a holdover councilman to the state Supreme Court, and lost. This left Tuxedo with a four-member Board consisting of two Republicans and two Democrats. They could not agree on whom to appoint to fill the fifth seat. So the Board met and functioned with one seat vacant for a year, until the next election.

During this year some important shifts took place on the Board. Party lines were soon forgotten. Ted Hoffman and Neal Martineau, after first skirmishing publicly, gained respect for one another. At Martineau's urging, the position of Town Attorney was opened for candidates outside the Town and a lengthy interview of candidates took place. It was Martineau's belief, with Hoffman and the others concurring, that at this time in its history the Town needed a Town Attorney with a proven track record and experience in zoning matters. Myron Mandel was chosen. He proved to be a key figure in educating the Board on the merits of a development like Sterling One.

Slowly but surely, Neal Martineau changed his public stance on Sterling One from doubt to belief in the project. He spent two weeks of his vacation trying to understand the project. He worked with Manny Emanuel, the author of the town ordinance, and he wrote several documents to the Town explaining the nature and merits of the development. Eventually, Hoffman, Martineau, and Sam Venezia came to believe in Sterling One as being best for the Town on all grounds: sociologically, economically, and environmentally.

In the meantime, however, opposition was gathering among the townspeople. Resistance was being organized. Some very wealthy opponents were hiring extremely effective lawyers. A period of dubious dealing ensued. The Planning Board, under the leadership of Peter Arrighetti, assured the Town Board privately that Sterling One was good for the town. But the public actions of the Arrighetti Planning Board went with the prevailing public sentiment against Sterling. And Fred Maute, sensing an opportunity to emerge a hero, was reassuring his friend and former running mate, Neal Martineau, that he favored Sterling One, while saying just the opposite to his constituents who feared the project.

In the year of the four-man Board, as a majority moved slowly to favor Sterling One — and while Maute was planning his moves — Sterling One's attorneys were examining the new zoning ordinance adopted after the moratorium. Clearly, it was designed to keep out the development proposed by the joint venture. Moreover, they were advised in March 1976 that Sterling One would have to pay the Town $63,000 just to review the project. Presumably this fee would be for a review, in part by Emanuel and Associates, who had just written the new ordinance.

Sterling One Amendments

The Sterling One attorneys rejected the request for fees and filed a demand for twenty-seven amendments to the ordinance. When these were rejected, they filed a lawsuit against the Town challenging the validity of the ordinance. Basically, Sterling One wanted to allow planned unit development (PUD) in the R-1 single-family zone, to increase the density for PUDs, to decrease the parking requirements, to relax housing types in the PUDs, and to permit shopping centers in PUDs.

More important, on Tuesday, November 8, 1976, Fred Maute was elected to the Town Board, giving the opposition to Sterling One a visible spokesman. In the meantime, Sterling One had received the first of a series of endorsements from regional planning agencies. In a letter to Town Supervisor Ted Hoffman, the Senior Vice President of Mid-Hudson Pattern, Inc., a private planning organization, said the project plans struck a desirable balance between economic and environmental considerations. And for the first time, Neal Martineau, who had doubted the project before his election, began to voice second thoughts publicly. He was quoted in the *Middletown Record* as saying:

> I feel there are two sides to the question. If these developers go away, we're not properly serving our present population because they're the ones who will have to foot the bill in the form of higher taxes.[5]

Martineau, on reflection after it was over, added wistfully:

> Finally I began to sound like Miles [Shanahan]. I began to say "You know, we're goddam lucky these people are willing to spend the fees for the best, the very best in the business on every single front." I said to them "We're going to have a piece of jewelry here. And we want to kick them in the face. What are we doing? This is insane."

These remarks suggested that by the end of 1976 there was a majority in favor of the project. And Maute had not yet revealed his opposition publicly.

After the Sterling One group filed its lawsuit, Hoffman, Venezia, Martineau, and Town Attorney Mandel proposed that the Sterling One group sit down with the Board and try to negotiate a settlement. Some of Miles Shanahan's advisors told him this was a mistake, that the residents of Laurel Ridge were becoming more vocal and intransigent, that Maute was not to be trusted. Shanahan believed, however, that there was enough support on the Town Board to work out a compromise and that undoubtedly the Town officials, faced with depositions and interrogatories, wanted

[5]*Middletown Record*, December 13, 1977.

to talk. So private negotiations were started. The lawsuit was not withdrawn but held in abeyance until the outcome of the talks was known. The parties met at the Conference Center and protests arose that the public was not allowed to participate. Some residents threatened a lawsuit even though New York State's open-meeting "Sunshine" law had not yet been adopted.

The tone of the conflict became increasingly emotional. The Tuxedo Conservation and Taxpayers Association (TCTA), a new group formed mostly from the village of Tuxedo Park, predicted in a letter to 1,000 people that the Sterling One proposal for changes in the amendments would increase the population to 165,000. One member of TCTA, Sazz Crosby, was quoted in the *New York Times:*

> Sazz Crosby liked Tuxedo Park just the way it is.
> She can look out the windows of her palatial home and see a terraced lawn, a clear blue lake, and waves of forested hills. Beyond the hills, largely undisturbed forests extend for miles in several directions.
> "This may sound nuts," she said, "but sometimes when I get sad, I open my window and I'm happy again. The whole area is special. It is beautiful and it is very sensitive land. It has become my friend."[6]

Another resident quoted in the same paper observed:

> It's the only place I know where there are no street lights, no sidewalks, deer in the front yard, raccoons on your patio deck and miles and miles and miles of hiking trails.[7]

Still the amendments were hammered out at the private sessions. Even Fred Maute appeared to go along, although he repudiated his alleged support almost the next day.

Neal Martineau described a meeting (to Richard Babcock) of the Town Board late in the night after what appeared to be the concluding meeting between Sterling One and Town officials:

> Now, here's what happened. This is the part you didn't see. It was late at night: 12:30 A.M. over in that awful town hall building. We were beginning to wonder what we would do about all this. We had heard your pitch. Maute was there. We went through two hours of this and it's 2:00 in the morning. Maute then says he had been calling Shanahan on his own without saying anything to us. Asking for this and that more. It was a total end run, pretending to speak for us. He had totally betrayed us. Then we said [to Maute] you did this without asking us. *And then I threw something at him.* [Emphasis added.]
> . . . And we never spoke again.

[6]*New York Times,* January 15, 1978, Section 8, p. 1.
[7]Ibid., p. 5.

Thus the two former allies, Maute and Martineau, split openly and for good as Maute revealed what he had secretly done. Likewise, a split took place throughout the Town, neighbor against neighbor. Even families split. And many people are not speaking to this day.

The tone of the Town was depicted in the following article in the *Middletown Record:*

> The Sterling Forest Corp.'s battle to construct a 3,900-unit housing development with the backing of the Chicago-based Urban Development Corp. has all the drama and comedy of the best of the afternoon soaps.
>
> Friendships have dissolved, political reputations are on the line and through it all the heroine, Sterling Forest, remains determined to build despite pressure from within her own family—homeowners in two corporation-constructed developments in the town—not to build.
>
> The battle has entertained Town of Tuxedo residents here since 1972, but the longest running soap opera in Orange County may soon reach its denouement. Within four months, town residents will probably know once and for all if the heroine finally wins.[8]

Basically, the eight amendments that were agreed on provided:

1. Sterling One agreed to add 200 acres to the 1,500 already included in the development.
2. Sterling One agreed to place a limit on the number of dwellings until a specified amount of new industrial was contructed.
3. No fewer than 5 percent of the dwelling units were to be single-family dwellings.
4. No fewer than 50 percent of the dwelling units intended by the developer were to be sold, not leased.
5. Not more than 10 percent of the multiple-family dwelling units were to be in structures higher than 2.5 stories.
6. In calculating density, each two-bedroom, one-bedroom, and efficiency unit was to be credited as less than 1.0 dwelling unit.
7. Lands in an R-1 single-family district were permitted to be included in a planned unit development as open space and were to receive credit when densities were calculated.
8. Accessory commercial, service, and nonresidential uses were to be permitted or required in planned integrated developments.

The amendments passed, most by a five-to-zero or four-to-one vote,

---

[8]*Middletown Record,* July 20, 1977.

with Fred Maute making long speeches and, according to the *Middletown Record,* labeling Hoffman and Venezia "the town clowns."

State and Local Politics

At last, the amendments held promise for Sterling One. But then a new obstacle appeared on the horizon: the State Environmental Quality Review Act (SEQR) — a rather typical National Environmental Protection Act-type law — was to come into effect January 1, 1978, and development of Sterling One would be subject to it. Technically, although this act would leave the final decision making with the local officials, it did enlist the state Department of Environment and Conservation. Sterling One decided to involve the state and other interested parties as soon as possible. Accordingly, a meeting was held the middle of September 1977. The state advised Sterling One that it was most concerned about treated sewerage discharge into the Ramapo River, the adequacy of available water supply, and the problem of traffic access along Route 17 through the Village of Sloatsbury and the hamlet in Tuxedo. (Sterling One had been trying to persuade the state to construct an exit and exit ramp from the Thruway at Route 210 that would avoid both bottlenecks.)

The rub with the Environmental Impact Statement (EIS) required under SEQR (much of which Sterling One had already addressed in the six volumes previously filed with the Town) was that under local law, it was to be reviewed by the Planning Board, not the Town Board, and members of the Planning Board were known to be strongly opposed to Sterling One.

An even more ominous prospect was looming. A town election was coming up in November 1977. Fred Maute had announced that he would run against Ted Hoffman for the position of Supervisor. Neal Martineau, unable by now to conceal his distaste for Maute, had announced that he would not run with Maute on the Republican ticket but would run as an independent, an act that caused the Town Republican Committee to announce that it was withdrawing support from Martineau. The campaign was short and bitter. Maute defeated Hoffman by a vote of 511 to 492 — 19 votes. Martineau and John McCarthy (an opponent of Sterling One) were reelected.

Three incidents suggest that Maute's victory could have been a defeat. First, rain started to fall in Tuxedo on election eve and continued all election day, creating what was described as a "hundred-year flood." Nick Rossetti of Sterling Forest spoke of his experience:

> Well, I mean they had, literally, they had that day, the 100-year storm.

I mean it rained from morning throughout and I don't know how many inches of rain and Route 17 was completely flooded out. . . .

The hamlet area . . . they were generally for us and they were for Hoffman and these were people whose basements started flooding and they didn't vote. They stayed home and all the people who were afraid to go out, I mean, the Democratic people, they had cars, they'd call people and offer to pick them up and that kind of stuff and the people would not move. They would not go. So he lost.

Another event was a touch more personal and — if one can detach oneself from the conflict — more amusing. Ted Hoffman had run a hard campaign, but the last weekend before the election he decided that he and his wife should go on a marriage retreat. Who knows how many votes he might have turned up had he pumped a few more hands that last weekend? Ten votes would have done it. Neal Martineau recalls the third incident:

The rain also keeps a trainload of Sterling Forest people from getting through to vote for Maute. From getting back out to vote. And there was some kind of shenanigan to keep the polls open for that train. When that train arrived there were guys — I was sitting watching it. It got through. It got through. Somehow God pulled the chain and said no more rain now. And it got through and guys dashed for their cars and went to the polls and *they kept the polls open* and they lined up and we lost the election. We were so far ahead when those guys on that train came through. We lost the election. [Emphasis added.]

So Sterling One's worst enemy, Fred Maute, was to become the chief honcho of Tuxedo, to take office in six weeks, on January 2, 1978. This also meant something else: the Town Board would be stymied, split two–two because Maute would vacate his councilman's seat when he moved up to be Supervisor. It would be Maute and McCarthy versus Martineau and Venezia.

For the six weeks before the new Board took office, Sterling One had a three-to-two majority on the Board. Three reviews of the project were pending, one under the recently enacted SEQR. The draft EIS had been prepared by Sterling One and submitted to the Planning Board for review. (Sterling One knew now that the Planning Board was death to its proposal.) A second review is mandated by the Town's zoning law. That application had been turned over to the Planning Board in June and a response had been due in September but no comment was yet forthcoming. A third review was required by the county under New York law. Sterling One looked with some hope to the action of the county.

All that was sought from these reviews was preliminary concept approval. Everyone recognized that even were this granted, Sterling One would have to return to the Town for a more detailed final site-plan approval. Nevertheless, Sterling One decided to try to get the three reviews completed before December 31.

Strange things were taking place. Not only did the State Department of Environment and Conservation ask for more time to review the EIS (although they had had it since September), but also for some obscure reason the State Attorney General sought to intervene on the Town's side. The Planning Board advised that it could not complete the review by the end of the year. So on December 21, 1977, the Town Board, by a three-to-two vote, amended the local ordinances to give it authority to review and approve the draft environmental study.

There was some justification for this act, although the appearance of game playing hurt the Town Board. It did have jurisdiction to grant or deny the special permit for the Sterling One proposal, and therefore it was the lead agency from the beginning. By this action, the Town Board was restoring to itself the authority that it never should have delegated to the Planning Board. The hearing on the EIS was, to say the least, a frenzy. Some idea of the emotional pitch was shown by the following account in the *Middletown Record:*

> During the hearing, Tuxedo resident Fritz Krieger was arrested and charged with disorderly conduct for a remark he made to Sterling Forest Development Corp. attorney, Arden Rathkopf. At one point, Rathkopf said his tape recorder had broken, and Krieger quipped, "Checkers ate it." . . .
>
> "This is the last act left in a black comedy," said Councilman-elect John J. McCarthy. "You're going to be remembered for rushing into this and ignoring the Planning Board, your best consultants."[9]

The *Record* went on:

> In a letter, Edgar P. Stegmann likened the passions aroused by Sterling I to lovers' passions. He said Sterling Forest Development Corp. is like a virile youth. The town, he said, could be viewed as an old maid given her last chance to bliss or a young, innocent maiden of whom the truth is trying to take advantage. "Look through your own eyes in deciding on this project, not the eyes of your suitors," he said.

The lame-duck Town Board granted the concept approval and adjourned. The process, after four years, had moved swiftly. Meanwhile, the state Supreme Court (trial court) had ruled that the amendments to the zoning ordinance that had been challenged by the TCTA were valid.

The meetings of the new Town Board under Fred Maute were predictable. Neal Martineau objected to the adoption of Robert's Rules of Order for fear they would give the Town Supervisor too much power

[9] Ibid., December 22, 1977.

in the event of a tie. Martineau also threatened that he and Sam Venezia might stop coming to meetings and deny a quorum.

Outcome of the Litigation

Even more contentious was the selection of an attorney for the Town. Fred Maute and John McCarthy believed that the attorney, Myron Mandel, was too sympathetic to Sterling One, but their suggestion for a new lawyer was vetoed by their opponents. And this was not a minor problem. The TCTA was pressing an appeal on its suit on the amendments. It had also filed a suit challenging the action of the lame-duck Board to give preliminary approval to Sterling One. Finally the attorneys for Sterling One had filed suit against the Town, contesting most of the conditions the Town had attached to its approval. These events fueled the existing anger and frustration and led to more acrimonious charges. McCarthy wrote a letter to the *Record,* which read in part:

> Look at who are the supporters of the Sterling housing project — a few contractors, architects, engineers, real estate brokers and agents, some merchants, and every wild-eyed liberal in the Tuxedo area, and, of course, the land speculators — the greedy, self-serving fast buck artists who don't give a damn for the taxpayers in the Monroe-Woodbury School District. These special interest groups want to mortgage your future to make a quick buck today.[10]

By this time the party was over for UIDC. Bob Merriam, one of the principals for UIDC, recalls:

> We had sort of always said to City Investing we'll go so far and then if it's going to go to protracted litigation we have no interest in sitting by and getting involved in that. And I think it was not long after that it looked like it was going to be a protracted litigation, and it was. And that's where Urban pulled out.

The only one of the lawsuits that reached any definitive conclusion was the TCTA lawsuit. On July 2, 1979, the Appellate Division, in a split decision, held that the lame-duck Town Board had acted improperly in granting tentative approval to the Sterling One petition on December 28, 1977. The Court held that they had acted without an opportunity to be fully informed. The one member who took most of the blame — unfairly, it is believed — was Neal Martineau, who had previously disclosed to the Town Board that his advertising agency had done

---

[10]Ibid., February 15, 1978.

some work for City Investing Company, Sterling Forest Corporation's parent. The Court observed:

> The vote was 3–2. The controlling vote in favor was cast by one Martineau, an appellant herein, who, in addition to being a Town Board member, was and is a vice-president of an advertising agency which numbers City Investing Corp. among its corporate clients.
>
> Sterling is a wholly owned subsidiary of City Investing Corp. It requires no feat of mental gymnastics to infer that if the application is approved, the agency will be a strong contender to obtain all the advertising contracts in the 200 million dollar project.[11]

The last paragraph is, we suggest, gratuitous. The true story follows.

The Untold Story of Neal Martineau

When the case went to the Supreme Court (trial court), Sterling Forest filed papers that were so voluminous they arrived in large boxes.

So did the opposition.

By now many sets of lawyers were involved: Sterling's lawyers, the Town lawyers, the objectors' lawyers. And so was one of the finest minds in zoning law, Arden Rathkopf, who wrote the definitive text on zoning law. The case filings were voluminous because it was the first large-scale development permit issued under the new SEQR law. So new judicial ground was being broken as well as everything else going haywire. The key issue on which the judge turned down the permit had nothing whatever to do with the SEQR law or any of the mound of technical appraisals it required. The judge turned back the permit based on the "aye" vote of Councilman Martineau.

Throughout Martineau's term on the Board, the record shows that every time there was a crucial vote, he read a statement before he voted. This statement had been prepared for him by Myron Mandel, the Town Attorney, and Neal Martineau's legal advisor on all Town matters. In the statement, Martineau would reveal that the parent company of Sterling Forest, City Investing, was a client of the advertising agency for which Martineau worked as a creative advertising writer. The statement set forth the relationship between Martineau's advertising agency, Martineau, and City Investing Company; namely, that City Investing was a corporate client and that advertising for City Investing stressed the

---

[11]*In Matter of the Tuxedo Conservation and Taxpayers Association* v. *Town Board of the Town of Tuxedo,* 418 N.Y.S.2d 638 at 639 (1979).

large corporate entities owned by City Investing: Rheem and Home Insurance.

At no time did City Investing's advertising even mention its real estate holdings in Tuxedo.

Nor did Martineau have anything to do with the City Investing account. As an advertising creative professional, Martineau's job was largely on package-goods business for General Foods' coffees and Lever Bros.' margarine and detergents. It was not his job to work on corporate business, or to solicit new business. Rather, it was his job to write ads and commercials, and supervise other writers and artists and producers—all mostly on food accounts.

Martineau's statement set this forth clearly every time he voted on a Sterling One issue. Martineau would ask Town Attorney Mandel if in his opinion he (Martineau) was free of conflict enough to vote. Mandel would say that in his opinion Martineau could vote, and he would vote.

The opposition seized on this and threw it into the court papers, never believing it would become the basis for reversal of the permit. The conjectures presented against Martineau were that this agency would get the Sterling Forest account once Sterling One was built and that the advertising budget would be 10 percent of sales, which were projected to be expenditures of $10 million. None of these conjectures were ever questioned, even though they were highly exaggerated.

The judgment handed down by the state Supreme Court fell short of saying that Martineau's vote for Sterling was in direct conflict of interest. It stated that Martineau's vote was an *appearance* of conflict—which, in Rathkopf's opinion, was in fact adding a new definition to conflict. To use his own words, "The judge is making new law." Sterling One was not willing to appeal this decision beyond the state Supreme Court, and so Martineau's side of the story never got told. And the judgment stands.

Conclusions

From a distance, it is possible to evaluate the Sterling Forest Corporation's efforts and find fault in a multitude of small and large ways. Certainly the name of the venture, "Sterling One," frightened some people who pictured a series of similar programs—Sterling Two, Three, and Four. Perhaps, as an official of Sterling Forest Corporation speculates, the corporation might have early on done more to win over the residents of Laurel Ridge and Clinton Woods:

> So I did nothing. As I said, this was not in our nature. But what we could have done if we had a long view, we could have buttered these people [in

Laurel Ridge]. Now whether that would have made any difference it's hard to say but we could have buttered them up. If Jerry Fix [an opponent] wanted something, give it to him. In view of the long range what we were doing—the cost—a few thousand dollars here and there and so on. There were a lot of complaints up there. And someone called and there was a hole on the road, there would be someone up there fixing it when we owned the roads. If they call about something that we didn't think we had responsibility for, we'd say we're sorry, this is yours. Sewer problems, water problems; they were ours and we would bend over backwards. So, perhaps we could have babied them along.

One thing that always puzzled us was the silence of the large corporations that were located in the Forest. None of them—IBM, Union Carbide, International Paper—ever said a word even though they employed about 2,000 people and only a handful lived in the Forest.

A Sterling Forest Corporation official says:

I went to them. I went to them and all I can say is what I've said then, is that these big companies, as companies and as heads are gutless wonders. . . . They, you know, IBM is so afraid of the public. . . . I remember very clearly that International Paper agreed that they need [Sterling One], they want it. They are in favor of it, but they can't take an official position.

This attitude seems typical among large corporations. It is hard to follow how offending people like Fred Maute, John McCarthy, or Sazz Crosby could have injured IBM or Union Carbide; nonetheless, it is generally true that the only groups who are willing to fight the neighbors are developers or landowners.

There were other theories on the decisions Sterling One made during eight years and at least a million dollars in expenses. It should have proposed a much smaller development, perhaps 500 units. The principals always maintained that the cost of the infrastructure—sewer, water, roads—required a much larger number of units, and probably that is correct. Unless the construction of 500 units could have given Sterling One some sort of vested right, it is hard to see how 500 units would have helped them on their way to 3,900 units. To lock in a vested right, they would have had to get some commitment from the Town on the entire package—so that little or no discretion would have been left to the Town. In addition, Bob Merriam of UIDC did not believe that would have made much difference to the opposition: "Well, some people criticized the size of Sterling One but I honestly have to say in retrospect that if it had been a thousand units, I don't think it would have made much difference. The opposition was to having anything happen."

This is reminiscent of Martineau's "teen-agers."

Manny Emanuel, the Town planner, thought Sterling One gave the Town too much credit for understanding the concept of Sterling One: "I had the feeling that they assumed that the community was more sophisticated about the concept of what was being proposed. . . . I think they felt they were being pushed — pushed too hard by the applicants at the time."

This theory seems questionable. The most uneducated, unsophisticated people of the community living in or near the hamlet were for the project because they foresaw more jobs and more business for the small shopping area. Moreover, those of us who have been in these battles know that the most bitter opposition will come from the lawyers, stockbrokers, and similar recent arrivals who have all the qualities that "sophistication" is supposed to provide.

One of the most persuasive arguments on what Sterling Forest Corporation should *not* have done was to develop Laurel Ridge, Clinton Woods, and Maplebrook in the early 1960s. These single-family detached houses were the residences of some of the most vocal opponents and their leaders. The housing style in those subdivisions lent an assumption on what other housing would be like, each with its own front and back yard. They were scared when there was a proposal for *attached* single-family units and garden apartments. Nick Rossetti and Neal Martineau believed these developments were a major error. Martineau said:

> It would probably have been smarter had they not put in the single-family dwelling neighborhood first because they are the ones who are liable to be the most conservative and want more single-family dwellings like themselves. Had there been a reasonable mix in the first, had the first development been a microcosm of what was to come so that you would have had a little tiny model of what a PUD was really like.

And Rossetti:

> Well, I think, without a doubt in my mind that the biggest mistake was putting up those residential subdivisions. Yeah, without a doubt. There are a lot of individual mistakes because there is the — proper amount of PR wasn't done, people were — people expected — you remember when we came in and we were then talking to the town. People would bring out brochures from the early fifties that showed tennis courts and swimming pools and all these amenities. . . . We should have said — someone should have explained to them that it's economics, that you don't have that kind of amenity package until you have an economic base to support it.

And perhaps some of the lawyers were right. Instead of bargaining, instead of believing that Fred Maute could be reasoned with, Sterling One should have aggressively pursued its rights in court. In retrospect, we as attorneys for the project should have urged a more aggressive stance.

After all, even when the lame-duck Town Council did give its approval late in December 1977, conditions were attached that Sterling One could not accept. It might have proved successful had Sterling One taken depositions of the opposition and pressed ahead with the experts as witnesses before a court rather than before a local Town Board or Town Planning Commission. This reasoning assumes that no concession by Sterling One would have changed the minds of the most intractable of opposition.

Martineau held to this belief: "As I look back on it I would say that you should have gone into court immediately and then be as thorough as you could possibly had been."

Some of the opposition looked upon the whole affair as a game. Maute was their leader and he played a hell of a smart game. An official of Sterling Forest describes a meeting between Matt Horan of Urban Investment and Maute:

> I talked with Fred Maute many times individually and I also talked with him with Matt Horan one night. . . . We were talking about the project and about what it meant and he had his differences of opinion but, gradually, finally, he admitted that the project would probably be the best thing for the area. You know, creating jobs, the economic base, that it wouldn't hurt the school district—all of this stuff. So, Matt and I were shocked. We thought, "Oh, my God, here's a breakthrough, and we said—so Matt said to him, "Does that mean you're going to vote for this stuff?" And he looked at us like we were crazy. And he said, "What do you mean?" He said, "Of course not. That's not politically expedient to do that." I don't know if these were his exact words, I don't remember that but it was just like, are you crazy? Of course not. I'm not going to vote for it.

So the neighbors won.

The land remains as it always has been: beautiful and virgin. Ironically, Fred Maute disappeared from the Town after being defeated for reelection. (A fuss erupted over his expenditures while in office.) Sterling Forest continues to pay about $500,000 in taxes. Businesses fail downtown in the hamlet for want of customers. The commuters continue to shuttle back and forth to New York City. Residents have to do their shopping twenty-five miles away. The high school has to import students to stay open. The hospital will probably close. Industries are pulling out. The Town lost the Reichold World Headquarters. (They went to Connecticut.) Rumor has it that IBM is leaving. International Paper has scaled way back. Not much else has changed. Miles Shanahan has retired. The new management has been trying to get some single-family housing around Greenwood Lake. It is about as tedious an effort as it was with Sterling One.

There are scores of "ifs" in this story, but the implacable fact is the tenacity of the neighbors, which is not much different than it has generally been in zoning.

What does all this suggest? We believe the one clear issue is whether, in a small town, the local officials are capable of bringing a detached judgment to such emotion-laden issues. And that is understandable. Were we residents of Laurel Ridge with those thousands of acres of open land, we too might fight to keep out any new development.

What appears to be needed is some system where, outside of the courts, there can be a review by an agency whose members do not reside in the town. Either there should be a system such as in Florida or Vermont, where developments of a specified nature (airports) or size (3,900 units) are reviewed and approved or disapproved by a regional commission, or there should be a state administrative agency to which an appeal might be taken. In the case of Sterling One, county and regional bodies did endorse the proposal, but their actions were not binding. Of course, political pressures never can be eliminated but one consideration would have been removed—the nagging question, "What kind of a nut is going to live *in a condo* next to me?"

3

Palm Beach, Florida: The Rich vs. The Very Rich

> *You can leave Florida — and enter Palm Beach — by proceeding north on Highway A1A. You can't miss it. The garish strings of Seven-11's and neon hotel signs vanish. Clean uncluttered streets of class take over. The structures behind the high walls of concrete and ficus are not museums, just "single-family" second homes to Palm Beachers.*
>
> "Insight Guides, Florida" (1982)

> *For the Town it's a matter of survival. The only way to keep Palm Beach as a community — a community that is known worldwide.*
>
> Town councilman upon the adoption of a Comprehensive Plan for the Town of Palm Beach

Palm Beach is, according to most observers, a unique place in the United States. Located on the southeast Florida coast on a twelve-mile-long barrier island sandwiched between the Atlantic Ocean to the east and a mile-wide bay named "Lake Worth" to the west, Palm Beach is blessed with a tropical climate and a tradition of wealth, which combine to create a haven of great elegance and beauty. It has also spawned innumerable, seemingly implausible stories, including a wealthy socialite's attempt to discredit his wife's reputation during a divorce proceeding by describing to a titillated audience her use of a herald trumpet during group sex and drug sessions in their home. "Only in Palm Beach" is not an uncommon refrain among those who have visited the Town.

Authors' note: In this case, Ross and Hardies were hired to represent the landowners.

History of Palm Beach

In part, Palm Beach is a product of its natural setting. The island is located far enough south on the Florida peninsula to be within the subtropical climatological zone, a clime of balmy winter days and lush tropical vegetation. So the island came equipped with all the essentials of a tropical resort: a wide inlet to the ocean, calm waters for safe harbor, and abundant recreational opportunities (the fish-laden Gulf Stream reaches its nearest approach to the continental United States, often less than a mile at Palm Beach).

As early as 1890, Palm Beach — or Palm Bay, as it was initially named (the U.S. Post Office rejected the name of Palm Bay because it was too similar to an existing post office station near what is now Cape Canaveral) — had become the winter home of the very rich. Robert McCormick, the Chicago industrialist of Harvester fame, constructed a large estate on the island that became a frequent stopover for wealthy visitors to southern Florida. One of those visitors was Henry Morrison Flagler, entrepreneur extraordinaire. Mr. Flagler, John D. Rockefeller's partner in the creation of Standard Oil Company, had retired from the oil business and plunged headlong into the tourist business in Florida. His hotels in Jacksonville and St. Augustine had become the standard for tourist facilities in Florida, and the railroad he built to get winter visitors to his hotels was opening up the state to rapid development. In 1893, Henry Flagler acquired several properties on Palm Beach and began three significant enterprises: an extension of his railroad to serve the area, a hotel, and a home. The hotel, the Royal Poinciana, was finished in early 1893, and was at the time the largest resort hotel in the world and the largest wooden building ever built. In the spring of 1894, the railroad was opened to West Palm Beach, a city Flagler established on the mainland side of Lake Worth as a "commercial town" to serve the needs of his wealthy visitors. His home, a marble mansion named "Whitehall," was completed in 1901 at a cost of $2 million and was furnished at a cost of $1.5 million. Without a doubt the Royal Poinciana and Whitehall set the standard for the future development and character of Palm Beach; almost immediately the Town became "the place to be for wealthy Americans and Europeans." Indeed, one society columnist in New York observed: "Not to go to Palm Beach is a serious thing from a social point of view. If you cannot go there, you should at all events say that you are going, and then retire from Society for a time."[1]

Flagler's tradition of wealth and grandeur carried on after his death,

---

[1] *New York Herald* (1920), as recounted in McIver, *Yesterday's Palm Beach* (Miami, Fla., 1976).

as mansion after sumptuous mansion was built in Palm Beach as one wealthy family after another tried to outdo its neighbor. Addison Mizner, a society architect from New York, became the rage and designed dozens and dozens of structures in a Moorish and Mediterranean style that set a visible character and standard that survives to this day. The stock market crash in 1929 brought estate building to a close in Palm Beach, but the Town and its character had been clearly established, and this character remained stable and unthreatened until the next great Florida land boom, a boom that commenced in earnest in the late 1960s.

This chapter is a story about growth management and Palm Beach, one that shows that even the wealthy are willing to be players in the zoning game. The uniqueness of Palm Beach is an integral part of this story. Palm Beachers think themselves unique and act to protect that status. For example, Palm Beach has always been a seasonal community, with residents, shopkeepers, and officials departing for Hyannisport or some other "in" place for the summer. Unlike other seasonal communities, however, Palm Beach has institutionalized its seasonality in its Charter:

> Once a comprehensive town plan is adopted by the town council, no material change shall be made therein or thereon, such as a change in classifications, etc. and no hearing shall be had on any such change or action of any nature or kind had thereon, *except during the months of December, January, February and March.* [Emphasis added.]

Palm Beach, a town that "knows better," regulates the dress of joggers, fingerprints its domestics, and controls surfboarding on its beaches.

To be fair, Palm Beach *is* a unique community, and its vulnerability to change as a result of the Gold Coast development boom that materialized in the late 1960s was perceived as beneficial by its citizens. Indeed, by 1965, landmarks like the Lido Beach Casino had given way to condominium projects and the few remaining parts of the island left undeveloped during the 1920s were being developed with a type of housing that many viewed as undesirable: apartments (Palm Beachers viewed the structures as high-rise even though the new buildings were generally only four to eight stories high).

Leach Case

For Palm Beachers, the threat of "condomania" was brought into focus when the Leach estate, an oceanfront mansion about five blocks north of Worth Avenue, the Town's exotic and world-famous commercial promenade, was proposed to be demolished to make way for an apartment project. The property was zoned for single-family residences; however, there had been a number of developments immediately to the south of the estate at higher densities. When the landowner's application for rezoning came before the Town Board, there was an outcry of concern about the Town's changing character. On that basis, the application was denied. The concern was that Palm Beach was letting its character erode and that before long it would be too late to save the Town's uniqueness. The ensuing litigation proved that the Town Board and an increasingly vocal populace were well advised to be concerned about Palm Beach's future. Confident of victory, the Town was shocked when the Court ruled against it:

> As a result of the growth of the community, the cumulative effect of the changes in the zoning ordinances and the variances granted in the City's zoning regulations, the character and use value as residential property of the plaintiff *has been materially changed.* To require that her property remain Residence A under the circumstances is arbitrary, unreasonable and discriminatory. [Emphasis added.][2]

The threat to the Town from the Court's decisions was more than the loss of a few oceanfront mansions, and it had dramatic political repercussions, as reported by the then Assistant Town Attorney, David Faust:

> The members of the Town Council, at that point in time, had all been in office for many years. Town Council meetings were very short, . . . but with the change that occurred as a result of the *Leach* case, which was the first of several focal points of land use controversies, we began to see people coming to the Town Council meetings or having concern. One of the people who began to appear on a regular basis at the Town Council meetings as a member of the public was Bob Grace. He would appear at every council meeting arguing against any kind of special exception or variance request that came before the Town Council if it had any possible impact.

Sloan's Curve

One area of the Town that was seen as particularly vulnerable to development was far to the south of Worth Avenue in the vicinity of Sloan's Curve, a double ninety-degree turn where the only north–south road on that part of the island shifts from oceanfront to lakefront. North of Sloan's Curve were estates designed by Mizner with gentle names like Tranquility and Deux Horizons (a not-too-subtle reference to the fact that the estate in question boasted unrestricted views of, and fronted

---

[2] *Town of Palm Beach* v. *Leach,* 185 So.2d 743 (Fla. 4th DCA 1966).

Sloan's Curve looking from the Lake Worth side toward the ocean, which lies below the dune line. (Photo courtesy of Ross and Hardies)

on, both the Atlantic Ocean and Lake Worth). To the south of Sloan's Curve was a largely undeveloped area that was dotted with a few developments, most of which were not single-family homes. A first new development south of Sloan's Curve was clustered near the Lake Worth Casino, a small municipal enclave of the City of Lake Worth almost three miles south of Sloan's Curve. It was obvious that the undeveloped lands between the Casino and Sloan's Curve were prime for apartment development. The prospects of repeating the mistakes of Hallandale, Hollywood, and Miami Beach became a subject of great political urgency. Long-time residents were joined by the new residents of the first few apartment buildings built in the area, who found an expanse of undeveloped land next to their own high-rise an understandably desirable amenity.

At the time, all of southern Florida was experiencing unprecedented growth, and concern for the environment and the future quality of life was an important issue at both the local and the state level. A gubernatorial study committee convened in 1971 reported that growth management was critical in southern Florida because exploding population growth threatened the entire state's "quality environment."

Palm Beach, unique in every other way, turned out to be no different on the growth issue, particularly when a developer proposed to convert the Palm Beach Par 3 Golf Course, located south of Sloan's Curve and one of only three golf courses in the entire Town of Palm Beach, into an apartment project. Frightened by the prospects of uncontrolled growth and an intuitive sense that developers were going to destroy the character of their community, the activists, now in control of the Town Council, called for new regulations that would prevent a reoccurrence of the much-maligned Miami Beach experience. David Faust, Town Attorney, recalls:

> What occurred was that Bob Grace and George Matthews were elected to the Town Council . . . on the premise that they were going to do something to control what they saw as a new development that was undesirable in Palm Beach. So what do they do? Almost immediately after they got elected and established their control they obtained authorization for the Town Manager to employ a land planner to come in and develop a land plan that would match their view of what should be.

Comprehensive Plan for the Town of Palm Beach

When a planning consultant was contacted, the new leaders wanted to know what they should do to protect the Town. The planner's response, not untypical in that day, was that the Town needed to approach the issue in a comprehensive way: it needed a comprehensive plan.

On October 20, 1969, the Town entered into a contract for the preparation of a Comprehensive Plan for the Town of Palm Beach. The succeeding sequence of events illustrates the best and worst there is to say about the zoning game and land use litigation.

To put it mildly, the Town Council was in a hurry, and eager to prohibit what was thought to be undesirable development. According to David Faust,

> The court had taught the Town in the *Leach* case that any hope that they had to limit height or densities would be adversely affected by what had already been permitted.

The Plan itself was published in final form in January 1970, barely three months after the planning effort was initiated. To many observers, particularly the owners of vacant parcels of land, the Comprehensive Plan appeared to be nothing more than an after-the-fact justification of a prejudgment that something had to be done to stop growth, no matter what the facts indicated. In its text, the Plan forecast a host of problems that would flow from apartment development, particularly south of Sloan's Curve and called for a revision of the Town's zoning ordinance adopted in 1947 and the downzoning of the land from as high as fifty-five dwelling units per acre to three to twelve dwelling units per acre. The zoning changes contemplated in the Plan were not limited to the area south of Sloan's Curve. Needless to say, the owners of affected properties were less than pleased and many complained to the Town leaders; however, only the Mayor seemed to be concerned. The threat of uncontrolled growth, amplified by the Court's ruling in the *Leach* case, urged the Council forward, without the advice of counsel, as David Faust later revealed:

> We were not involved in any of the political activity that occurred. We were not consulted with respect to the employment of new land planners or the entire process. The first time we got involved as lawyers was after the plan had been pretty well formalized and we were called upon to look at various aspects of the proposed zoning ordinance that was in the process of being completed.

On the other hand, the owners of vacant land that was targeted for downzoning saw the Plan as a poorly conceived overreaction to a minor traffic problem. One landowner said:

> There is such a thing left in this country as property ownership, and the fact that you can confiscate property by zoning to a certain extent, but I think that the town should have studied the situation a lot closer than what they have done apparently and should have given it a lot more thought.

Defense of the Plan

The draft Comprehensive Plan triggered vocal sentiments on both sides of the issue. Not surprisingly, the citizen activists were not particularly sympathetic about the developers' plight, and at a public hearing on the ordinance one speaker said:

> Reports are that there are 12 apartment buildings now on the drawing board to be erected on South Ocean Boulevard. The many millions invested by property owners far exceeds the few million dollars of speculative investments in locations where these apartments are proposed.

Most residents saw the Plan as critical to maintaining the Town's great charm and beauty, and they responded emotionally: "It is essential to the preservation of the Palm Beach we love, of its character that made it world famous, that the Town Council enact the Comprehensive Zoning Plan now before it."

If not, the plan's proponents argued, the "evil condominium" would clog the Town's streets, strain its sewers, overextend its police and fire services, and "erode its charm." Even the specter of urban blight was unabashedly forecast if the plan were not adopted. The proponents' fears were summarized at a public hearing by a citizen:

> If some modification in the growth pattern is not provided by the town council, the population on this island could grow to 100,000–120,000 people which is a gross population density of 30 to 40 people to the acre and which in other locations has proven to downgrade the quality of living. After all, population density is one of the main contributing factors to slums and ghettos and obviously if Palm Beach, the island we live on, is loaded up with more people, you can expect the quality of life to deteriorate; you can expect real estate and improved real estate and improved land values to deteriorate.

Old-time Palm Beachers were not the only people concerned that high-rise buildings would destroy the quality of the Town. Newcomers, particularly those in the developing parts of the Town, were also concerned about a tidal wave of growth. A resident of one of the recently developed high-rise apartment projects made it clear that he believed Palm Beach had grown enough already: "I believe this section [south of Sloan's Curve] already has reached enough density and we want no more multi-family residents in the area."

Perhaps most eloquent and least egalitarian were the words of the Chairman of the Board of the Palm Beach Civic Association, when, at a public hearing, he lamented on the costs of growth to accommodate "unwanted friends."

> Palm Beach is a unique distinctive town of great charm and beauty. Its well-kept, well-groomed body is the creation of the architectural genius of Mizner, Fatio, Major, Wyeth, and Volk. Its soul is the spirit of the people who live here, giving it an atmosphere of simple elegance, of elegant simplicity. . . . It is of the greatest importance to Palm Beach's world-wide image, to its quality of living and to the general health and welfare of its people, that its face be not disfigured, nor its body mangled, nor its charm dissipated, nor its character blackened by the invading forces who care nothing about the beauty of its body nor the purity of its soul.

One of the attorneys representing the landowners later reflected candidly about the real issues behind the growth threat:

> To be blunt, I think there was then, and still may be, a substantial amount of prejudice in Palm Beach. Dick Babcock and I were walking on Worth Avenue one day and heard one Palm Beach matron say to another, "You see more of them here now than ever before." Dick and I looked around expecting to see blacks. But there weren't any—everybody in sight was white. We could only conclude that the two ladies had a more discerning eye for ethnic and religious characteristics than Dick or I. Frankly, I think that was a part of it—when they talked about it not being like Miami Beach they didn't mean just the high-rises, they meant the demographics of the growth as well.

And so it was that the Town Council voted to adopt a plan that its own manager admitted might be less than ideal:

> While the plan is not perfect, we have to start somewhere and I think we should start with the new plan and go as far as we can to retain both the land values and the quality of the environment.

Challenge to the Plan

The landowner response was swift and sure. Thirty-three suits were filed challenging the Plan and its implementing regulations. The suits involved parcels as small as a single filling-station site and as large as all the vacant tracts south of Sloan's Curve; collectively they challenged literally every element of the Town's Plan.

Richard Babcock was called in by a local attorney who felt he might be getting in over his head. He represented a well-known Chicago resident, Lester Crown, whose wife's family owned land up and down the East Coast including three parcels in Palm Beach, the largest of which was twenty-five acres just south of Sloan's Curve. Starting with a copy of what he immediately nicknamed "the 90 day-wonder," Babcock zeroed in on what he characterized as the "hurry-up" character of the Plan. His critique revealed that the Plan was not something to be proud of. The questions he penned in the margins of the Plan indicated its shortcomings: "By when?" "What other?" "What is social structure?" "What degree?" "What was test for suitable?" "What study?" "Which ones?" — and so on.

Moreover, Babcock's reactions were backed up by an expert planner who was brought in to review the Plan. In a painstaking review of the Plan and its preparation, the consultant discovered that little time had been devoted to the collection and organization of data; in fact, data collection and alternative growth plans were completed and delivered to the Town within thirty days of the onset of the study. Babcock and his experts did not believe that the planning effort was legitimate and theorized that the Plan was nothing more than an after-the-fact justification for a preconceived idea and not a real planning effort. He said:

> The period from the execution of the contract for the Plan to the presentation, completion of the data assembly and the presentation of the first draft plan was something like three weeks, perhaps four. It was done with enormous speed. During the course of the litigation, we examined the town's files and we found this marvelous letter from Ernst Bartley who had been asked to do this job for the town. He had written back saying that he would be happy to be of assistance but that it was his view that they didn't want

a comprehensive plan because they had already decided on their planning objectives and what they needed was a planning report. And if they wanted him to prepare that he would be happy to do so. The document came back to haunt them because it indicated that their planning objectives were well formulated long before they did the plan itself.

In addition, Walter Blucher, a distinguished planner and lawyer, hired to give the plaintiff's case a little "gray beard," characterized his reaction to the Plan at trial as ranging from "astonishment to mild shock to a little sadness."

Impact of the Sunshine Act

While the planners, engineers, and appraisers dissected the plan and its impact on properties south of Sloan's Curve, the lawyers sparred with each other in front of the judge assigned to the cases. One of the challenges presented by the landowners was a claim that the plan and its implementing regulations were invalid because of alleged violations of Florida's Sunshine Act.

The landowners' claim was that a citizens' advisory group formed to assist planning consultants had met with the Town's planning consultant in private during the planning effort. And, indeed, the group had met in private; however, the Town's response was that the advisory committee was not a decision-making body and therefore not covered by the Act. The Town Attorney had not been consulted in regard to the committee's activities and the possible application of the Sunshine Act to its meetings; nevertheless, the Town was unconcerned, even when the lawsuits were filed because, as the attorney later recalled, "The state of Florida law at that point in time was somewhat ambiguous on that subject. We had complied with the plain language of the law according to an attorney general's opinion, so that gave us some comfort."

In July 1971, the trial court held a pretrial hearing for all the consolidated cases challenging the plan and bifurcated the matter into two elements: the Sunshine Act violation and the substantive challenges to the Plan. The Sunshine Act count was set for a hearing in November and, after five days of testimony, the Court took the matter under advisement. In the meantime discovery proceeded on the substantive challenges, and Crown's lawyers continued to focus on the "hurry-up" character of the Plan, spurred by discoveries of internal memoranda such as the following directive in the planning consultant's file: "Based on our conclusions and local expectations, I hope that you will be going through this first stage (Inventory, Analysis, Alternatives) as lightly as possible."

In early 1972, the trial court ruled in the Town's favor on the Sunshine Act count, setting the stage for the first of the plaintiffs to go forward on its substantive claim; the preparation for trial was very thorough and extremely expensive. The matter was set for trial and the parties prepared themselves for what was destined to be a battle royal. The witnesses were prepared with care. Babcock recalls his "woodshedding" of planner-lawyer witness Walter Blucher. Blucher had always been voluble, and Babcock feared that Blucher would be long-winded. He told Blucher that he would be sitting next to the local attorney and if he pulled on his right ear, that meant to break off his testimony. At the conclusion of Blucher's testimony, Babcock's ear was red and sore.

Trial on the Plan

For Babcock, his partner (R. Marlin Smith), and their local counsel, the matter was simple — the Plan was a sham and inflicted heretofore unheard of economic injury on their client. For Town Attorney Faust, the matter was less clear. First, the purpose for the Town's action was unimpeachable — change was in evidence everywhere and the courts had already told the Town, "Don't let your community character change, or it will be too late." Second, the Plan that had been produced was "graphically beautiful and textually it read well." Third, the Plan almost immediately won an award as an outstanding plan. Nevertheless, when Faust began to prepare his defense, he found himself in an unenviable position. Much later he admitted that the Plan's conclusions were virtually unsupported by research or other evidence:

> Almost immediately after discovering that there was some difficulties with the conclusion that there were problems with providing adequate water supply for drinking water for a large population and sewage facilities supposedly were scant and traffic problems and so forth, I saw that if I had any hope for proving the validity of the plan I had to begin on several fronts developing some kind of expert testimony or alternatively some kind of factual basis to support the conclusions that the planners had included in the plan which the town had adopted.

Property Value

Leaving nothing to chance, the plaintiff's attorneys called three economic witnesses: a local appraiser who just happened to be the well-respected former county tax assessor, a regionally recognized appraiser, and a nationally known land economist. Their testimony was consistent and compelling — the reduction in density reduced the value of the plaintiff's property by a range of $5,775,000 to $6,612,000. The Town of Palm Beach countered with a single local appraiser, who testified that the loss in value was "only" $2,835,000.

The plaintiff's post-trial brief of course highlighted this issue: "We know of no case in this country during the half-century of zoning where a rezoning has so suddenly imposed so great a loss upon a single property owner."

Using words such as "killed," "calamity," "dramatic," and "confiscation," the plaintiff was able to demonstrate that the rezoning produced dire consequences. (The plaintiff coyly suggested in his brief that "confiscation is a term that should not be used frivolously. In this case, it is hard to avoid.")

As for the integrity of the Plan, the plaintiff focused on the claimed "need" for reduced densities south of Sloan's Curve. According to the Plan, future growth in that area under the prior zoning would have resulted in a population increase from about "9,000 to between 40,000 and 65,000 persons." The Plan contained no explanation of how these projections were compiled, even though it was clear that this threat of uncontrolled growth was a major focus of the Plan.

Population Projection

Tony Wiles, the planner hired by the plaintiff, testified that he could find no explanation for these projections in the Town's planning program but that he had carefully calculated, on a lot-by-lot basis, the maximum number of units that could be developed south of Sloan's Curve under the old ordinance. As the plaintiff stated in his brief,

> Plaintiff did the homework that the Town should have done. This was done through careful field surveys, use of the 1970 census data and a calculation of allowable densities based on the provisions of the pre-1970 ordinance. . . . Mr. Wiles testified that under the old zoning ordinance the *maximum saturation* south of Sloan's Curve would be a little less than 25,000 persons. He added that the *probable* population would be considerably smaller and that the number of units per acre actually constructed under the old ordinance was substantially less than the permitted units per acre. [Emphasis in original.]

His testimony was devastating to the Town's position because the population projection he developed was slightly less than 25,000 persons, far less than the 40,000 to 60,000 the Plan had forecast. The contrast between the Plan's vague assertions and the plaintiff's expert testimony was dramatic and was reiterated in the plaintiff's post-trial memorandum:

> The document [the Plan] has no substantiation for these incredible estimates. The Town's expert planning witness offered no explanation. The

Town did not call any other member of the planning team to explain these figures. No Town official appeared to show how these threatening figures were reached. The most crucial issues in the case, the rationale for all that followed — and silence.

Traffic

The other thrust of the plaintiff's planning case involved the much-ballyhooed traffic issue. One of the few subjects on which the plaintiff and the defendant agreed was that the Town of Palm Beach indeed had a traffic problem and that development south of Sloan's Curve would exacerbate the problem. What the parties did not agree on was the solution to the problem. For the Town, the obvious answer was to cut densities: "limiting in a reasonable manner the increase in population will give the Town needed time to handle pressing sanitation, traffic, parking and other problems."

The plaintiff's counterattack, was that route A-1A was already congested, and that any development, including development permitted after the downzoning, would exacerbate this congestion. Therefore it was argued that A-1A should become a four-lane highway regardless of the densities permitted.

The plaintiff's position was bolstered by a curious phenomenon. The plaintiff's lawyers, in the course of their investigation, had noticed a peculiar characteristic of Highway A-1A: the posted speed limit signs said, reasonably enough, "Maximum Speed 35 MPH." But a second sign affixed below that sign proclaimed "Minimum Speed 25 MPH." The State Highway Department claimed to know nothing about the sign. But they suggested that these signs were posted by the Town to keep the tourists from going too slow while rubbernecking the mansions. That helped in the plaintiff's response to the suggestion that high-rises were the cause of the traffic.

Decision on the Plan

After a ten-day trial, the Court took the matter under advisement and on April 28, 1972, issued a written decision. After reciting that the Town of Palm Beach is a "unique community residential in nature," the Court noted that "although there is no evidence of an impending crisis, . . . the trend of population movement is northward from Dade to Broward Counties, and the citizens of Palm Beach, to put it mildly, are seriously concerned over a duplication here of the development there." Echoing the Town's self-description of beauty, tranquility, and internationally famous resort, the Court reviewed the plaintiff's assault on the Town:

> Plaintiff has made a vigorous attack upon the entire Comprehensive Plan and Ordinance with a very impressive array of expert witnesses. And while the assault on parts of the plan and ordinance reflects error in some basic facts and conclusions, on the whole, looking at the reasons, purposes, and goals precipitating the plan and ordinance, the Court finds they should not be declared invalid in their entirety.[3]

Nevertheless, the Court found that as applied to the plaintiff's property the "Comprehensive Plan and Ordinance are unreasonably restrictive and ordered the Sloan's Curve property rezoned to no more restrictive than R-D (40 dwelling units to the acre)."

To the public, it appeared that everybody won as the *Palm Beach Daily News* trumpeted "Judge Upholds Town Zoning Plan." The Town Attorney was more sanguine: "I am pleased with some of the rulings and less pleased with others." And one councilman was brutally honest: "I'm not happy about it, and I don't think a lot of people in town will be happy about it. I think it is unfortunate the judge has decided to become a land planner."

The Town appealed the decision.

Appeals

Sunshine Act — Appeals Court

While the substantive validity of the Comprehensive Plan and zoning ordinance was on appeal, the Sunshine Act challenge was also on appeal and on May 30, 1973, the Fourth District Court of Appeals reversed the trial court and held that the Planning Advisory Committee was subject to the Sunshine Act:

> The adoption of the zoning ordinance in question was, in our view, tainted by the previous "steps in the dark" as evidenced by the appointment of and deliberations by the Citizen's Planning Committee which admittedly never gave notice nor conducted public meetings.[4]

The Town petitioned the appellate court for a rehearing, or in the alternative, to certify the Sunshine Act question to the Florida Supreme Court. The petition for rehearing was denied, but the basic Sunshine Act issue was certified to the Florida Supreme Court:

---

[3] *First Bank & Trust Co. of Boca Raton* v. *Town of Palm Beach*, Circuit Court No. 70C 3415.
[4] *IDS Properties* v. *Town of Palm Beach*, 279 So. 353 (Fla. 4 DCA 1973).

Whether a zoning ordinance adopted by zoning authorities and the Town Council after public hearings is rendered invalid under the §286.011, F.S.1971 [F.S.A], Government in the Sunshine Law, because of the nonpublic activities of a citizen's planning committee which committee was established by the town council and acting on behalf of the council in an advisory capacity participated in the formulation of the zoning plan.[5]

Town Strategy — New Ordinance

Cleverly, the Town was not content to merely await its fate in the state Supreme Court and began to "plan" for any outcome. Recognizing the distinct possibility that the invalidation of the 1970 ordinance for violation of the Sunshine Act might be sustained by the Supreme Court, the Town decided to readdress the planning and zoning issues. A new planning consultant was hired and a moratorium was announced to ensure that developers could not take advantage of any "grace period" that might result if the Supreme Court affirmed the new zoning ordinance's invalidity.

The ultimate result of this effort was a new zoning ordinance (1974) carefully tailored to the lessons learned in the Sloan's Curve case. The new zoning ordinance limited density on the Sloan's Curve parcels to eighteen units to the acre, far less than the R-D zoning the trial court had conferred upon the plaintiffs.

Sunshine Act — State Supreme Court

On May 1, 1974, the Florida Supreme Court ruled that the Sunshine Act was violated, and that the zoning ordinance adopted by the zoning authorities and the Town Council after public hearing was rendered invalid because of the nonpublic activities of the citizens' planning committee. This decision confirmed that the Town was wise to protect itself against the eventuality of a grace period.

For the landowners, the news from the Supreme Court, a victory on paper, was not in fact good. The Court held that the 1970 zoning ordinance was void *ab initio* (from its beginning), and therefore the effect of the invalidation was to resurrect the original 1947 zoning ordinance. To the landowners, voidness *ab initio* was a disaster because their 1972 judgment to build at forty units to an acre, a judgment that was predicated on the revised ordinance, was, as a matter of law, as if it had never existed.

A string of victories suddenly turned pyrrhic as the Town's new (1974) ordinance, now the legal operative instrument, limited the Sloan's Curve

---

[5] *Town of Palm Beach* v. *Gradison*, 296, So.2d 473, 474 (Fla. 4 DCA 1973).

property to eighteen units to the acre, less than half the density the trial court judge found to be reasonable. Obviously, the Town's new planning consultant, educated by the best planning attack money could buy, believed that the new density would be "fairly debatable" in the face of another attack.

Substantive Validity — Appeals Court

At that point the landowners had been at it for more than four years, had expended untold thousands of dollars, and had been told by a court of competent jurisdiction that the original downzoning had a "horrendous" impact on land value and that every legitimate objective of the Town could be accomplished with a limitation of forty units to the acre. Yet the Town's official position was that the 1974 ordinance, with its eighteen-units-per-acre density, controlled.

Arguing to the appellate court that "it just can't be so," the landowner's attorney urged the appellate court, in the Town's appeal from the decision on the substantive validity of the 1970 zoning, to hold that the trial court's decision had created a cognizable right and that the right to develop forty units to the acre should be sustained. Unfortunately for the landowner, the appellate court saw what it described as a "critical, anamolous, unforeseen and intervening event" in a different light:

> The chain of events has left a field of irresolution. We think it can only find correct solution and afford proper process across the board by a new look and new adjudication at the trial level, prosecuted by those who may be aggrieved.

Strategies after Appeal

The landowner unsuccessfully petitioned the Florida Supreme Court for review, and then faced the reality of doing it all over again. Ironically, the "unforeseen" circumstances of the ordinance's voidness had indeed been forecast by, of all persons, the trial judge, who upheld the validity of the ordinance against the original Sunshine Act challenge:

> It certainly would be ironic if having decided in favor of the Town and proceeding now to trial with respect to the other counts, if the appellate court reverses and all of this time spent on trying the merits of the zoning case went to waste.

The Town, of course, had suggested that the time and expense of actually trying the merits of the zoning cases should be deferred until the Sunshine Act appeal was complete; however, the landowners were adamantly opposed to any delay.

No shrinking violet, the landowner's attorney added a count seeking $6 million in damages against individual Town Council members, Zoning Commission members, the Town Clerk, and the Town building official. The Town and its officials, no less timid, saw the suit as a "shotgun charge in a wild attempt to intimidate," defended in earnest, and eventually convinced the trial court that the public officials named in the count were immune from suit and that the only proper issue was the zoning question. Inadvertently, the landowner had helped the Town to solidify its resolve to defend itself, as observed by one of the named individuals:

> I hope the outcome will serve as a reminder of future Council members not to succumb to threats and pressure. This is still a unique town only because we have the guts to stand up and keep it the way it is. I hate to think that policies would be determined by such threats.

Outcome — The Town

By this time, the battle over Sloan's Curve was almost six years old, and time had overcome the combatants. The 1974–75 recession in southern Florida had run its course, and low- and medium-density development in Palm Beach had become very profitable; in fact the landowner was offered, according to published reports, $3 million more than the most optimistic appraisal under the pre-1970 zoning. The battle over Sloan's Curve had been won not by the eloquence of lawyers, but by time. The matter finally ended in February 1978, when the Town approved a development proposal for the property under the density provisions of the 1974 ordinance. After eight years of expensive litigation, development commenced at less than half the density permitted under the 1974 zoning and less than one-third of the density the trial court had found to be a reasonable minimum in 1972 (forty units per acre).

To the Town of Palm Beach, the fray was well worth the time and money invested in the litigation. The actual development of property south of Sloan's Curve has been limited to five stories in height, and to far less density than permitted prior to 1970 and far less than the trial court ordered in 1972. As David Faust observes:

> We were always of the opinion that time was on our side and that the longer final disposition this case took, the better off we would be in terms of winning our objective. In large measure, we felt that these cases ended up with us as the winners in a context of what has been finally come to be built

Sloan's Curve, looking south-southwest. (Photo by Davidoff Studios)

on this property. We even have a single family house in Sloan's Curve development, and we have townhouses.

Unique in many ways, yet ordinary in its zoning battles, Palm Beach did display a distinctive capability in the defense of its zoning ordinances. Faust again:

> I don't know of any town that has been so willing on almost every issue when sued to defend it with vigor and to approach compromise and settlement as an exception rather than a rule as in Palm Beach.

It was this resolve that was a vital element of the Town's success. According to Faust,

> There are other communities around here that have not had the same resolve and have become easy pickin's. There are places I know that immediately start quivering the minute a suit is threatened and you can negotiate very easily with them to get what you want to have. . . . We just go a little further south to South Palm Beach developed subsequently and there is an example, of one of the Miami Beach style developments.

Outcome — The Landowner

In contrast, it is hard to believe the experience is viewed with favor by the landowner. Time is, after all, money, and time was indisputably wasted as the litigation worked its way laboriously through the courts. The implications of eight years of dispute undoubtedly weigh heavily on the landowner's mind. Yet, his attorney said:

> I think in the end you have to say our client won in the sense that all three parcels of land were sold for a very, very substantial income at over what the investment in them was. Even considering carrying costs in the meantime. And it was that the landowner had not simply sat on the sideline. Because he then would have been struck with four units to the acre on the biggest and most valuable parcels. He probably could not have made the same economic gain we ultimately did.

Conclusions

In retrospect, it is possible to suggest that the story of Sloan's Curve is just another dispute between the "I've got mine's" and the next person in line, or as the plaintiff's brief put it, "Bosun, pull the ladder up, I'm aboard." Some of the supporters of the downzoning (those who described future newcomers as "unwanted friends") were residents of the few high-rise buildings that slipped in before the Town could change the rules. These people assuredly answer the description of the "last man on board." Two of them testified at trial in support of the Town's position and described the threat future development posed to the tranquil, utopian character of Palm Beach; however, on cross-examination, one of them conceded his opposition to high-rise buildings and reflected, in part, that "I guess I'm just selfish." The other testified that he hoped the area south of Sloan's Curve would remain just as it was when he moved into his apartment in an eight-story condominium.

As noted in *The Zoning Game*, it is a curious phenomenon that the titans of industry who abhor government regulation and place full-page ads in the *Wall Street Journal* extolling the virtues of the marketplace are among the most zealous devotees of zoning. And perhaps that is all the Sloan's Curve case involved: a simple zoning fight between the rich and super rich.

Palm Beach can hardly be said to have suffered a material change in character as a result of new growth and development, and indeed it is hard to imagine a more insular place secure from the ravages of uncontrolled growth. It is true that the owners of McDonald's stock have replaced the Dodges, but the Town is still safe and secure. The Town has traffic problems however; most authorities conclude that the problem is attributable not to growth and development on the island, but to the increased popularity of the island to gawkers and tourists and the general increase in population in Palm Beach County.

Sloan's Curve today is different from when the Town of Palm Beach enacted Ordinance No. 3-70 in 1970. The Sloan's Curve property has been developed with a series of townhouses and mid-rise apartments that are handsomely landscaped and appealing to the eye. A guardhouse and guard now stand as another exclusive element of the Town of Palm Beach. To the south of Sloan's Curve, there is very little undeveloped land, and with the exception of the golf course and Phipp's Park, the area is an undisrupted row of mid-rise condominiums. Yet, traffic along A-1A seems no worse than it was in 1970. It is very hard to tell what effect the growth and development of the south beach has had on the quality of life. Indeed, other than the conversion of vacant land into developed land—a process that was inevitable under any of the alternatives ever considered—it is difficult to see any significant change that has resulted from the area's growth and development.

This story, seemingly a testament to the inefficacy of land use litigation, could be summarized as follows: The old guard controlled the Town; the nouveaux riches were the interlopers. The nouveaux ("I've-got-mines") wanted their carefully chosen paradise protected from any more apartments and somehow persuaded the old guard to take up their cause—at great, but politically inconsequential, expense. Palm Beachers, like other Floridians, feard the heavy winds of change in the late 1960s and felt helpless to respond to rapid growth and its attendant problems. When the "I've-got-mines" called for help, the effort gave the old guard something to do about the problem and, notwithstanding the facts or merits, they did something.

And so did the plaintiffs. And yet in the final analysis, the controlling influence was time. All the plaintiffs' witnesses and all the plaintiffs' attorneys could not overcome time. As Town Attorney Faust candidly puts it, "I think honestly that time is one of the best weapons that you have on your side if you are defending a public side, and is one of your vulnerable points if you are on the private side."

There is an irony to this story that is often ignored by the pundits who look at Florida and its astounding growth. Growth management, Florida's slogan of the 1980s, is the focus of vast public resources in a curious reversion from the pioneering views that predominated Florida just a few years ago. In the 1950s and even the early 1960s the talk in Florida about growth involved its promotion, not its control. Where the long-rumored "east Disneyland" would be located was a major topic for community leaders around the state, as each tried to outbid each other for what was viewed as desirable growth and development—a far cry from the issue of the 1980s megagrowth, as Florida receives 4,000 new residents a week.

4

Grand Central Station: Beware the Establishment Aroused

> *"Cursed be he that removeth his neighbor's landmark." And the people shall say, "Amen."*
>
> Deuteronomy 27:17
>
> *Europe has its cathedrals and we have Grand Central Station.*
>
> Philip Johnson
>
> *Let us now praise Grand Central.*
>
> Jacqueline Kennedy Onassis

There are few examples of judicial reversal of direction to match Justice William Brennan's two opinions, less than four years apart, in *Penn Central Transportation Co. v. New York City,* 438 U.S. 104 (1977), and in *San Diego Gas & Electric Co. v. City of San Diego,* 450 U.S. 621 (1981). One may search the tea leaves for an explanation but the hypothesis most favored here is that in the former case, the courts were heavily swayed by the incredible campaign mounted in 1975 by the Committee to Save Grand Central.

Both cases raised the issue of whether government regulation went so far that it was not only invalid but that damages should be paid to the complainant as well — a "taking." In *Penn Central,* the railroad alleged that the Landmarks Law of New York City that denied it the right to erect a fifty-five-story office building over the Grand Central Station at 42nd Street and Park Avenue involved a "taking" under the Fifth and Fourteenth amendments of the U.S. Constitution. In his opinion Brennan addressed this problem and conceded that it was too difficult for the Court to develop any "set formula" for what constituted a "taking." Consequently, while the Fifth Amendment (Just Compensation Clause) is "designed to bar Government from forcing some people alone to bear public burdens which, in all fairness and justice, should be borne by the public as a whole," the *determination* (of when fairness and justice dictates such action) is made "upon the particular circumstances of the case," based on an ad hoc factual inquiry.

Brennan, speaking for a majority of the Supreme Court, went on to conclude that there had been no taking.

In the *San Diego* case, the electric company owned 214 unimproved acres. Most of it had been zoned industrial, and some was in an agricultural "holding" zone. In accordance with California statutes, the City was obligated to establish an open space plan, which it did, placing the company's land among the City's open space areas. The plan acknowledged that the company intended to build a nuclear power plant on the property. The company sued the City, alleging a taking and asking over $6 million damages. A trial court found that the City had taken the property, and a jury awarded San Diego Gas & Electric Co. over $3 million damages. The California Appellate Court upheld the award. The Supreme Court of California set the judgment aside and sent the case back for a new trial.

On appeal, four members of the U.S. Supreme Court concluded that the appeal must be dismissed because the California judgment was not final.

One justice, William Rehnquist, concurred but added: "If I were satisfied that this appeal was from a final judgment or decree of the California Court of Appeals, . . . I would have little difficulty in agreeing with much of what is said in the dissenting opinion of Justice Brennan."

Brennan's dissent (in which Justices Potter Stewart, Thurgood Marshall, and Lewis Powell joined) was, to put it gently, a shocker. He held there had been a "taking." Measure the following language in *San Diego* by the facts in the *Penn Central* case:

> Moreover, mere invalidation would fall far short of fulfilling the fundamental purpose of the Just Compensation Clause. That guarantee was designed to bar the government from forcing some individuals to bear burdens which, in all fairness, should be borne by the public as a whole. . . . If the regulation denies the private property owner the use and enjoyment of his land and is found to effect a "taking," it is only fair that the public bear the cost of benefits received during the interim period between application of the regulation and the government entity's rescission of it. [Citations and footnote omitted.]

Brennan had no difficulty in taking in *San Diego* despite his acknowledgement in *Penn Central* that the judgment was essentially ad hoc. Indeed, under the ancient "harm" or "benefit" dichotomy, it is hard to see where the "harm" was in another fifty-five-story office building in midtown Manhattan and easy to see where the "benefit" was to the public in preserving Grand Central.

There is one more interesting contrast between the two opinions. In *San Diego,* the City made considerable fuss about the policy considerations that should influence the Court, particularly on the consequences to the municipal fiscal budget. Brennan, however, dismissed these arguments: "But the applicability of express constitutional guarantees is not a matter to be determined on the basis of policy judgments made by the legislative, executive or judicial branches." And in a footnote in reference to the *Miranda* rule, he wrote:

> Such liability [by municipalities] might also encourage municipalities to err on the constitutional side of police power regulations, and to develop internal rules and operating procedures to minimize overzealous regulatory attempts. After all, if a policeman must know the Constitution then why not a planner? [Citation omitted.]

If policy cannot enter into consideration when "express constitutional guarantees" are at stake, why did Brennan, in his *Penn Central* opinion, immediately following the statement of the issues discuss the recent widespread legislative movement to encourage or require preservation of buildings and areas with historic significance? He said:

> Not only do these buildings and their workmanship represent the lessons of the past and embody precious features of our heritage, they serve as examples of quality for today. "[H]istoric conservation is but one aspect of the much larger problem, basically an environmental one, of enhancing—or perhaps developing for the first time—the quality of life for people." [Footnotes omitted.]

Later, in responding to Penn Central's arguments, he observed: "Agreement with this argument would, of course, invalidate not just New York City's law, but all comparable landmark legislation in the Nation. We find no merit in it."

If the above observations are not "policy," then Penn Central Co., reading Brennan in *San Diego,* must wonder why it is cursed with being "a Grand Beaux Arts building" and not just another 412 acres of "open space."

Grand Central Station. (Photo by Walter Smalling, Jr., National Register/Courtesy of Municipal Art Society)

Background

Grand Central, when it was completed in 1913, was an engineering marvel, with ramps between its two levels of walks and Park Avenue circumnavigating through and around the station. It was a monument to the Vanderbilts, occupying forty-five acres between 42nd and 46th streets and Lexington and Vanderbilt avenues.

There was a station on part of that location. The latest model had been rebuilt in 1871 with an open cut leading trains into the facility. In 1902, a serious accident killed thirteen people in the cut. In May 1903, the New York legislature passed a law forbidding steam trains from entering Manhattan. But the railroad was a jump ahead and had already decided to have a limited competition to build a new station and to make use of two new concepts: steel frame and electricity. The architectural firm of Reed and Stem of St. Paul won the contest; "but," as Deborah Nevins in her chapter in the superb book *Grand Central Terminal: City Within the City*, says, "corporate and family connections would decree that their role was to be only as collaborators with the New York firm of [Whitney] Warren and Wetmore.[1]

Nevins adds one more interesting sidelight: "In the original Warren and Wetmore plan there was a 20-story tower that was abandoned. But it was part of the conception in the architectural drawings that later became a 'landmark.'"

During oral argument before the U.S. Supreme Court, Daniel Gribbon, attorney for the railroad, was asked by Justice Stewart:

Q: Mr. Gribbon, back in 1911, one plan considered was a 20-story tower on the property, was there not.

A: Yes. Over the terminal. . . .

Q: Has anything along that line been suggested to the [Landmark] Commission here at this point?

A: No, your Honor, nothing that small has been suggested simply because it would be an inefficient utilization of land. . . . I must say there is not any suggestion in the action taken by the Commission that even that would satisfy. Nothing is going to satisfy because they want the air to roam freely over Grand Central Station.

What would the Commission do, were that proposal submitted?

There were forty-two tracks on the express level, and twenty-five on the lower or suburban level. In its heyday, the station saw 63 million passengers and 550 trains. Today, by contrast, in addition to the suburban traffic, there are exactly eleven Amtrak trains, and Amtrak is considering consolidating all its services at the Pennsylvania Station. As we shall see, the decision in *Penn Central* may be a victory for preservationists in general, but it may be forty years too late for the Grand Central Terminal. Nevertheless, in the 1970s, long after its days of glory had vanished, the structure evoked enough emotion to mobilize sentiment among those who count in Manhattan. Indeed, this tale may be one of those instances where lay efforts did, in fact, have a significant impact on the opinion of the courts.

---

[1]Deborah Nevins (ed.), *Grand Central Terminal: City within the City* (New York: Municipal Art Society of New York, 1982), p. 15. She continues: "Soon the Reed and Stem firm's disassociation with the project would become an affair.

"On November 12, 1911, Charles Reed died. On November 16, the day after the funeral, Wetmore, originally trained as a lawyer, wrote to the railroad suggesting that Warren and Wetmore have sole responsibility for the terminal from then on. In December a new agreement was drawn up without consulting Allen Stem. Stem eventually sued Warren and Wetmore for their share of the architectural fees, and the case was decided on July 17, 1916, in favor of Reed and Stem. Stem and the Reed estate were awarded $219,000, which included interest. The case was appealed in 1919, the earlier decision was upheld, and the case was appealed again in 1920. In this second and final appeal, Reed and Stem again prevailed, and were awarded $500,000. This included

The story starts in the early 1970s with three separate applications filed seriatim by the noted architect Marcel Breuer to the New York Landmarks Commission to erect a fifty-story-plus building over the Terminal. The Commission turned them all down, observing at one point "to balance a 55-story office tower above a flamboyant Beaux-Arts facade seems nothing more than an aesthetic joke."

The railroad went to court, and New York Supreme Court Justice Irving Saypol's opinion in January 1975 invalidated the landmark ordinance as applied to Grand Central. He held the designation as a landmark invalid and reserved a decision on the award of damages. At this time there came to the attention of an officer of the Municipal Art Society of New York (MAS) a recommendation by the Corporation Counsel's Office of the City of New York that the City not appeal the decision. The memorandum reported that if the City did not appeal, Penn Central would waive its claim for damages. The Corporation Counsel urged such a course of action. Brendan Gill of *The New Yorker,* one of the directors of the MAS, puts it more gently:

> As I recollect the City had the tendency to drag its feet on this thing. The City wasn't sure what position it wanted to take. So we had to buck up the Corporation Counsel. We had to urge them, at the beginning at least, to fight the good fight because there was a question of whether the City was going to lose an enormous amount of tax revenue.

Dorothy Miner, now attorney for the Landmarks Commission and formerly a legal researcher in that office, recalls more vividly:

> [I]t was the First Assistant Corporation Counsel who came to visit the whole [Landmarks] Commission and said that there could be this settlement after the adverse decision provided the Commission agreed not to file a notice of appeal, or to pursue an appeal. There was this threat hanging over of very high damages and at that point, of course, the City hadn't reached the actual hysterics of '75, but it was getting toward this whole bankruptcy issue and then as it got around to '75 everybody was very nervous. . . . Anyway, the Commissioners decided they did not want to accept this offer of Penn Central on the damages and that they did want the appeal to be pursued.

---

2 percent of the building cost of the terminal and 1.5 percent of the cost of the Biltmore Hotel, for which they had done preliminary work. In that same year Whitney Warren was expelled from the American Institute of Architects, presumably as a result of his actions after Reed's death. Nonetheless, Warren and Wetmore maintained their very profitable New York practice."

The Role of the Municipal Art Society

The Municipal Art Society, a "big-name" prestigious organization now located in the Villard Houses on Madison Avenue, swung into action. It formed an organization known as the Committee to Save Grand Central. At first the Committee consisted largely of the staff and members of the society, but when it called for help, more people volunteered. Jacqueline Onassis telephoned to ask what she could do. Former Mayor Robert Wagner became chairman, and among the members of the Committee were Jimmy Breslin, Brendan Gill, Philip Johnson, Congressman Edward Koch, Bess Meyerson, George Plimpton, William H. Whyte, Helen Hayes, Celeste Holm, Anita Loos, Mrs. William Paley, and Gloria Steinem. There was also a National Committee of Preservationists from Texas, Utah, Maine, Illinois, Michigan, Georgia, and Massachusetts. The *Chicago Tribune, San Francisco Chronicle,* the *Dallas Herald,* and the *Boston Globe,* to mention a few, ran major stories on the efforts to save the terminal. Distinguished volunteer legal talent was also associated with the Committee. These included Bernard Botein, former Presiding Justice of the Appellate Division, Whitney North Seymore, Jr., United States Attorney for the Southern District of New York, Francis T. P. Plimpton, diplomat and former President of the Association of the Bar of the City of New York, and Samuel I. Rosenman, Counsel to Presidents Franklin D. Roosevelt and Harry S. Truman.

No one was quite sure how the new Mayor, Abraham Beame, would react. He was not in the same tradition (some might say of wine and brie) as former Mayor John Lindsay. The Committee sent out a mailing asking for money and urging the recipient to contact Mayor Beame:

> Next, write or wire Mayor Beame immediately (See enclosed sample suggestions.)
> Urge your friends to contact the Mayor. Have the organizations to which you belong pass resolutions to support and send a copy to the Mayor.

The mailing worked. On March 2, 1975, Beame announced that the City would appeal Justice Saypol's decision, presumably reversing the recommendation of his legal advisors.

Then the Committee's work really began. In addition to the amicus brief to be filed on its behalf, an enormous publicity drama was performed. J. Walter Thompson, the large advertising agency, volunteered to help. A storefront was opened on Vanderbilt Avenue. Guided tours were organized to go through the terminal. Press conferences and television interviews became almost a weekly diet. Committee volunteers sold the usual tee-shirts and trinkets. Money was raised to put floodlights on the terminal. A made-for-TV movie was put together, a montage of old movie scenes showing everyone who was anyone arriving or leaving Grand Central Terminal on the *Twentieth Century Limited.* The response was remarkable. Brendan Gill again:

> And Grand Central is really a genuinely loved public building in New York City after 1913 to the present day. . . . People have become attached to it and we found that there was an emotional basis for our appeal that was based upon, as we thought, fact. Nevertheless, it turned out that a lot of people did care. Partly because there had been so many movies made there. It was where so many people had set forth on happy journeys. It was the occasion for many honeymoons beginning on the way to Niagara Falls. All kinds of strange things turned up. It turned out that people in all the hotels had spent their wedding nights like Scott Fitzgerald at the Biltmore. It figures in the fabric of New York City both artistically, culturally, romantically, in a very strong way. So from that point of view we had a stronger case than we even supposed we had.

The committee organized an enormous rally on April 15, 1975, at the terminal. Dick Cavett was master of ceremonies and the celebrities included Benny Goodman, Henny Youngman, Tony Randall, Lionel Hampton, and the cast of *Grease.*

The *New York Daily News* quoted Kent Barwick, Executive Director of MAS, as saying:

> We chose April 15, income tax day, purposely. We feel that since the tax dollar is being used to subsidize the railroad the railroad does not have the fight to flout the public interest. The people of our city and our country want this building saved.[2]

On December 15, 1975, the city secured a reversal in the Appellate Division that was affirmed in the Court of Appeals. The Committee was elated, particularly because the Appellate Division quoted widely from their brief, including mention that "[u]rban landmarks merit recognition as an imperiled species alongside the ocelot and the snow leopard." It was in the Court of Appeals opinion that then-Judge Brietel added his comment that "society as an organized entity, especially through its government, rather than as a mere conglomerate of individuals, has created much of the value of the terminal property." Nowhere in the briefs had this concept been put forward. It was an observation that upset many who foresaw Justice Rehnquist pouncing on that when the case reached the U.S. Supreme Court. In a footnote to the opinion, Justice Brennan felt obliged to disown Brietel's venture into a neo-Henry George theory, and in the oral argument Justice Stewart asked Mr. Gribbon, attorney for the railroad:

[2]*New York Daily News*, April 16, 1975.

Q: As I read over the briefs filed by your brothers and sisters on the other side, my impression is that none of them really tried to defend the basic reasoning of the—that part of the reasoning of the Court of Appeals; would you agree with that?

A: I believe that is a fair statement, Mr. Justice Stewart. That is the way I read those briefs. They all back away to some degree and come forward with a further explanation of why the decision should go against Penn Central.

Q: The Court of Appeals really is a statement of Henry George's single tax, is it not?

A: Yes. But I submit it is not a statement of sound constitutional law, as many of Henry James' things were, not necessarily sound—

Q: George.

A: George. I am sorry. James would be different.

The Committee's efforts did not cease with the victories in the Appellate Division and the Court of Appeals. Someone—perhaps Margot Wellington, then Executive Director of the Municipal Art Society, or an executive of J. Walter Thompson—thought up a train ride from New York to Washington with whistlestops along the way. Of course, they would have to compromise: someone pointed out that no train went from Grand Central to Washington. So the Committee settled on Pennsylvania Station.

There was a nice irony in this. A decade earlier, before the landmark law was enacted, a few lonely persons had picketed in front of Penn Station just before it was effectively destroyed. Margot Wellington, former Executive Director of the MAS, observes:

> People were so upset about losing Pennsylvania Station. Of course I always say that the job of the preservationist has been made so much easier by mindless developers. Not good ones but mindless ones who have wantonly destroyed things like the Metropolitan Opera House and Pennsylvania Station—great—great New York City monuments. In their place they put up trash. That's where the idea of preservation came from. It's like trading Aladdin's lamp for a little junky, brand new tinny lamp and people began to understand that very well.

The MAS set a date and prepared for a going-away rally at the Terminal. It would be "The Grand Central Express." Then the lawyers dropped the bomb: the Supreme Court had set oral argument for the day after the train was scheduled to go to Washington. Would this appear to be too flagrant an attempt to lobby the Court? They decided to go ahead, but they changed the name to "The Landmark Express." As Wellington says:

The Municipal Art Society's "Landmark Express," April 16, 1978. Jacqueline Onassis and Joan Mondale were among the celebrities involved in the campaign to save Grand Central Station. (Courtesy of Municipal Art Society)

We whistlestopped. We went to places like Newark, Philadelphia, and Wilmington, Delaware. People came out and the Mayors were there and we got down to Washington and there was Joan Mondale and there was [Senator] Moynihan and there was Jackie and everyone else. J. Walter Thompson said that they have never in their lives done anything in the whole history of the agency to generate as much footage or print ever. They were so excited, they had a party for our Board and for the Committee leaders and they had cut out all the clippings around the world and pasted them up and they ran all the video programs that were made. And we even got letters from Turkey. We got letters from everywhere you can imagine—Australia—wherever.

It was quite a party. McDonald's donated the food. The MAS paid $14,374 to rent the train and recouped the money from fares. The *New York Times* reported:

Musicians played Mozart and Scott Joplin tunes during the trip, and Mr. [Brendan] Gill added to the cacophony over the train's loudspeaker system, leading a disharmonious chorus of passengers singing a "Save Grand Central" song to the tune of "Tipperary." It went:

"Let's make a grand stand to save Grand Central, the greatest landmark site of all.
It's a great part of New York City, like the lights of old Broadway.
Let's make a grand, grand stand for Grand Central, for the good old U.S.A."

Among the other passengers were Philip Johnson, the architect, and Henry Geldazhler, the city's Cultural Affairs Commissioner. At Union Square in Washington, Senator Daniel Patrick Moynihan, Democrat, New York, and Joan Mondale, wife of the Vice President, were among those on hand to welcome the train.[3]

Kent Barwick, now President of MAS and then head of the Landmark Commission, comments:

> I was not the architect of the trainride. I was the architect of the original committee. But by the time we got to the trainride the cast had changed and I was over here on the governmental side and other people were — it was controversial. But the die was cast. We'd been public all along. We had the entire cast of Broadway shows dancing and sports figures and it was too late to turn back. It was to demonstrate the national purpose.

When asked what connection she saw between all the hoopla and the Court's decision, Margot Wellington replied:

> Did the lawyers tell us what the connections were between tee-shirts and legal decisions? Several of the attorneys that I have spoken to at that time who had had dealings with the Supreme Court, and I believe Whitney Seymour also said that, said, you know, of course, none of these kinds of tactics is going to change a legal opinion of a Supreme Court Justice; however, a great deal of the foundation work of the decision is done by these brilliant young clerks that come out of the law schools, all of whom are a great deal closer to young passions and youthful thinking than the gray eminences. The knowledge of a national sentiment for preservation and the knowledge of a national sentiment for the preservation of Grand Central is something that will have an effect on the Clerks and it's going to creep into the decision somehow. . . . And, in fact, there was a recognition in the decision.
>
> It was surely the kind of whipping up not only of the Municipal Art Society's side but every other preservation group doing all the rabble-rousing. You can't rabble-rouse unless you can have strong legal arguments when you are in court. There are three elements in this kind of thing: the public education process, there was a public rabble-rousing process, I mean you have nothing else to do but whip up the emotions of people, and there was a process that dealt with the city of New York, the agencies.

---

[3]*New York Times,* April 17, 1978.

Asked how she evaluated the MAS effort, Wellington said she felt that it was merely an intensification of their typical effort in the realm of public education:

> The Municipal Art Society has always been the kind of organization that keeps a lot of balls up in the air at one time and thinks that that's good use of its energy. So it's always been known as simultaneously a force for public education, while it's also a force pushing on political structures.

Conclusions

Few, if any, decisions that have reached the U.S. Supreme Court have aroused as many emotions as Grand Central Terminal. No one can argue with any persuasiveness that the hoopla was the direct cause of the result in that case. At least no lawyer would be willing to make that admission. Yet the rationale in the opinion turned old doctrines upside down, such as that any regulation that tends to offer a benefit rather than prevent a harm to the public is the occasion for compensation not regulation, or that the concept of "average reciprocity of advantage" must exist in all efforts to control design. And when Leonard J. Koerner, Corporation Counsel of the City of New York, rose to argue for the City he was pitched dozens of questions, most of which can only be described as gopher balls. For example:

> Q: You say as this case comes to us, we must judge it on the basis that Grand Central in its present use is profitable?
>
> A: Must be. And that, Your Honor, is the essence of this case and that the appellant has ignored the lengthy trial and the two findings of the Appellate Courts.

And yet, if most of the "hard" arguments appear to run against the preservationists, what was left to be said for the terminal? What indeed except the hype that the Municipal Art Society put forward?

But was it worth it? The MAS bucked up the New York Corporation Counsel's Office when it was about to toss in the towel. It led Justice Brennan to start off his opinion with a recitation of the scores of cities and states whose landmark legislation would be in jeopardy if the decision went contrary.

Indeed, Mr. Gribbon, on behalf of the appellant, Penn Central, started off his argument before the Court as follows:

> Perhaps I should be intimidated legally, if not physically, by the sheer number of governments and organizations on the other side of the question presented on this appeal. There have come to the support of the appellee,

the greatest city in the world, three other major cities, the nation's two largest states. . . . In addition, 20 civic organizations, all highly respected, and finally the United States has had sufficient interest not only to file a brief but to participate in the argument.

But we repeat, was the battle worth the effort? Certainly. According to Brendan Gill, "If you save a building for 20 years, that is a victory." The terminal stands as it did in 1913. The opinion had a profound impact on the preservation movement across the country. It cut back the threat of "taking" at a time when municipal finances were at their nadir. And yet, if you go inside the Grand Central Terminal "it just ain't what it used to be." This is not the depot from which the red-carpeted *Twentieth Century* departed with its cluster of Hollywood stars. There is no honeymoon express to Niagara Falls. The glorious skylights have been painted over since World War II. True, the famous Oyster Bar remains, but so much else is just plain junk. A Merrill Lynch substation is posted in the center of the massive lobby, like some crustacean on the seafloor. A series of off-track betting windows take the place of ticket booths along half the south wall. Tacky shops line the entrances to the main lobby. An enormous Kodak color photo lines the east wall, not too bad in comparison with its various commercial associates.

When it was suggested to Gill that there were a lot of junk boutiques in the concourse, he responded:

> And a lot of junk people, more or less, go in there to get warm. They have had to close it for the first time. They close it at night. They shut off the toilets, no one can go there to pee anymore which is a scandal because we need it to pee in, for Christ's sake. There are hundreds of thousands of people going through there. They closed all that down with the result that poor helpless, homeless people pee on the premises to the extent that they can and make everything worse.

The Vanderbilt entrance is a mess. It looks as though it has been a substitute for the closed urinals. Hugh Hardy, in his chapter in *Grand Central Terminal,* laments:

> No longer two stations in one, nor blessed with 63 million passengers on 550 trains a day, Grand Central has become (with the exception of eleven Amtrak trains) merely one large train station servicing 500,000 pedestrians who use an unparalleled resource with all the ceremony of eating fast food. Bedecked with jarring commercial displays and third-class retail activities, its taxi ramps used for parking, its corridors made urinals, its platforms unwashed, and its roof in disrepair — this is not the stuff of urban grandeur.[4]

---

[4]Nevins, *Grand Central Terminal,* p. 136.

72 · *The Zoning Game Revisited*

"We think Marcel Breuer really has it licked now."

Drawing by Alan Dunn; © The New Yorker Magazine, Inc.

The truth of the matter is, a shopping center the terminal is not. Yet hundreds of thousands of people pass by on 42nd Street, Park Avenue, and Vanderbilt Avenue. Scores of thousands more march through the terminal on their way to or from Stamford or Greenwich, Connecticut, or by the subways that disgorge their daily loads. But they all have to be at work by 8:30 A.M. or catch the 5:20 P.M. commuter train to Connecticut. Who has time to do more than drop off film or pick up aspirin?

Hardy continues:

> It has been sly of time to leave the terminal's grand concourse, never designed for such things, as a repository for billboard displays, second only to Times Square in the mammoth scale of their commercial messages. These extravaganzas are not without charm. They offer the public information, give stock news, and provide seasonal displays. They form part of the terminal's present architecture and contribute important revenues. And while outraged protests of aesthetic vandalism need to be balanced by economic reality, what would it be "worth" to stand in the grand concourse and see the Chrysler Building illuminated at night, or have sunlight stream through the terminal's south facade, replacing the commercial slogans and redundant clocks? If we are to allow such amenities to replace current necessities, we must establish a new economic strategy for the terminal's survival.[5]

One problem is the lessee. The Metropolitan Transit Authority (MTA) leases and manages the terminal. The MTA is a beleaguered public institution charged with running railroads, both subways and commuter lines—and not very well in the public view. A James Rouse or Donald Trump, MTA is not—nor should it be. It is hard to see how the interior of the terminal can ever be anything but a depressing experience as long as it remains a train station with few if any long-distance trains and commuters just as eager to get out as if it were a parking lot.

Hugh Hardy again:

> Natural light, which helped generate the terminal's design, today is excluded from its skylights because of leaks, World War II blackout precautions, and current fiscal austerity. The six-story walls of glass, which once permitted startling views, are too grimy to offer more than shadows of the city beyond. The waiting room has become a limbo, stripped of its carved oak benches to discourage loitering, hacked up by new access routes at its eastern end, shorn of its connections to other levels along its south wall. Its original light-colored ceiling is stained dark brown, and its resplendent windows are rendered dimly translucent by dirt. It is a forlorn remnant of past magnificence now used to house a newsstand and a candy store.[6]

---

[5]Ibid., p. 137.
[6]Ibid.

Nor is the picture of the exterior much better. The problem with landmark designation, if it is in a strong market area, is that nothing prevents development around the landmark. And that is what has happened to the terminal's environs. (The FAR of the Terminal is 2.0; the permissible FAR in the area is 18.0.) You cannot see it. Margot Wellington is probably right: the notion that you can walk the Manhattan streets and expect to see the tops of buildings is a Chicago or Los Angeles viewpoint but certainly not a New York City viewpoint. The terminal is a bug engulfed by glass and steel sequoias. It is more an architectural anomaly (not at least an "aesthetic joke") than a historic structure, surrounded by an excrescence of a Hyatt Hotel, the outrage of the Pan Am Building, and the Philip Morris Building. Incidentally, Philip Morris did purchase 3 percent of its air rights from Grand Central for its headquarters, which occupies the site formerly occupied by the art deco airline terminal at a price said to be about $30.00 a square foot, high even for midtown Manhattan.

Deborah Nevins warns: "[T]he terminal is still not safe from destruction. We must understand that misuse and brutal alteration can destroy it in a manner almost as complete as any planned physical demolition."[7]

Misuse? The terminal is now operated by a public agency, which in turn is being prodded by the MAS. The MTA has had a ninety-nine-year lease to operate the terminal since 1970. (They are the folks who raised graffiti to new heights on the New York subway cars.) The MAS insists that the MTA wants to change the quality of the interior, and Kent Barwick alleges that the situation has improved since five years ago. A very small restaurant on the Vanderbilt balcony is the latest experiment.

Whether the Grand Central Terminal was worth saving is another question. Any lawful effort that can keep down densities on Manhattan's east side is meritorious. Certainly, if you can gain permission to look down out of the 32nd-floor windows on the northeast corner of the Philip Morris building, the terminal is a gem squatting there amid the turmoil of the island's heart. But the interior is squalid. And the Supreme Court's opinion is a hollow victory for New York City, even if it is a triumph for preservation. But, to paraphrase Justice Brennan, if a policeman must know the constitution, then why not a preservationist?

Clearly, the reason that the Committee to Save Grand Central was able to raise such wide support across the country was due to pure nostalgia — the recollections of thousands of people who remembered the grand days, that one trip with dad or mom in the twenties. How many of the stars of TV, radio, and screen the committee enlisted actually

[7]Ibid., p. 10.

had used Grand Central? It no longer is the place of arrival or departure for great trains. (But, it might be rejoined, neither does George Washington enjoy Mt. Vernon.)

In another generation, no one will be around to recall the halcyon era and probably the same effort would not evoke the emotions. If it were tried, it probably would be a picket line of a half-dozen architects and art critics such as paraded futilely in front of Pennsylvania Station.

Within twenty years, another effort predictably will be made to desecrate this grande dame and it probably will be successful. (In the euphoria of victory, it should not be forgotten that three of the youngest justices—Burger, Rehnquist, and Stevens—dissented.) Is Brendan Gill correct?: "If you can save a landmark for twenty years that is a success."

5

San Antonio: Politics Makes Strange Bedfellows, or Everything You Ever Wanted to Know about Aquifers

> *Plaintiffs . . . herein seek damages, in at least, the sum of Seven Hundred and Fifty Million and No/100 Dollars ($750,000,000) against the City of San Antonio and the six (6) individual council members named herein.*
>
> *Plaintiff's Original Complaint: Application for Preliminary Injunction, Permanent Injunction and Damages. Civil Action No. SA-77 CA 174, United States District Court, Western District of Texas, San Antonio Division.*

TOTAL AQUIFER BAN 'NO BUENO'

> *Headline of the San Antonio Light,*
> *June 30, 1977*

Unlike those paragons of modern Texas, Houston and Dallas, the City of San Antonio is rich in tradition and character. First established in 1718, the City has a long, colorful history including the famous Battle of the Alamo. The Alamo, located in what is now downtown San Antonio, was one of many Spanish missions established in the area in the early 1700s, and was the site of the famed siege where a small band of Texans and Davy Crockett briefly held off Santa Ana's horde during the war over Texas's independence from Mexico. The Alamo, as histor-

Authors' note: Ross and Hardies were brought in as attorneys for the City of San Antonio.

Riverwalk, San Antonio. (Photo by Chuck Beckley)

ically and culturally important as it is, is not, however, the City's only tourist attraction. The "riverwalk," an improved river channel complete with arched stone walkways and Texas-style gondola barges, is a notable tourist attraction and a unique urban resource. The riverwalk, which winds around and through the downtown area, was constructed during the Great Depression and has served as a tourist magnet every since with its walks, stately trees, and handsome landscaping. Indeed, the riverwalk is a focal point of the City's entire being. At Fiesta time (a springtime carnival of Texas culture and history that starts with a pilgrimage to "Remember the Alamo"), mariachi bands float along the river past crowded sidewalk cafes and restaurants as thousands line the river to celebrate the traditions of south Texas.

Growing with Grace

San Antonio is far more than just a tourist stop in southern Texas. It is, and has been for many years, an active participant in the great sunbelt growth game. As a result, the one-time battlefield of Davy Crockett is now the eleventh (some say the tenth) largest city in the nation. For San Antonio, the economic prosperity that comes with growth has been problematical, because growth involves change and San Antonio's traditions resist change. The conflict between growth and those traditions is a fascinating story of contrasts and transition. Indeed, the recent history of San Antonio could be described as a tale of two cities—a traditional city of wealth and gracious living and a modern, urbane city of diverse racial and cultural character. The old city—the one of grace and wealth—is still there, but a variety of events have conspired to integrate it into a new aggressive, growth-oriented city that advertises itself as "growing with grace."

The contrasts are many. San Antonio is located at the southern edge of the Texas "hill country," where rolling hills and stone outcrops provide dramatic relief from the flat plains of southern Texas. Land to the north of downtown San Antonio is hilly while land to the south is flat and chronically subject to flooding. Not too suprisingly, San Antonio's growth has been affected by its geographic location. Growth and development to the north has been sprawling, expensive, and white, while growth to the south has been sparse and Mexican-American. There are other contrasts, as well. San Antonio, as an old city, has a reservoir of turn-of-the-century houses that rival the historic architecture of any city in this nation, and yet the city is also the home of some of the least attractive tract housing projects in the nation. Miles and miles of uninterrupted homes in grid-square subdivisions give contemporary meaning to the label "shot-gun houses." One large-scale developer from Florida who visited a calvacade of homes in San Antonio put it bluntly: "Criminies, don't they know what a tree is? It's insane to let people live in those little boxes."

There are also political contrasts. Although the majority of the adult population of San Antonio has always been Mexican-American, between 1955 and 1973, 77 of 81 City Council members were representatives of a predominantly "Anglo" (San Antonian for white) political action league. Fully 75 percent of the councilmen during that period lived on the north side of the City. Then in 1976, the City under pressure from the Department of Justice, acting pursuant to the Equal Voting Rights Act of 1965, was divided into ten single-member districts. The result was dramatic—a nine-member Council of six Anglos, two Mexican-Americans, and a black became an eleven-member Council (the Mayor is still elected at large) with five Anglos, five Mexican-Americans, and a black. This is the story of an innocent little land use issue that got caught up in this political transition, an issue of vital importance that received little government attention until a fateful election in 1977.

Edwards Underground Aquifer

The little land use issue involved water, potable drinking water for over a million souls. San Antonio draws its potable water from the Edwards Underground Aquifer, a karst limestone formation that underlies the hill country to the north of the City. The aquifer, a limestone formation over 175 miles long and 5 to 40 miles wide, provides San Antonians with virtually unlimited quantities of water that requires almost no treatment before consumption. The trouble allegedly was that the aquifer was in danger of pollution. According to those who were concerned, the acquifer was threatened because it is replenished by surface water that percolates through porous limestone from recharge areas at the surface, and these recharge areas lie directly in the path of San Antonio's sprawling Anglo growth toward what developers called the "great northwest."

Concern about the integrity of the aquifer originated in the mid-1950s, when a severe drought in southern Texas raised fears that the aquifer might not be able to support unlimited mining of water to serve the needs of San Antonio's rapidly expanding population. Springs fed by the aquifer stopped flowing at the peak of the drought, and environmentalists were legitimately concerned about what steps should be taken to protect the City's source of potable water. The state legislature responded by establishing the Edwards Underground Water District for the purpose of "protecting, conserving and recharging the underground waterbearing formations and for the prevention of waste and pollution." The District was not a regulatory body, however, and its principal role since its inception has been to monitor and study the aquifer.

Public concern about the aquifer's future was not abated by the District (and its monitoring and study activities), and several public and private groups continued to pursue the recharge issue in a variety of forums. In 1967, the Texas Water Quality Board was established with jurisdiction over permits for point-source discharges throughout the state, and the environmentalists immediately directed their attentions to this Board. Although the Board responded with a general order governing discharges in the recharge area, it did not have authority over land use, a major issue with environmentalists because of the increasing concern about the pollution potential of development runoff. At about the same time, a City of San Antonio task force was formed to consider a number of issues, including landfills and septic tanks in the recharge area. The task force ultimately recommended to the City Council that septic tanks should be banned. Unfortunately for the activists, most of the recharge area is located outside the corporate limits of the City of San Antonio and was therefore beyond its zoning and subdivision controls; the area under the greatest growth pressure, however, was within the City's extraterritorial jurisdiction, where subdivision controls could be applied.

San Antonio Ranch

The somewhat abstract nature of the debate over the aquifer was transmogrified in 1971, when a development consortium proposed a new 8,000-acre community in the very center of the recharge area. The San Antonio Ranch was proposed under the 1968 Housing Act, and its developers applied for an $18 million grant from the Department of Housing and Urban Development (HUD). The City of San Antonio, apparently oblivious to or unimpressed by the recharge issue, at least in its political persona, welcomed the new community with open arms and endorsed the developer's funding request and signed contracts to provide municipal services to the project. Environmental groups, however, were not so receptive.

Litigation: Environmental Impact

Under the National Environmental Policy Act (NEPA), an environmental impact statement (EIS) is required in conjunction with a grant application, and HUD requires that the developer prepare a draft EIS. When HUD published the San Antonio Ranch developer's draft EIS, the environmentalists were outraged that the document did not even mention the aquifer or its potential pollution. In response, a coalition of environmentalists (the Sierra Club, Citizens for a Better Environment, and the League of Women Voters) filed a lawsuit in federal court challenging the sufficiency of the draft EIS. At a hearing on a preliminary injunction in front of Judge Adrian Spears, several deficiencies in the draft EIS were noted and the developer was given six months to revise the EIS. The coalition of environmentalists (now joined by the Edwards Underground Water District and Bexar County) was still dissatisfied with the revised EIS, and a trial eventually took place in April 1973.

The focus of the trial was the sufficiency of the draft EIS, and although the trial court apparently understood the environmentalists' concern (among the many arguments pressed by the activists was the claim that the draft EIS failed to evaluate the best available alternative — no development and public acquisition of the recharge area), the Court ruled that the EIS did satisfy NEPA's minimum requirements.

The environmentalists appealed. In *Sierra Club* v. *Lynn,* the Fifth Circuit Court of Appeals affirmed the trial court on the grounds that the draft EIS was sufficient, as a matter of law. The environmentalists filed a petition for a writ of certiorari with the U.S. Supreme Court; however, the case was disposed of on the basis of a newly issued Supreme Court opinion on the sufficiency of draft environmental impact statements.

"Super Mall"

In the meantime, the City of San Antonio had been busy. The Anglo City Council, receptive to visions of economic prosperity, rezoned a 129-acre northside parcel of land for what was to be called the "super mall." The site was located in the recharge area, and there was much concern about whether the development, if carried out in accordance with the Texas Water Quality Board's order (substantially amended in 1973) would still pollute the aquifer. The Council's five-to-four vote in favor of the mall was a stinging defeat for environmentalists, particularly for the Aquifer Protection Association (APA), a new group formed in 1974. The APA decided to take the matter to the voters in a referendum to repeal the mall zoning. The mustering of a popular majority to overturn zoning granted by a duly elected City Council would, in the ordinary course of events, be a most difficult task; however, as subsequent events were to show, water pollution was not the only political issue alive and well in the City of San Antonio.

Communities Organized for Public Service (COPS)

In August 1974 (coincidentally the same month that APA was formed), a new political group was formed in San Antonio: Communities Organized for Public Service (COPS). A Mexican-American organization, COPS was created to demand public services for the long-overlooked south side. Organized along the pragmatic lines of Saul Alinsky's theory of "power to the powerless," COPS did its homework about the public service problems plaguing Mexican-American neighborhoods. Ironically, the principal issue for COPS was also water—not drinking water, but flood water. The City of San Antonio found itself confronted by an organization that had its facts, figures, and objectives clearly in order: "Stop spending tax dollars on the Anglo north—it's our turn." And COPS knew how to get attention. In a very short time, peaceful demonstrations, including long lines of Mexican-Americans flooding Anglo banks to change dollars into pennies and vice versa or jamming department stores to "just look," led to pledged support for a $46 million bond issue for drainage improvements. But COPS had bigger things than the drainage issue in mind, at just the time that APA was looking for support to overturn the super-mall zoning. Although the ultimate objectives of APA and COPS were very different, the goal they both sought had a common element: to divert growth and development and its attendant expenditure of public funds away from the north. The APA wanted to protect the aquifer, and COPS wanted "a piece of the action" — or better public service for their people.

Almost 50,000 people signed a petition to overturn the super-mall rezoning. (This was more than double the 20,000 signatures that the environmentalists had previously assembled in support of a petition to purchase the recharge area.) Eleven thousand of the signatures were collected by COPS in just seven days. When the referendum was held in January 1976, the super-mall zoning was crushed by a four-to-one margin, with voters in Mexican-American precincts voting more than sixteen to one in favor of rescinding the zoning. The development community was shocked as they realized that times were changing in San Antonio.

In 1977, it all came together. The developers of San Antonio Ranch, confident from their victory in federal court, were ready to proceed with their plans. Fresh from its victories with the drainage bond issue and the mall referendum, COPS was now a major political force in the City. And APA, reinforced by what it saw as a public mandate to protect the aquifer, was once again demanding a moratorium on growth in the recharge area. Moreover, the new City Charter was in place, with single-member districts for councilmanic elections. When the new Council took office, its composition was much changed and the environmentalists' demand for aquifer protection was supported by the new majority's intention to put a hold on the north side and to direct the City's attention to the south side.

Moratorium on Development

For years, APA had demanded a moratorium on development over the recharge area so that a planning program could be put in place that would redirect growth into the City center and the south side. The new Council members, committed to serving the entire community, saw their election as a political mandate to look into the City's growth policies, and thus they were receptive to the idea of a moratorium both as a substantive matter and as a bold political statement that "things have changed here in old San Antonio." A consultant was hired to study the impact of development on the aquifer, and a moratorium on development was adopted until the study could be completed.

The decision to adopt a moratorium was not without debate and discussion. Some councilmen were concerned about the legality of such a step, while others were concerned with the politics of the move. Others still were wary that the moratorium was too much for the City to take on. Henry Cisneros, an up-and-coming politician and a Mexican-American holdover from the previous Council, tried to forge an alliance for a moderate response to the demand for a moratorium; however, the "moratorium 6," as they would be later known, went for it "all." The moratorium was simple and straightforward. It prohibited the issuance of building permits in the recharge area, the processing of rezoning applications for land in the recharge area, the processing of any plat application for land in the recharge area, and the extensions or connections of city services to land in the recharge area.

Litigation: Encino Park Venture

The developers were apoplectic, particularly the developers of the San Antonio Ranch, who had been working on their project for almost six years and up until that point had the City Council's approval for their project.

The developers' anxiety did not, however, prevent them from filing two lawsuits, one in state court and one in federal district court, seeking to invalidate the moratorium and demanding $750 million in damages in each court. The theory of the lawsuits was simple: the moratorium was unlawful (in many different ways) and the plaintiffs were grievously damaged by the City's action. The federal case was filed in the name of one large-scale developer, the Encino Park Venture, by the same attorney who had represented the San Antonio Ranch in the NEPA litigation and was assigned to Judge Spears, the same judge who had decided the NEPA case.

The federal case proceeded immediately to a hearing on a motion for a preliminary injunction in front of a magistrate appointed by Judge Spears to take evidence in the matter. At the close of the hearing, the magistrate advised the parties that he would make his findings and recommendations in "due time" but he went on to say, "I personally find section 4 of this ordinance most atrocious." His findings of fact were no more generous as he found that (a) tests indicate that there is no pollution of the water in the aquifer, (b) studies prove that development near the aquifer has not caused pollution, (c) existing regulations will prevent pollution of the aquifer, and (d) developers had committed large sums of money to their projects and would sustain substantial damages if the moratorium were allowed to continue in effect. The magistrate's view was not surprising to the City Attorney, who had just submitted an opinion letter to the City Council questioning the constitutionality of the moratorium.

> Pursuant to Council member Dutmer's request for a written legal opinion relative to whether certain provisions of Ordinance 48106 [the moratorium] are contrary to existing state statutes, the answer is *yes*.

Judge Spears, agreeing with both the magistrate and the City Attorney, ruled that the plaintiffs would suffer "immediate and irreparable harm" if the City were not enjoined from

> (1) Enforcing in any way Section Four of Ordinance No. 48106, concerning the construction and installation of all sewer, water, gas or electric service extensions or connections in the areas covered by said Ordinance; (2) enforcing Sections One, Two and Three of Ordinance No. 48106, whenever such enforcement would interfere with the obtaining of building permits, zoning changes, or plat approvals urgently and immediately needed under the terms of any contracts already effective as of the date on which this Order is entered.

The parties agreed to a temporary injunction in the state court proceedings given Judge Spear's action on the preliminary injunction in the federal case.

City Strategy

In response to the judge's order, the City Council decided it ought to get some help and a call was placed to Richard Babcock's office in Chicago. Mayor pro-tem Henry Cisneros, all along a moderate on the moratorium issue, explained the situation to Charles Siemon and invited him to meet with the City Council to discuss defending the case. Siemon flew to San Antonio on the next available plane, and was met at the airport by the Mayor's driver with a copy of the moratorium ordinance. On the way to City Hall, Siemon quickly read through the ordinance and confirmed his worst fears: that the ordinance was beyond help. At this meeting with the City Council, Siemon described the background of his firm and its experience in land use matters; as a result, the firm was hired to defend the City. (Later, the press would nickname us the "windy city mouthpieces.")

A week later Siemon, now reinforced by Babcock, met with the City Council to advise them that the ordinance could not be defended and that the best defense would be to adopt a replacement ordinance. The present ordinance was factually unsupportable and noticeably contrary to a number of well-established principles of law. The only solution was for the Council to prepare a valid moratorium ordinance as soon as possible, *before* the federal court could hold a dispositive hearing on the plaintiff's motion for a permanent injunction.

The strategy we recommended was to fend off the litigation and prepare a new moratorium that responded to several critical points: (a) vested rights, (b) a relief in the event of hardship, (c) a substantive basis broader than water quality (general policy issues), and (d) a distinction in the moratorium in response to the City's limited authority in the extraterritorial jurisdiction.

At a meeting, in private "executive session" to outline this strategy, we strongly suggested that it was desirable to maintain secrecy. This strategy was necessary to avoid a rush to trial on the existing moratorium, at least until the new ordinance could be prepared and adopted, thereby mooting the current difficulties. In the meantime, the lawyers would go on defending the pending actions as if nothing had happened, a suggestion that was seemingly agreed upon. The morning paper made it clear, however, that mum was not the word. Under a banner headline announcing *"Total Aquifer Ban 'No Bueno,' "* the *San Antonio Light* reported that we had advised that "a total construction moratorium over the Edwards Aquifer Recharge Zone is not legally possible, and modifications should be made to the existing city ordinance."[1] The paper went on to detail the City's tactical plans complete with a schedule of events.

Northside Independent School District

To make matters worse, the Northside Independent School District filed its own action in the federal court. The heart of the school district's action was that the effect of the moratorium was to reduce the value of affected lands during the effective period and therefore had reduced *ad valorem* tax revenues upon which the school district depended. This in turn prevented the school district from carrying out a long-planned expansion in the recharge area. The City responded to the school district's action, which was consolidated with the pending *Encino Park Venture,* with a motion to dismiss on a number of relatively esoteric grounds. One such claim was that since the school district was a political subdivision of the state, it had no standing to raise federal questions in a federal court against another political subdivision of the same state.

The magistrate assigned to the case concluded that the school district did not have standing to raise the federal questions; however, the Court adopted the findings of fact from *Encino Park* in case the district

[1] June 30, 1977, p. 1.

TOTAL AQUIFER BAN 'NO BUENO'

Headline from San Antonio Light, *June 30, 1977.*

judge were to find that the school district did have standing. Despite our recommendation to file objections to these findings, the City chose not to file objections because the magistrate's result was favorable to the City. Unfortunately, Judge Spears reversed the standing issue, and after observing that "no objections were filed by the defendant to these findings and conclusions," lowered the boom on the City once again:

> This Court finds a substantial likelihood that the moratorium will be found unduly oppressive at a subsequent trial on the merits, given the end for which it was passed. It is stated in Ordinance 48106 that continued development over the Edwards Aquifer "may cause pollution" and that "the City has no assurance that any given development will not degrade the quality of water." . . . However there appears to be no present danger to the City's water supply warranting the passage of the present ordinance, given the harmful result its enforcement would bring. There is a substantial likelihood that the challenged moratorium is sufficiently unreasonable as to be unconstitutional, in violation of Fourteenth Amendment due process.

There was one piece of encouraging news in the Court's order. During the proceedings, we made much ado about the damages claim alleged by the school district. Given the collective damage claims of the various plaintiffs for more than $1.5 billion, the City notified the Court that there was substantial precedent that damages would not be an appropriate remedy. The trial court agreed, providing the City with some sense that its exposure might be limited to injunctive relief:

> The City has cited persuasive authority to the effect that a municipality is not liable in damages for the enforcement or attempted enforcement of an ordinance which is not "unreasonable or void on its face" in which category the instant ordinance belongs.

New Moratorium

In the aftermath of the Court's order, we began to prepare a new moratorium ordinance, an ordinance designed to avoid the deficiencies of the first ordinance. The first of these deficiencies was to broaden the justification of the ban beyond the water issue. The Court obviously believed that there was no real threat to the aquifer. Moreover, the City's engineering consultant had admitted in a deposition that his study was unlikely to generate significant new information about the aquifer and its sensitivity to pollution by land development in the recharge area (an Assistant City Attorney reported that Siemon gasped audibly at that point in the deposition); therefore, it was recommended that the ban be placed in the context of the City Council's more general mandate for a truly comprehensive plan for the City. The preamble to the new ordinance was expanded to serve a host of identified public needs:

> It is essential that the issues of the protection of the City's water supply and growth in areas that may eventually be annexed to the City be considered as part of a comprehensive review and articulation of the City's land development and growth policies.

Chastened by the Court's criticism of the first ordinance (Ordinance No. 48106), the authors of the new ordinance left nothing to chance and included a very clear policy statement of purpose and intent in the ordinance:

> a. It shall be the policy of the City of San Antonio to defer development decisions, the installation of public utility infrastructure and the commitment of land to particular kinds of use in the Edwards Aquifer recharge zone and drainage area until the City's on-going study of the hydrological properties of the aquifer and the relationship of those properties to the location, character, and magnitude of development is completed, and a comprehensive plan for the protection of the potable water supply of the City of San Antonio and a rational and reasonable pattern of growth for the City can be adopted.
>
> b. It shall, however, also be the policy of the City of San Antonio to permit development to proceed where a developer is able to demonstrate that the proposed development, individually or cumulatively will not have an adverse effect on the quality or quantity of water in the Edwards Underground Aquifer and is unlikely to impair in whole or in part the goals and objectives of the comprehensive planning process.
>
> c. It shall further be a policy of the City of San Antonio to permit the completion of those developments where because of prior acts of government, there has been good faith, detrimental reliance, such that it would be inequitable to delay completion of the proposed development until the comprehensive planning process if concluded.

Similarly, the new ordinance did not lump the City's powers together (recalling that a portion of the recharge area was in the extraterritorial area where the City's zoning power did not extend), the ordinance set out a careful separate statement of prohibition for building permits, rezonings, plat approval, and water service.

Another major area of reform involved the question of vested rights. The initial moratorium had been interpreted as basically requiring that all development in the recharge area cease, even when a project was 95 percent completed. Not too surprisingly, the Court was concerned about the breadth of this total building ban and its impact on pre-existing contractual rights and enjoined any enforcement of the ordinance. A key section of the new ordinance provided for the recognition of claims of vested rights.

> Developers who claim vested rights to develop may . . . submit an application for development approval during the effective period of this ordinance. In determining whether the applicant has vested rights, the City Council shall consider whether the applicant has demonstrated:
> a) an act of an agency of the City of San Antonio
> b) upon which the developer has in good faith relied to his determinent,
> c) such that it would be inequitable to require the applicant to delay development during the time this ordinance is in effect.

If a landowner could demonstrate that he met the criteria by way of a carefully proscribed procedure, then he would be allowed to proceed with development.

Natural Resources Disclosure Statement

In addition, the draft ordinance allowed development during its effective period if a landowner could demonstrate that the development, by itself or cumulatively, would not have an adverse impact on the quality or quantity of water in the aquifer. By filing a Natural Resources Disclosure Statement (affectionately known as "NRDS"), a landowner could be granted approval if the required element of a NRDS demonstrated no adverse impact. Finally, the ordinance provided for a periodic review every six months to ensure that its continued enforcement was in the City's best interests.

Impact on Development

For developments like the San Antonio Ranch and Encino Park Venture, the new ordinance (Ordinance No. 48484) fell far short of ideal, but it was a great improvement over the previous ordinance. Both developers ultimately applied for and received approval for incremental approvals under the vested rights provision because of their prior approvals and their reliance expenditures.

The Northside Independent School District was less enthusiastic, presumably because it had not previously secured development approval and therefore would not qualify for a determination of vested rights. The school district pressed the federal court to proceed. The Court took the new ordinance under advisement and on November 18, 1977, entered an order that effectively put the litigation to rest over the objection of the school district. Advised that the developers and the City had reached a "détente" in regard to the new ordinance, the Court deftly avoided upsetting the situation by severing the school district from the *Encino Park Venture* case and then abstaining on the grounds that the new ordinance left the school district's complaint to turn on an unresolved question of state law.

The Court's order of abstention was, in and of itself, comforting to the City in that it eliminated a threat to the uneasy truce between the developers and the City. Nevertheless, the Court provided further comfort and went on to observe that the new ordinance was a reasonable exercise of police power:

> In an effort to avoid the clear constitutional deficiencies from which the first ordinance suffered, the present Ordinance recognizes the need to protect the "vested rights" of developers and others. . . .
>
> This Court cannot immediately conclude that the present Ordinance No. 48484 is not "reasonable and realistic." It is true that previous proceedings revealed no very great likelihood of immediate danger to the Edwards Aquifer from continued development over the recharge zone. . . . *The present Ordinance is significantly more reasonable in its* operation. Justification for the previous ordinance was based almost entirely upon the need to prevent pollution of the Edwards Aquifer, whereas the present law is supported both by this rationale and by the need to slow immediate expansion over the Aquifer until the City can prepare "a comprehensive review and articulation of the City's land development and growth policies. . . ." [Emphasis added.]

Aquifer Study

For the moment the hostilities had been quelled, and the City could turn to the task of translating political rhetoric and emotion into programs and reality. The aquifer study, ill fated from the outset, suffered delay after delay but was finally released in the summer of 1979. The study contained two very interesting but disappointing findings, according to one of the environmental activists:

There was a risk of pollution. And that, if the City continued development on the recharge zone, they were running the risk of polluting the aquifer. The problem with limestone aquifers is that they don't renovate themselves. So if you pollute it you have to abandon it. Then the other thing they said was a problem . . . was that the aquifer moves and if the City uses regulatory power to limit development on the recharge zone, they would be liable to suit from people who would have been regulated because in reality the water that would enter the recharge zone within the City's jurisdiction was not the water that San Antonio would be drinking because it would go in and move downstream and therefore we would be protecting San Marcus. And that was an improper use of the regulatory powers.

To the environmentalists, the study was a disappointment because it did not contribute significantly to the knowledge about the aquifer and led to very little reform. Essentially, the report left the City in the position of being legally powerless to take regulatory action:

> The report did suggest other regulations, namely what you could do with the subdivision regulations in relation to the way the drainage was managed. Since it was done for flood protection anyway, you could do it for other reasons and not be challenged. And they suggested what some of those might be. . . . The city did not pursue that at all. A little aside was that a guy from [Texas] A&M got a class to pursue that and take it one step further and produced a little booklet with some suggested ways to handle this. The City did participate in that. They allowed personnel to be part of that exercise. They even agreed to bear the cost of printing a short report, but again nothing else happened. Everybody was still upset.

More Studies and Reports

In the spring of 1980 the City's Planning Department completed a major review of available information and concluded that the City could not, on its own, protect the aquifer and recommended that the City petition the Texas Department of Water Resources for more stringent controls for the recharge zone. The City, according to most observers, was rapidly maturing as a progressive sunbelt growth area and had learned a lot from the moratorium experience, as later recounted by Jane Macon, an Assistant City Attorney when the aquifer litigation was initiated. Macon was elevated amid the litigation when the City Attorney (who had declared the moratorium invalid and recommended against its approval) resigned.

> We got . . . a lot of the growth/no-growth questions resolved and worked through before we were truly faced with some major growth problems. . . . And I think the moratorium had educational effects on the City of San Antonio. One, the whole issue was put under a microscope which it prob-

ably would have never been put under but for the lawsuit and but for the work that was done by the lawyers.

And the City was beginning to pull together, rather than apart. Macon again:

> We worked hard on economic development, . . . and one of the things we found was that when we're promoting the City we have a lot of private sector people who go with us at their own expense to help promote the City. . . . And how do you get people to be so high on the City of San Antonio? I think maybe that some of that is tradition. There's really a total commitment. It's not just the Council, it's not just the Mayor or the manager [who is] supposed to solve the sanitary problems. It's all of us together.

This philosophy began to work on the aquifer issue as well. In the fall of 1981, the City sponsored a series of workshops in a regional-management approach to protecting the aquifer; however, another issue began to play a role in the aquifer question — water quantity. The City's staggering growth resurrected the surface water-supply issue, and a new municipal task force was appointed to investigate the problem — whether it was cost effective to look to another source of water rather than protect the aquifer. The debate over the aquifer, it seemed, was to be endless and indeed the task force's recommendation was still another study — of the regional economics of a regional water-supply strategy.

New Regulations

Then in 1983, without worrying, the Texas Department of Water Resources promulgated a revised set of regulations for the recharge area including a permit requirement for all developments larger than five acres. More important, the new regulations required a "Water Pollution Abatement Plan" to mitigate pollution potential and a detailed geological and hydrological analysis as a part of the permit process. No one suggests that the new regulations guarantee the integrity of the aquifer; however, even the environmentalists are encouraged by the new initiative:

> It prohibits cattle feed lots, it prohibits any kind of toxic waste. . . . It specifies very carefully the type of sewage connections that are required. . . . All development of more than 5 acres had to have a permit . . . and when you apply for the permit, you have to include something called a water pollution abatement. . . .
> And then the interesting part is if your plan is approved, that is if the subdivision or whatever the development plan is including the water pollution abatement is approved by the TWR, the existence of this plan has to be entered on the deed record as a covenant to the property. And any

change in the development from the plan that is so filed requires a new approval, you have to back through the process and get it approved.

What it all means is hard to tell. The City surely learned from the litigation—no one likes to be sued for $1.5 billion. And the replacement moratorium showed the way for decision-making processes that accommodate reasonable expectations. Yet the government took six years to react to the obvious need for further protection and the progress, significant as it is, is still viewed by long-time participants as "something from nothing," but only something.

6

Sanibel Island: A Paradise Lost and Saved

> *The piece of coast that trends east and west is the beach of an island called Sanibel. This place is further remarkable for a great number of pine trees without tops standing at the bottom of the Bay like which there is no spot in the whole extent of this coast. The northernmost entrance is likewise remarkable for a singular hammock, or grove of pine-trees standing very near the beach and the only one of its form and kind in all these parts.*
>
> Romans R, *Instruction to Mariners* (1769), as recounted in Elinore Dormer, *The Sea Shell Islands* (Vantage Press, 1975).

Sanibel Island is still remarkable along the southwest coast of Florida. Its topless pine trees and singular hammocks are, however, no longer its most notable feature. Sanibel is, according to serious shell collectors, one of the great shelling beaches in the world, and each year thousands and thousands of visitors do the "Sanibel Stoop" along the Island's white sand beaches in search of the Island's abundant shells. The Island is also the home of the J. N. ("Ding") Darling National Wildlife Refuge, where more than a million visitors a year have an opportunity to view several hundred species of birds by simply driving through the heart of the 4,750-acre wetland refuge on a one-way shell road. There are few, if any, places in the world where the average citizen has such easy access to ecological treasures.

Sanibel lies just offshore the City of Ft. Myers in Lee County, Florida, one of the fastest-growing areas in the nation and the "resplendent" home of Cape Coral, a 58-square-mile subdivision of "cookie cutter" lots,

Authors' note: Ross and Hardies were attorneys for the City.

an earth scar that is literally visible from the moon. Unlike the rest of the barrier islands along the southwest coast of Florida that lie parallel to the Coast on a north–south axis, Sanibel, which is about twelve miles long tip-to-tip, is oriented along an east–west axis. The orientation of Sanibel is suggested by some as the reason for the exceptional shelling on its white sand beaches.

The Island is not all white sand beaches. Indeed, Sanibel's beaches, which are classified by scientists as low-profile, low-energy beaches with dunes or sand drifts of less than five feet, are limited to the Island's southern edge. The balance is a mosaic of freshwater wetlands, ancient sand dunes or ridges, tropical hardwood hammocks, and mangrove forests. Bald eagles, roseate spoonbills, herons, egrets, and a host of other birds reside on or visit the Island, as do alligators, sea turtles, and other tropical fauna. The Island has little relief with ridge lines only five feet above mean sea level, exposing even the most developable lands to flooding in almost any sort of hurricane.

Sanibel's Growth

Prior to 1963, Sanibel and its sister island of Captiva were accessible from the mainland only by boat or by car ferry, and consequently the islands were largely undeveloped. A scattering of houses and cottages served as winter homes for the faithful following of visitors, many of whom were noted conservationists, including J. N. ("Ding") Darling, founder of the National Wildlife Federation. In 1963, a causeway was extended across San Carlos Bay from the mainland to the Island, and Sanibel began, slowly at first, to become a part of the most recent of the great Florida land-development booms. Sanibel has experienced many traumas during its 5,000-year geological history, not the least of which was a 1926 hurricane, which overtopped the island with fourteen-foot waves; however, direct automobile access to the island signaled a change of epic proportions.

In 1960, the last time a hurricane graced the "Seashell Island" (more than nineteen storms have made landfall near Sanibel this century), there were only 300 dwelling units (including cottages and motel rooms) on Sanibel. By 1974, the number of residential units on the island had increased to over 4,000, and the first beachfront "condominiums" had been completed. Building permits for more than 500 dwelling units were issued by Lee County in 1974 alone, and concern about growth and the future of the Island were major topics of discussion among Sanibelites.

Concern about growth and development on Sanibel had in fact been a volatile subject long before condominiums began to spring up along

Sanibel's secluded beaches. When the causeway appeared to be inevitable, despite strong local opposition, a group of Island activists persuaded the Florida Legislature to create a "Sanibel Island Zoning Authority." Unfortunately, the Act creating the authority was struck down by the courts as unconstitutional, leaving the Island's future in the hands of the Board of County Commissioners of Lee County, a body that subsequent events would reveal was either incapable of or uninterested in planning and managing for Sanibel's future.

During the late 1960s, residents of the Island intensified their efforts to persuade Lee County to prepare a comprehensive plan for the county's barrier islands, including Sanibel. After several years of political debate, including a major dispute over a proposed trailer park, Lee County actually hired a planning consultant to prepare a plan for the Island. The result of the planner's deliberations, which was released in 1968, was something less than Sanibel residents had hoped for. The plan called for high-rise condominiums along the Gulf beach and a four-lane bypass through the heart of the "Ding" Darling Wildlife Refuge. Sanibel residents were outraged at the plan they had demanded the County to prepare and, in a perverse turn of events, lobbied for its rejection. Ultimately the plan was rejected; however, the bulk of the Island was zoned for high-density residential and commercial use. The zoning applied to Sanibel by Lee County would permit as many as 35,000 dwelling units on the Island.

Sanibel-Captiva Planning Board

By this time, the residents of the islands were well organized and had formed the Sanibel–Captiva Planning Board, Inc. The Planning Board proposed a number of zoning initiatives to the County. Some of these proposals were accepted (thirty-five-foot height limitation and a density limitation of twenty-two units) but many were not, and the inhabitants' frustration with the County's failure to plan for and control growth did not abate. A comprehensive planning effort for the islands that would have reduced densities to 15,000 dwelling units was prepared by the Sanibel–Captiva Island Planning Board, but no action to implement its terms was ever taken by the County. As one activist in the Sanibel planning effort put it, Sanibel residents feared that the causeway would be the ruination of the Island; in fact, it took ten years before it made an appreciable difference. According to Porter J. Goss, former Mayor of Sanibel:

Sure there was a dramatic difference where the rape and scrape went on in one big subdivision, but that was just one isolated area. In other words, the thing didn't ignite instantly, it sort of hung fire until the early 70s, when it started to ignite. And it was quite clear, that when that ignition took place the county government was standing there with cans of gasoline ready to really turn it into a hot conflagration.

Simply put, the County's perspective was that it was business as usual on Sanibel, and construction on the island increased 72 percent in 1973. Condominiums were springing up all along the Island's once-secluded beaches, and the County's disregard of the residents' pleas created in the residents' minds the specter of Sanibel turning into another "Miami Beach," an east coast barrier island described by one appellate court in Florida as the "concrete Himalayas."[1] Interestingly enough, historical descriptions of the environment and economy of Miami Beach bear a striking resemblance to the undeveloped Sanibel:

> Growth of Miami Beach in three decades has been phenomenal, in large part, if not entirely, due to its attractiveness to those who would escape business cares, the rigors of northern winters and the ravages of disease. Situated on a narrow peninsula between the Atlantic Ocean and an arm of it known as the Biscayne Bay, blessed with a warm climate and fanned by the southeast trades, it has become known as one of the earth's principal vacation places.[2]

Incorporation

Clearly, the citizens of Sanibel concluded, there had to be another way, and in mid-1973, several organizations joined forces to carry out a study of three alternative approaches: work with the County, establish a special zoning district for the Island, or incorporate the Island as a new municipality.

Working with the County was viewed as no alternative at all, according to Goss, who led the study effort:

> I mean to the point where one Commissioner sent out a letter to all the constituents on Sanibel using a developer's stationery. That is a comment not only on the closeness of the County to the developers but on the stupidity of the Commissioners and how out of touch they were.

Special zoning districts had fallen into disfavor in the State of Florida; thus the only real option seemed to be incorporation. When a straw vote at a community meeting on Sanibel supported incorporation, a new group

---

[1] *City of Hollywood* v. *Hollywood, Inc.* 432 So.2d 1332,1335 (Fla. 4th DCA 1983).
[2] *City of Miami Beach* v. *Ocean and Inland Co.*, 3 So.2d 364, 365-6 (Fla. 1941).

was formed, the Sanibel Home Rule Study Group. The study group employed a consultant to prepare the legislation necessary to create the city. The preamble to the proposed Charter of the City of Sanibel said it all:

> Whereas, residents of Sanibel Island in Lee County, Florida, desiring to have the rights of self-determination to the fullest extent allowed by law, in the planning for the orderly future development of an Island Community known far and wide for its unique atmosphere and unusual natural environment, and to insure compliance with such planning so that these unique and natural characteristics of the Island shall be preserved, do seek the benefits conferred on municipal corporations by the Constitution and laws of the State of Florida.

In May of 1974, the Legislature enacted House Bill 4001, which established the City of Sanibel subject to approval by a referendum of the Island's residents. And after a series of last-minute maneuvers failed to derail the incorporation drive, the Board of County Commissioners set the incorporation referendum for the November general election. On November 5, 1974, the City of Sanibel became a reality. Nevertheless, Lee County officials had one more "bite" of the apple and responded to the City's establishment by issuing $10 million worth of building permits for beachfront condominiums during the forty-one days it took to elect and seat the first City Council.

The success of the incorporation drive is attributed by many to a relative newcomer on the island, Porter Goss. Goss, then 35, had been recently retired because of medical problems from the Central Intelligence Agency, where he had been a political analyst. Almost immediately he became involved with the group trying to save the Island, and it was he who was selected Chairman of the Home Rule Study Group. All CIA employees are pledged to secrecy about their training and experience, and therefore Goss's background and experience in regard to politics and influencing local affairs will never be known; however, it hardly can be considered a mere coincidence that the drive for political independence found new strength at the same time he became active in the movement to save Sanibel. Goss (as it turned out) was but one of the number of former federal government officials who had retired to Sanibel, including several individuals who had apparently also served in the CIA. Another key actor was Vernon MacKenzie, a retired federal administrator who many described as the "father of federal programs for air- and water-quality protection" because of his pioneering work as a deputy surgeon general of the United States. Goss himself considers Vernon MacKenzie's extensive technical knowledge about government a major factor in the success of the effort. In any event, Goss, MacKenzie, and their compatriots brought a wealth of experience to the Island, and the success that was achieved is largely attributable to their efforts.

One key element in the drive for incorporation was extensive media coverage of the Sanibel situation, coverage that was achieved through a new paper on the Island, *The Island Reporter*. Later events would confirm that Goss, who provided coverage of the incorporation effort for *The Island Reporter*, was also a principal in the new paper and that some of the paper's staff had also been CIA employees. Goss dismisses suggestions of bias and believes that the facts, not any pro-incorporation perspective, made *The Island Reporter's* coverage so important.

Comprehensive Plan

On December 16, 1974, the City Council of the City of Sanibel assumed responsibility for the health, safety, and welfare of the Island by implementing the City's charter mandate for a comprehensive plan. Goss, the highest vote-getter in the councilmanic election, was elected Mayor. Vernon Mackenzie, Francis Bailey (a long-time resident of Sanibel and proprietor of Bailey's Store, an island landmark for years), Charles LeBuff (a field biologist for the Fish and Wildlife Service and Director of Project Caretta, a sea turtle conservation group), and Zee Butler (an ardent civic activist) rounded out Sanibel's first City Council. To give themselves time to gain control over the Island's future, the Council adopted a ninety-day moratorium on the issuance of new building permits. The moratorium eventually would be modified and extended until July 19, 1976, when the City would finally adopt its new comprehensive plan.

There were a number of distractions as the new City learned the ropes of municipal governance. One of the more notable was a lawsuit challenging the validity of the City's incorporation. While the lawsuit itself was not particularly threatening, it prevented the City from borrowing money for operating expenses, a critical need because tax revenues would not be available until late 1975. Commercial banks, not surprisingly, were hesitant to loan money to a city whose very existence was being contested in court. Nevertheless, the spirit that created Sanibel came to its rescue and, within seventy-two hours, residents pledged to purchase $250,000 of tax-anticipation notes.

Most veterans of Sanibel's early days suggest that Sanibel ironically is indebted to Walter Condon, the developer who challenged the incorporation, for the suit brought Island residents together in support of the new city. As Porter Goss says:

> If there hadn't been a Walter Condon we would have had to invent him and we should put a statue to him at the end of the bridge because it was clear that he was able to give us a focal point for a sense of outrage and

Dunes Subdivision under construction, Sanibel Island, October 1974.

to provide credibility to what we were doing and to show that the threat to the Island was real.

In March of 1975, the City Council selected William Roberts, of the Philadelphia environmental planning firm of Wallace, McHarg, Roberts and Todd (WMRT), as a planning consultant. Many of the City's planning commissioners and councilmen had read Ian McHarg's *Design with Nature* and felt its theme was responsive to the island's circumstances. Fred Bosselman, our former partner, was a subcontractor on the WMRT team, and Charles Siemon was assigned to the project. The planning team commenced their work in earnest in April, and by the end of the month, citizen task forces were fanned out all over the island to collect data and opinions about various issues. The WMRT work program called for three phases: a general data report, a series of alternative levels of growth, and finally a plan. When the data report was completed, the planners presented the growth alternatives accompanied by an impressive array of graphically portrayed background data.

The planner's analysis presented four growth alternatives: 2,000, 4,000, 12,000, and 20,000 additional dwelling units. Each level of growth was characterized by its impact on various public services, the environment, and the quality of life on the Island. The planning consultants recommended level one, and the Planning Commission agreed: what Lee County had zoned for 35,000 dwelling units was to be reduced to 6,000 units. The developers were very obviously upset with this recommendation.

Not surprisingly, the Sanibel planning effort was met by an army of lawyers employed to protect landowners' and investors' development expectations. At each public hearing on the draft plan, planning commissioners, who were dressed in slacks and sport shirts, were challenged by lawyers clad in pinstripes and sharkskins. The sight of a lawyer in a three-piece suit suffering through a tropical heat wave underscored the sharp contrasts that had to be reconciled in the planning process. In retrospect, many people suggest that the threat to the planning process posed by these legal dragoons was an important element of the Plan's ultimate success. One councilman observed that "the more these people bellowed and hollered and did their thing, and were mean and nasty, the more sympathy the City Council had and the more support the City had and the more fuel the City had to accomplish what needed to be done."

Pre-Plan Litigation–Vested Rights

Even though the adoption date of a comprehensive plan had been put off from December 1975 to sometime in 1976, many property owners or developers concluded that there was no reason to wait until a plan was complete before filing their lawsuits. Several landowners, sure their dreams of development were not going to be acceptable to the new City, filed legal challenges to the City's moratorium. At first, the City did not fare too well and a large condominium-hotel, the "Sundial" project, was found to have vested rights to complete its future phases as originally planned. The City's defense in the *Sundial* case focused on the so-called red flags doctrine, which holds that vested rights are not acquired when "warning flags" of a change in land use controls are flying. Unfortunately, the Florida Supreme Court receded from the red flags doctrine and the City lost in the trial court. The City appealed the trial court judgment and hired Bosselman and Siemon to assist in the appeal. The City's position was simple: *Sundial* was a precedent-setter, and the City had to do whatever it could to undo the decision. Ultimately, after all briefs had been filed, the developer and the City compromised their respective positions and the matter was settled without entry of a precedental holding. The pattern had nevertheless been set, and the City of Sanibel found itself confronted by a parade of landowners and developers who found their plans and expectations for development frustrated by the new Plan and now claimed "vested rights."

It had always been anticipated that the principal legal issue in the planning effort would be the "taking issue." Indeed, Bosselman had been selected, at least in part, because he was the principal author of the book *The Taking Issue.* Most of the litigation that actually ensued, however, focused on claims of vested rights, a subject Siemon would later conclude was much ignored in planning law.

In part, the landowner's reluctance to press their claims of a "taking" was a result of their unwillingness to take on the substantive elements of the planning program and its carrying-capacity analysis. The City's principal justification for reduced densities was a policy decision that every resident on the Island should have a realistic opportunity to evacuate in the event of a hurricane. Because only a limited number of automobiles could be evacuated across the causeway during the twelve-hour period projected to be available for evacuation, the Plan limited future population to a number that could be evacuated safely. In contrast to the vague justifications for density found in most zoning ordinances, hurricane evacuation capacity represented a clear and objective measure of appropriate densities. Moreover, the City's meteorological consultant, Dr. Robert H. Simpson, the "father" of modern hurricane meteorology, was himself a significant deterrent to "taking" litigation because his knowledge and reputation were unassailable.

More importantly, a vested rights suit involved a *de novo* judicial proceeding free from the cloak of a "fairly debatable" rule.

The Plan

The draft plan was presented to the City in December of 1975. It divided the island into a series of ecozones, and allocated densities and uses according to the developmental tolerance of each category of land. Mangroves and other wetlands were assigned densities of one dwelling unit per thirty-three acres, while gulf-front properties were slated for five dwelling units per acre. Residential densities were further adjusted on the basis of availability of public services and distance from the built-up or established part of the City. The western, undeveloped part of the island, where the "Ding" Darling Wildlife Refuge was located, was allocated significantly lower densities than lands in the eastern, built-up sectors.

During the first seven months of 1976 all attention was focused on the planning process as the Planning Commission and then the City Council laboriously discharged their responsibilities under Florida's new Local Government Comprehensive Planning Act. The LGCPA, as it is affectionately known, was adopted in May of 1975, further complicating an already complex planning effort and subjecting Sanibel's Plan to the role of a "guinea pig" as the first plan approved under the new act. The public hearings were long and often contentious as landowners decried the economic disaster they were sure the Plan would produce. Slowly the Plan moved through the procedural maze required for approval, and on July 19, 1976, it was adopted by the City Council.

Councilmanic Election

Notwithstanding the adoption of the Plan, opponents continued to invoke visions of economic disaster and promised to take the matter to the voters in the fall when four councilmanic seats would be up for election. Although confident that the Plan was right for the Island, the incumbents were concerned that the Plan's impact on year-round residents (still a large part of the electorate) might result in a strong anti-Plan ticket. Significant opposition never materialized, and the three incumbents who stood for re-election ran unopposed—a tacit endorsement of the Plan. The election of the fifth Councilman, however, constituted the Good Housekeeping Seal of Approval for the planning effort. Vernon MacKenzie, the former U.S. health official who contributed so much to the Plan, had resigned his office because of poor health. Two candidates filed for MacKenzie's seat—Duane White, the Chairman of the City's Planning Commission, who had shepherded the Plan through the Commission, and an outspoken opponent of the plan. The opponent of the Plan was originally a supporter of the planning effort, but had become disenchanted when she learned that her plans for a trailer park on her land were going to be inconsistent with the Plan. The former chairman of the Planning Commission's platform (in Florida you have to resign to run) was the Plan, and his election with 70 percent of the vote was a clear victory for the Plan and its proponents.

Post-Plan Litigation

In the aftermath of the Plan's adoption, more than a dozen significant lawsuits were filed. The claims were strikingly similar and for the most part alleged that a developer or landowner had relied on some County approval in making substantial expenditures on a development. Most of the suits followed the theory of the *Sundial* case and alleged prior approval by the County — in some cases nothing more than a phone call to some County official — and expenditures in reliance on the approval.

Fortunately for the besieged city, now fortified with the lesson learned in *Sundial,* the first post-Plan vested rights case was decided in its favor. The City had by this time retained Bosselman and Siemon to handle the new litigation. The suit, which involved a proposed mobile home park, was patently modeled after the complaint and judgment in the *Sundial* case. The difficulty was that the developer had not received a rezoning from the County prior to the City's incorporation, nor had building permits been issued. Moreover, the only "hard" reliance expenditures that could be offered were lake excavation costs carried out by the developer's predecessor in title, before the alleged government approvals. The turning point in the litigation, however, had very little to do with vested rights law.

Under examination by the City's counsel, the developer admitted that the legal instrument that purported to give him an interest in the property prior to the incorporation of the City (upon which he claimed a vested right) had actually been prepared by his attorney at the same time as the complaint in the lawsuit in November 1975, one year after the City's formation. The developer initially testified that he was "sure" the lease had been executed prior to the City's incorporation but, when confronted with irrefutable evidence that it could not have been, he admitted that the lease had been backdated for the purposes of the litigation.

The "evidence" that exposed the backdating was the signature of a witness who, as it turned out, had been the City Attorney's secretary in 1974 and had not gone to work for the developer's attorney until mid-1975. Moreover, a local attorney, called as a witness on the developer's behalf, testified that it was a common practice to backdate legal instruments in Lee County and that he did it "all the time." Clearly, the Court's esteem for the developer was not enhanced by this witness. Vested rights in Florida are controlled by equitable principles, including a requirement that one who seeks equitable relief must come to the court with "clean hands," a status that the developer was no longer able to claim. The Court denied the developer's claim that he had a right to develop a trailer park nonwithstanding the newly adopted plan.

The victory was important to the City and its new Plan, and a sense of confidence that Sanibel would be conserved, if not saved, began to grow in the County. The victory did not deter aggrieved landowners from pursuing their litigation, however, and the City was actively involved in litigation for four years after the Plan's adoption. Nevertheless, many of the cases were settled as landowners reassessed the City's resolve and chose to compromise rather than fight. Not every case had a happy ending. In one case involving a very large golf-course subdivision, the developer, a popular Lee County resident, was killed in a private plane crash just weeks before trial. The equities of the developer's claim of vested rights shifted dramatically in the hands of his widow and a compromise was quickly reached prior to trial.

Property Value Increase

While the "vested rights cases" plodded forward in the courts, a phenomenon was underway on the Island that had been forecast by the City's economic consultant, but was doubted by many observers, including almost all local developers and bankers. The law of supply and demand drove the value of a Sanibel dwelling unit up dramatically. Two years after the Plan was in place, the appraised value of properties on the Island had doubled despite a sevenfold reduction in density. The first sign of this phenomenon, later to be described in an esoteric land economics paper entitled "Comprehensive Planning as Just Compensation," was a series of land acquisitions by an aggressive developer on the Island. The developer had come to Sanibel only two years before the incorporation drive and had opposed the Plan's adoption because he believed the proposed severe density restrictions would destroy the Island's tourist-based economy. Nevertheless, when the Plan became law, the developer took advantage of a clustering provision and developed a sixteen-unit condominium on the beach at the previously unheard of density of five dwelling units per acre. (The nominal density prior to the plan for such projects was 22 dwelling units per acre.) The project sold out almost immediately at prices that were three times the price of condominiums on the Island at the time the City was incorporated.

The increase in values did far more than comfort Island residents and landowners; the City used this market strength to defend itself in the vested-rights cases. In one case, the developer of a subdivision originally had planned to develop a large number of lots. After receiving preliminary plat approval, improvements were put in place for the project and Phase I was opened up for lot sales. When the City was formed and a moratorium declared, lots in the subdivision sold for about $10,000. Under the new Plan, the total number of dwelling units permitted on the site was reduced and the developer claimed it was "highly inequitable" to deprive him of his right to complete his project as planned. The City's evidence showed that the reduction in the number of units permitted would not lower the developer's expectations because of a rise in land values triggered by the Plan. In fact, the evidence showed that the Plan actually increased the per-square-foot value of the developer's land. Two lots valued at $10,000 each prior to the Plan could be combined under the Plan and were appraised at a value of $25,000.

Commercial Zoning

The Plan was not impregnable. During the planning process, the City leaders had little trouble being tough with reduced residential densities for environmental protection, and in large measure, the policy recommendations of the planning consultants were understood and followed. The story was a little different, however, when it came to commercial zoning along the Island's major east–west road, Periwinkle Way. Under Lee County zoning, both sides of the road had been zoned business along most of its length. The planning consultants recommended that commercial uses be clustered at nodes along Periwinkle Way as a means of facilitating traffic movement along this critical roadway. The planners recommended that nonconforming uses between the nodes be phased out over time, or at least in the event of abandonment or destruction.

For business interests along Periwinkle Way that were classified as nonconforming it was "the end of the line," and some of the environment's staunchest supporters spoke against the Plan. The commercial cluster and nonconforming use issues, of course, were not as clear to the public as the environmental issues. Scattered commercial uses along Periwinkle Way were a part of the Island's character; nevertheless, the possibility of a corridor of continuous curb cuts constituted a real threat to the Island's quality of life. Traffic congestion was already a major seasonal problem, and engineering solutions that had been considered, including a bypass through several thousand acres of wetlands, were seen as unacceptable. Eventually, political "pressure" won, and the City, attempting to strike a "balance between public and private interests," adopted the node policy but grandfathered in perpetuity all nonconforming uses, even if abandoned or destroyed.

Predictably, a landowner, sandwiched between two of what the City now called "lawfully existing uses," brought a lawsuit challenging the residential zoning applied to his previously commercially zoned property. The case was unusual because the plaintiff, John Goode, was the City's building official who, in an ironic twist of fate, had to "resign to sue." Sanibel's leaders were in a dilemma. On the one hand, it made little sense to maintain commercial zoning on the property, which fronted on the Island's major east–west road and backed up to a mobile home park; on the other hand, it was an assault on the Plan. The City defended with vigor. Unfortunately—or fortunately, depending on one's perspective—the trial and appellate courts had little trouble seeing through the City's defenses and the zoning was invalidated.

> The city forcefully argues that the trial court failed to accord proper credence to the City's comprehensive plan. The court, however, did afford proper credence by weighing the plan's protection of the public health, safety and welfare against the harm caused to Goode by the plan's application to his property. . . .
>
> . . . As noted, Goode purchased his property prior to consideration of the City's new zoning plan. And, while diminution in value does not by itself invalidate an otherwise valid zoning ordinance, we cannot ignore the testimony before the court which showed a decrease in value, from $105,000 for Goode's property as commercially zoned, to $17,500 for it as residentially zoned property.[3]

In the meantime, the City of Sanibel had become a reality and the real estate market responded to the City's strict control of its future. Understanding that the Island's character would endure, the pace of development (albeit consistent with the requirements of the Plan) astounded even the most ardent believer that good planning is good business. Available land was being developed at an incredible rate at a density that just two years before had been described as impossible. The City leaders, confident of their ability to deal positively with the situation, adopted a "rate of growth" ordinance. Under the ordinance, if the number of building permit applicants exceeds the specified allocation of permits for a specific period, the applicants are rated according to a complex formula that favors high-quality, single-family residences. Those earning the highest rating were allocated permits for the period. As a result, the Island had effectively controlled not only the character, location, and magnitude of growth, but its pace.

---

[3] *Town of Palm Beach* v. *Gradison,* 296 So.2d 473 (Fla. 1984)

Mariner Point, Sanibel Island, October 1974.

"Wulfert Woods"

As the Comprehensive Land Use Plan moved toward its first five-year review in 1981, the last important piece of Plan litigation was beginning to get serious, and the parties were talking of a trial date in the "near future." The case involved a 415-acre parcel of land located at the western tip of the island far to the west of the causeway. It was, by far and away, the largest tract of privately owned, undeveloped land on the Island. The property, which comprised a mosaic of wetlands and uplands, was the site of an early settlement during the ferry boat and farming days on Sanibel. In fact, the property was the site of the "singular hammock near the beach" described in the 1769 *Instruction to Mariners*. The property had been purchased by seven Chicago investors just prior to the drive for incorporation of the City. According to the complaint the landowners filed, Lee County zoning would have permitted 4,050 dwelling units on the parcel, while the Plan saw this area, remote from the built-up section of the Island and home of an endangered bald eagle, as a place for fewer than 100 dwelling units.

The property and its owners' plans for development were well known to the City and had been a well-visited issue during the planning program. The allocation of densities was carried out in accordance with very clearly defined policies and standards under the Plan: the more remote the land, the less intense the development. And the greater the available services, the higher the density. The plaintiffs' (or, to be more precise, the plaintiffs-to-be's) property was remote in every sense of the word.

Like other landowners, the investors employed counsel to represent their interests. Unlike other landowners, however, the landowners' attorneys came from Chicago. (It has never been made clear whether Chicago counsel was selected because the investors were from Chicago or because the City's planning law consultants were from Chicago.) And unlike the other attorneys, Chicago counsel pursued a course of aggressive and hostile pressure including open and often-repeated attacks on the Plan's precepts and the integrity of individual members of the Planning Commission and the City Council. As one part of their opposition to the draft Plan, the investors and their attorneys presented a development plan for their property to show "those environmentalists" on Sanibel just how the property would be developed if "properly" planned. Far fewer than 4,000 dwelling units the investors originally claimed a right to develop, this scheme called for 1,600 dwelling units, a golf course, a lodge, a marina, and a shopping center. The development plan was received with polite nods but little enthusiasm, and was euphemistically named "Wulfert Woods" (one wag asked what woods would be left after the proposed development was completed). Presented by the landowners' planner, the project was equal to more than one-half the total number of dwelling units the Plan's carrying capacity analysis indicated could be accommodated on the entire Island. When questioned about hurricane evacuation, the owner's representatives stated that the project could be evacuated by boat if necessary. When asked about water, they said that they would desalinate if potable water was not otherwise available. When asked about sewage treatment, they said they would "handle it," and when asked how, they said, in effect, "We'll figure something out." They did not respond at all to the question of why the development plan included properties owned by the Sanibel-Captiva Conservation Foundation, a local environmental group. The fact that the City's Planning Commission did not respond favorably to "Wulfert Woods" was apparently quite unsettling to the investors and their esteemed counsel from Chicago.

What happened next seemed to indicate, from the City's perspective, that the landowners had decided to intensify their effort. Florida is a state that carries "doing good" to its illogical extreme. Alert to the potential for abuse and excess in government, public interest groups in Florida had, as they have in many other states, worked hard to "open up" government and make it accountable. As a result of this movement, the "Sunshine Act" and the "Public Records Act" had become law. The first requires that *all* meetings of government bodies be public. The second provides that any citizen has the right to examine, and copy, at reasonable times and at cost, any public record. Conceived as a shield against the abuse of governmental power, these two acts became arrows in Chicago counsel's quiver, as he submitted lengthy requests for all kinds of documents, many irrelevant to the planning effort or in some cases nonexistent, and made repeated allegations of meetings outside the "Sunshine." Interestingly, the landowners' theory that the Plan was invalid because of alleged Sunshine Act violations was derived from a landmark case decided by the Florida Supreme Court in the Palm Beach matters.

These allegations appeared with increasing frequency in public hearing remarks and in a series of letters that were to become legendary. Typical of the style and nature of this phase of the City's citizen input process is the following opening paragraph of one of the many letters that the investors' counsel sent to the City:

> It is the position of our clients that action of the City of Sanibel and of its officials, agents, consultants, advisors and employees in failing to provide adequate and appropriate responses to their inquiries, petitions and requests and to hold full and fair public hearings concerning these matters and to provide for public inspection of all appropriate public records is con-

trary to the laws of the State of Florida and the United States Constitution and the Florida Constitution and may very well have seriously jeopardized and infringed on the constitutional and statutory rights and interests as property owners in the City of Sanibel.

The City, however, was not intimidated and the parties seemed to drift farther and farther apart as each letter from the landowners' attorney got longer and longer. The following is another excerpt from the voluminous correspondence:

> We have received your letter of July 9, 1976 concerning our letter of June 25, 1976. By now you should have received our letter of July 8, 1976, which confirms certain of our requests for the review of certain studies, surveys and supporting documents.
>
> It is our position that in our letter of June 15, 1976 we specifically note that in our estimation your answers fail to properly respond to the questions which we have posed in our letter of May 26, 1976 to you. Your letter of June 25, 1976, which you refer to in your letter of July 9, 1976, fails to cure those problems which we have previously noted in our letter of June 15, 1976 with regard to our previous letter dated May 26, 1976.

The City's ultimate response, a letter from Mayor Goss to counsel, was, according to later revelations, not well received. He said:

> It seems apparent to me that you have received adequate answers to all of those questions posed in your various letters except to those questions that you specifically asked the City to refer to the City Attorney for review and in regard to these, the City Attorney's response to these questions will be presented at a hearing of the City Council on Monday, June 14. It appears to me that the City has been extremely courteous in responding to your many letters and *I can only conclude that your dissatisfaction with these responses reflects certain erroneous interpretations of Florida law in which you apparently persist.*
>
> . . . As you have previously been notified, speakers are limited to 15 minutes and are requested to use that time to summarize previously submitted written material, such as that which you submitted to the City on June 4. As is typical with legislative hearings before local elected officials, there are no elaborate procedural rules since the purpose of the hearings is to obtain the views of the public regarding proposed legislation. *Beyond this, I can only recommend that you speak clearly and distinctively and, if possible, concisely. [Emphasis added.]*

Relations did not improve, and on July 18, 1977—one year after the adoption of the Plan—all seven landowners filed a seventy-three page, eight-count complaint (a ninth count was added in January of 1979) against the City, all past and present members of City Council, the Planning Commission, and the City's planning counsultant. The appendices to the complaint, mostly copies of the ponderous correspondence between the City and the investors' counsel, ran to hundreds of pages and was over three inches thick when filed. According to the complaint, the City of Sanibel (a) had taken the landowners' property, (b) denied the landowners equal protection of the laws, (c) violated the Local Government Comprehensive Planning Act, (d) violated the Sunshine Act, (e) violated the Public Records Act, (f) misspent tax proceeds and should be required to recover funds paid to the planning consultant, and (g) should be ousted from jurisdiction over the plaintiffs' lands.

The City defended its position with vigor and moved to dismiss the complaint. Its motion to dismiss described "Plaintiffs' complaint" as prolix, confusing, repetitive, and replete with conclusions, evidentiary matter, and immaterial statements." The plaintiffs' memorandum response to the City's motion to dismiss was no less strident and the battle was clearly joined.

The Estuaries Project

In the meantime, the Sanibel planning effort was beginning to have an impact in Lee County beyond the city limits. The astonishing rise in land values on Sanibel had impeached the local development community's attack on planning as financially disastrous, and Sanibel residents began to "export" planning to the rest of the County. City officials served on the Southwest Florida Regional Planning Council and were instrumental in inspiring a "can-do" attitude for planning at the regional level. One focus of the Planning Council's attention was a "small" project planned for the mainland side of San Carlos Bay (the bay that borders Sanibel's northern coast and across which the much-maligned causeway extends) and Estero Bay. The "Estuaries" was to be a new community of 26,500 dwelling units built on a 6,400-acre assemblage of lands that was largely wetland. The project would lie immediately between Sanibel and mainland hurricane shelters and therefore the Estuaries constituted a real and practical threat to the City and its land use plan. The City actively opposed the project and encouraged the Planning Council to learn from Sanibel's experience.

The planning advocates who opposed the Estuaries project had little trouble stirring up concern about the proposed development. Not only was the project planned for the heart of Lee County's most productive estuarine ecosystem, the property had also been the subject of a long-standing dispute over ownership of the wetlands on the proposed development site. In Florida, submerged lands belong to the state unless conveyed to a private person. The ordinary demarcation between public and private lands is the mean high-tide line—everything seaward of the line is public. In wetlands areas, the line is difficult to locate because wetland plants impede the flow of tidal waters. After the State of Florida suffered an adverse ruling in a case involving the mean high-tide line in a mangrove forest, the state reached a boundary agreement with the owner of the Estuaries parcel concerning the dividing line between public and private ownership. When the agreement was executed by the state's Governor and Cabinet, sitting as Trustees of the Internal Improvement Trust Fund, local environmentalists were outraged because the boundary line was far offshore and in effect gave the landowner thousands of acres of land that the environmentalists felt were state lands. Already agitated, the environmentalists wasted little time in joining the fray.

One state official described the Estuaries project as a "new day" in environmental planning because it left intact approximately 2,800 acres of tidal red mangroves (coincidentally, the same land area the environmentalists believed was public land) but the project was soundly criticized in the regional impact report prepared by the Southwest Florida Regional Planning Council. Because of its size, the project was a development of regional impact (DRI) under the State's Environmental Land and Water Management Act. The act, an adaptation of Article 7 of the American Law Institute (ALI) Model Land Development Code, required that applications for development approval be submitted to local government, but provided for preparation of an impact assessment by a regional planning council. In addition, the act provided that local government decisions would be appealable to the Governor and the elected Cabinet. According to the assessment, the project—which involved, in addition to 26,500 dwelling units, 11 separate shopping centers, 4 marinas, 5 boat basins, 3 golf courses, and 28 acres of tennis courts—would have major negative impacts on Lee County's economy, public facilities, and environment.

The site did not lend itself particularly well to the proposed project. Situated on environmentally sensitive Estero Bay, the property was home to a bald eagle nest and was largely wetland. Of the 6,484 acres, all but 1,800 were subject to periodic tidal inundation, and only 526 acres of the 1,800 acres of nontidal lands were true uplands. The assessment was particularly critical of an environmental engineering solution to surface water runoff that the developer proposed. The so-called interceptor waterway was a long canal that would be developed at the seaward edge of the project. According to its designers, the waterway would receive polluted runoff from the project and then assimilate the pollutants through photosynthesis in the canal. Then, incoming high tides would bring in fish and other organisms to feed on the plant growth, thereby treating the project's pollutants. According to the Regional Planning Council's consultant, the waterway was nothing more than an excuse to "dredge and fill" as usual and would rapidly become polluted by runoff waters because the photosynthesis capacity of the waterway was far less than that estimated by the developer.

The magnitude of the project and its impact on the Estero Bay was well illustrated by the projected annual pollutant loadings from the project — 2,400 tons of suspended solids, 106 tons of biodegradable oxygen, 12 tons of nitrogen, 3 tons of phosphorus, 80,000 pounds of lead, 100,000 pounds of zinc, 30,000 pounds of copper, 10,000 pounds of chromium, and 7,000 pounds of nickel. In one set of proceedings, an attorney for the developer challenged the accuracy of these figures because they were based on studies conducted in downtown Orlando, a city setting. The expert's response to the question of whether it was valid to compare the Estuaries to downtown Orlando was a classic: "In fact the Estuaries will produce more pollutants than those produced by downtown Orlando." Of course, the facts of the Estuaries case were only a part of the story because the project was proposed to be developed in Lee County, the land of "development opportunity" and home of the "revolving door" planning department. Nevertheless, the County's planning staff agreed with the Regional Planning Council and recommended denial. The hearings before the Board of County Commissioners made it clear, however, that the outcome was still in question. Leaders of the business community, energized by the prospects of fortunes to be made from serving the project, extolled the virtues of the project. The environmentalists countered with equally passionate concern for the future of the County. The Board, caught squarely in the middle, struggled with the politics of the issue as well as a staggering body of scientific facts and analysis. The Commission's difficulties were hysterically underscored when a recently married member of the Commission asked about the interceptor waterway and inadvertently used the word "orgasm" instead of "organisms." The gales of laughter, however, did little to relieve the tension of the proceedings.

Eventually, the Board of County Commissioners, by a three-to-two margin, denied the application. Under the DRI process, the County was obligated to specify what changes would make the project eligible for approval, and the County did so. The total number of dwelling units that could be developed was reduced to 13,000 units, and the dredge and fill of tidally influenced wetlands was eliminated.

The developer appealed to the State's Land and Water Adjudicatory Commission (the Governor and Cabinet), and a full *de novo* hearing was held. The City of Sanibel intervened in the proceeding through its City Attorney, and Bosselman and Siemon, hired at the City's recommendation, represented the Regional Planning Council. The hearing, characterized by detailed testimony by many scientific, planning, and economic experts, was most notable for its transcript, which struggled vainly with hundreds of technical terms and scientific names. The findings and recommendations of the hearing examiner that the "proposed development would have an adverse impact on the ecology and economy of the area and that the appeal should be denied" were adopted by the Adjudicatory Commission; however, neither the hearing officer nor the governor and cabinet were particularly impressed with Lee County's planning record, and Governor Reuben Askew openly chastised the County's record on planning.

Askew's words were not to be the final disparaging remarks about the County's planning record. The First District Court of Appeal, on appeal from the Adjudicatory Commission's decision, declared the permit denial to be a "taking."

> One cannot possibly read the record in this case, nor the challenged order, without concluding that the principal reason for the denial of Petitioner's application was to preserve mangroves which presently serve as a protective buffer for the Estero Bay Aquatic Preserve, adjacent bay systems, and public fishing grounds. Petitioner has been denied the right to use its property because that use would deny the public certain free benefits.[4]

The County, now somewhat aware of the need to plan for the future, had felt quite vindicated by the Adjudicatory Commission's order. The First District's decision was shattering news.

An appeal was immediately lodged with the Florida Supreme Court, an appeal that was ultimately decided in the County's favor in 1981 in what is now regarded as a landmark case in planning law. The case established that

> [a]n owner of land has no absolute and unlimited right to change the essential natural character of his land so as to use it for a purpose for which it was unsuited in its natural state and which injures the rights of others.[5]

For Florida, with its abundant natural resources, the opinion was hailed as provenance. More importantly, the Supreme Court's comforting analysis of very restrictive land use controls fortified Sanibel's position in the Wulfert Woods matter.

Settlement of Wulfert

In the meantime, the hostilities between the Sanibel Bayshore Association and the City were occupying most of the City's attention. Depo-

---

[4]*Estuaries Properties, Inc.* v. *Askew,* 381 So.2d 1126 (Fla. 1st DCA 1980).
[5]*Graham* v. *Estuaries Properties, Inc.,* 399 So.2d 1374, 1382 (Fla. 1981).

sition after deposition revisited the history of the City and its planning program in painful detail. Then, not too long after the Supreme Court's momentous decision in *Estuaries,* an opportunity for compromise appeared. What happened was that the plaintiffs discovered what they could do with their property—the City had hired a design team to prepare plans that met all the land use Plan's requirements as evidence of the Plan's reasonableness. Eventually, a settlement stipulation was worked out and the books on the planning phase of Sanibel's history was closed. The number of units the plaintiffs were allowed to develop under the agreement still exceeded what many citizens wanted on the west end of the Island, but resolution of the final challenge to the Plan had great legal and symbolic meaning. *The Island Reporter,* by then sold to others, reported:

> Sanibel's last major land use confrontation—in the words of Mayor Porter Goss—was settled Monday when a compromise was reached in the six year old Wulfert Point lawsuit.
>
> "It's the end of an era in the development of this community," said Goss, "and a benchmark moment in Sanibel's history."[6]

Conclusions

In 1976, Porter Goss told a writer for *Sports Illustrated* that

> Sanibel is a perfectly extraordinary demonstration of democracy in action. The people were dissatisfied. They made it known what they wanted in a meaningful way, and now, at long last, we've got control of our own destiny. . . . It is the will of the people that we preserve the unique natural assets of the island, and we plan to see that their mandate is carried out.[7]

And, indeed, the mandate has been implemented. Sanibel is not the pristine spit it was before the causeway was installed, and yet it is pleasant and beautiful, and a very desirable place to be. Moreover, Sanibel stands as a monument to communities who face the challenge of preserving and protecting the quality of life that made them attractive.

Indeed, although the success of the planning effort on Sanibel is attributable to the exceptional people and unique circumstances of Sanibel that spawned the Plan, Porter Goss's formula for a successful planning effort suggests universal application:

> What I think you need first of all is a community consensus that you need

[6]July 15, 1982, p.1.
[7]"Eden Fights Back," *Sports Illustrated* (February 3, 1975), p. 35.

a plan. That is to me very important. . . . Number 2, once you've achieved a momentum to do something, you've got to get the "knowhow." And that, of course, involves legal advice. The third ingredient that is vital is community flavor.

Lee County, on the other hand, is still in an evolutionary state in regard to planning. A comprehensive policy plan was actually prepared and adopted in 1979; however, the County Commissioners refused to adopt a land use map, which relegated the plan to virtual uselessness. The evolving need for a plan did not die, however, and in 1983 the County once again embarked on a major planning effort. Although the plan itself has been adopted, the effort is not yet complete. Nevertheless there is reason to believe that Lee County has in fact turned the corner on planning.

Goss, who had retired from politics on Sanibel, was appointed to the Board of County Commissioners by Governor Bob Graham to fill a seat vacated by a political scandal. Goss's agenda as a commissioner is focused on a meaningful comprehensive plan for Lee County, and even a casual observer of the Sanibel experience would have to conclude that Goss is very likely to succeed. This is particularly so because he is joined on the Board by another pro-planning member, Roland Eastwood, former Executive Director of the Southwest Florida Regional Planning Council. It was Eastwood who had been a steadfast and courageous opponent of the Estuaries project in an unplanned county. When the Lee County Plan is adopted and implemented, the cycle will be complete, and somewhat ironically the citizens of Sanibel will have achieved a thirty-year-old goal: responsible planning in Lee County.

7
Sioux City, Iowa: Don't Tell Us Where to Build a Shopping Center

> *I will not allow big business to dictate where this City's economic growth is to take place.*
>
> Mayor William Gross

> *The arguments the Council has for voting against the proposed shopping center are based on nothing but their own personal feelings and probably a few of their friends.*
>
> Mrs. Virginia Erwin

Waterloo, Fort Dodge, Mason City, Cedar Rapids, and Sioux City—all have the ring of Meredith Willson's *The Music Man*. Unfortunately, none of them is River City and the story of one—Sioux City—does not end as joyously.

Sioux City, Iowa, is at the confluence of the Missouri, Big Sioux, and Floyd rivers. Across the river to the southwest is Nebraska and just northwest is South Dakota. Interstate Route 29 runs north-south from Sioux Falls, South Dakota, through Sioux City and south on to Omaha. Sioux City has a population of about 80,000 and a shopping market of about 127,000. It has been a marketplace for the great western Iowa and eastern Nebraska farms for over one hundred years, since

Authors' note: Ross and Hardies represented Sioux City in this case.

the demise of Chicago as a slaughterhouse, it has provided hogs and cattle for the markets to the east.

History of Sioux City

Sioux City history is a microcosm of the history of the upper plains. The first white man to be buried there was Sergeant Charles Floyd, a member of the Lewis and Clark expedition in 1804. The Floyd memorial still stands. It is said to have been the first historical landmark registered by the U.S. government. The period from 1854 (when the town was laid out) to 1880 is full of the usual tales of Sioux (really Dakotah) Indian conflicts, French traders, and scalawags in the form of itinerant traders. One story is of a white trader who married an Indian only to discover that by tribal custom the marriage automatically also wed him to the bride's three sisters.

The following brief account of Sioux City picks up the chronology:

> From 1920 until 1952 Sioux City was quite a complacent, wealthy, meatpacking and agricultural center. Population growth in this period was practically non-existent and physical improvements were few and very poorly planned. A series of disasters . . . brought about the now famous Sioux City Study sponsored by the Ford Foundation. This study was made by 600 people from all walks of life sitting down in living rooms in small groups. . . . All of the small groups were then brought together, their findings analyzed and a set of goals established. Out of this the Council-Manager form of government was established.[1]

Sioux City itself, like many of its peer towns—Waterloo and Mason City, for example—suffered from the post–World War II obsolescence that hit much of the north central United States. These towns, developed in the era of the buggy and the streetcar, could not compete with the changes the automobile brought, the desire of the new homebuyer to escape urban life, and the eagerness of the federal government to encourage those new centrifugal forces.

As the urbanized area spread outward and mobility increased, one consequence was the debilitation or death of many central business districts (CBDs). The commercial services followed the migration of their customers. The core of the urban area was left with vacant stores, unused infrastructure, and usually a virtually empty, trash-littered $1 million parking ramp.

---

[1] John Schmidt, *Historical Profile of Sioux City* (Sioux City, Iowa: Sioux City Stationery Company, 1969), p. 15.

Background of the Conflict

This is an account of how Sioux City, Iowa, tried to turn this around, of the bitter conflict between the town and a major shopping center developer that spilled over into its judicial arena, of the way the quarrel split the City, and, one could argue, of the City's eventual failure to achieve its goal of a revitalized CBD.

It started back in the mid-1960s when money flowed like tap water from the federal government for downtown rehabilitation projects. The CBD in Sioux City was obsolete and threatened with extinction and the City sought some of these readily available funds in the belief that pouring money on the CBD would restore the mercantile vitality of the bygone days of the trolley.[2] The City caused three blocks to be cleared and persuaded J. C. Penney to build a new store and found a developer to build a Hilton Inn. (Both are still there, although the Hilton has passed through at least three different owners.) Of course, it designed a three-block pedestrian mall and even constructed two second-floor passageways to connect the new buildings. Prospects began to look good, particularly when contrasted with other Iowa cities, where CBDs were rotting away and whose populations were seemingly indifferent to this dismal condition.

Metro Center, Inc.

In the early 1970s (August 20, 1973, to be exact), six Sioux City businessmen formed a development company, Metro Center, Inc., to acquire additional renewal land from the City and to continue the rebuilding process. This effort eventually ended in a fiasco that came under investigation by both the Internal Revenue Service and the U.S. Attorney's office. It is hard to conjecture what their real motive was. Certainly none of the organizers had any experience in major development. One appraisal of this group was offered by an attorney and former member of the Sioux City Plan Commission:

> They were babes in the woods. They didn't know enough to pour piss out of a boot. They may have thought they knew what they were doing and

---

[2] Sioux City had an extensive trolley system, operated in its last incarnation by the City Service Company. The system reached a peak of 56.8 track miles before it began to decline and for about ten years, from 1891 to 1901 or thereabouts, actually boasted an elevated section across the Floyd River marshland. In somewhat reduced size, the trolley system survived World War II and expired in 1948 when the Service Company replaced the trolleys with buses. See Central Electric Railways Association, *Iowa Trolleys*, Bulletin 114 (Chicago, 1975), pp. 147–150.

there are people who feel that they got undercut, but Christ, it was easy enough to undercut them because they were neophytes.

Each of the men put in $10,000. Howard Weiner, a former member of the City Council, later became chairman of Metro. Some members of the company clearly saw an opportunity to make money out of the renewal contracts. Frank Audino, one of the partners who was in the construction business, said: "Our prime business is construction, and that's what we look after first. That's how we make our money." Audino was paid $107,500 (and later filed a lien for $238,821). Another partner, Robert McIntosh, an architect, was paid $54,000 (and later filed a lien for $245,946). It was McIntosh who was quoted by the *Des Moines Register* as saying: "We all had various motives for joining." For McIntosh and his partner, "it was the architectural fees."[3]

Things appeared to start out swimmingly for Metro. The company signed a renewal contract with the City on February 4, 1974. Then within a year Brandeis, a major midwest department store chain, signed a letter of intent to put a store on one of Metro's downtown blocks. When the City approved the plans for that block, Metro negotiated a mortgage and purchased the land from the City for $198,000. At that point, the City had spent $2.3 million in local and federal money to acquire the block, to relocate businesses, and to demolish buildings on the block.

Meanwhile, trouble was gathering.

General Growth Corporation

General Growth Corporation, a large shopping center developer from Des Moines, had bought sixty acres in the unincorporated area adjacent to the Sioux City line and had taken an option on nineteen acres adjacent to as well as inside the City. General Growth was the operator of twenty-two shopping centers throughout the midwest. It had approximately 7 million square feet of enclosed space and was just completing a large center in Sioux Falls, South Dakota. In the late 1960s and early 1970s, shopping centers were booming. There were about 140 regional centers in Iowa alone. A regional center is generally defined as one having more than fifty stores, including at least one major department store. As reported by the *Des Moines Register,* such centers have at least 350,000 square feet of enclosed space and are supported by a population of more than 150,000.[4] By 1978, this explosion had virtually stopped, but in 1973

---

[3]*Des Moines Sunday Register,* December 24, 1978.
[4]Ibid., January 9, 1977, p. 12.

there was still a vacuum to be filled in some cities, and General Growth saw an opportunity in Sioux City.

The Conflict

Sioux City's municipal officials were, to say the least, not enthusiastic about the prospect. By 1974, the City had invested about $18 million in its CBD and the idea of a competing major shopping center was not welcome. Not only would a second development threaten the viability of the CBD but both General Growth and Metro would be competing for major retailers such as Sears, Montgomery Ward, and Brandeis.

The City decided to resist. As one strategy, under an established policy, it could refuse to run sewer and water to the area General Growth had purchased outside the City. Moreover, should General Growth ask that the property be annexed, it would be automatically zoned as residential pending a public hearing under the provisions of the zoning ordinance. So General Growth was not likely to request annexation. Without city water and sewer General Growth had to request premission from the State of Iowa to put down its own well and install a package sewer plant. The Iowa Water Quality Commission granted permission over the City's objection. Nevertheless, General Growth continued to plan a center that would span the city limits line.

There was a more serious problem for Sioux City. Under its existing zoning ordinance drafted in the early 1960s, the nineteen acres inside the city limits were zoned for light manufacturing (ML), and in this industrial district commercial enterprises—including a shopping center—were permitted uses. Sioux City, unlike many other municipalities, had failed to remove the pyramidal or "pour-over" concept from its zoning ordinance. At that time, the City had a plan for the CBD, adopted in 1966, but no stated policy.

City Strategy

Faced with the General Growth acquisition of acreage in the City, Sioux City had to take action without being too obvious. The City Council could amend the text of the ordinance to remove the permitted commercial uses from the ML zone. One problem was that if it took that course, the Council would create an estimated fifty-two nonconforming commercial uses. The other problem was that with General Growth requesting entry, the amendments would appear as a direct effort to preserve and protect the CBD from competition. Nevertheless, the Council directed the City's staff to prepare such an amendment and submit it for a public hearing. In the meantime, Planning Director John Curfman and his staff were issuing statements that the policy of the City was to protect the 540 acres of vacant and available industrial land for industrial use. On July 5, 1974, the *Sioux City Journal* reported, "Curfman said the changes would help preserve for industry a rapidly dwindling supply of industrial development land inside the city." Unfortunately the same article had a boldfaced subheading that stated "Zoning Amendments also Seek to Protect Redeveloped Downtown Area from Competition."

General Growth, in the meantime, had filed for a building permit for the nineteen acres inside the City. The response of the City was to stall. The Plan Commission held its hearing and voted ten to one that the Council not adopt the amendments. The Council reconsidered. The *Journal* (July 11, 1974) reported:

> The council, in remarks opening the meeting, conceded in the words of Councilman Jan Albertson that it might be guilty of poor timing in proposing the zoning changes now. Albertson said it might not be prudent to change the zoning ordinance while the action "is under the cloud of General Growth."

So the Council, under pressure, came up with a new, more subtle tactic. An ordinance, to be known as the Interim Development Ordinance, was proposed and passed, which required specified developments to obtain their building permits through the Council:

1. all apartment developments over 80 units anywhere in the City,
2. any proposed mobile home developments,
3. any construction within a quarter-mile of identified interchanges, and
4. all commercial development over 100,000 square feet.

The ordinance was to be in effect until March 1975, by which time, the Council instructed the Plan Commission, the Commission was to have drafted a comprehensive revision of the zoning ordinance.

General Growth's Response

Nice try, but it did not fool General Growth. The company's president, Stanley Richards, told the Council:

> Mr. Mayor, you are going to have to convince major retailers interested in coming to your downtown that they shouldn't come to Sioux City unless they come into the downtown.
>
> Department stores today, either downtown-oriented, or not downtown-oriented, are not going to be dictated to as to where they have to go to make a buck.

Connolly, General Growth's attorney, accused the City of "willfully scheming" against General Growth and of acting like a "hanging judge." General Growth then threatened litigation.

On September 27, 1974, General Growth issued a press release to Sioux City, which said in part:

> On or about Tuesday, October 1st, our general contractor will file a full and complete set of building plans with the City of Sioux City for construction of a Younkers department store containing approximately 100,000 square feet of space and located entirely within the City limits. The application for the building permit will supplement the original filing of foundation and structural plans which was initially made with the building permit application dated July 1, 1974.

The lines were being drawn.

And General Growth was not an easy opponent. Margaret Prahl, a City Council member, one of the foremost opponents of the shopping center, and now a lawyer in Sioux City, recalls that she was advised to give up because the opponent was so tough. She describes General Growth in this way:

> They made it clear that they would pull no punches and they would get their shopping center one way or another. Were they political? Yes. Were they conspiratorial? Yes. Were they above board when they had to be? They did everything they needed to do to win. And I don't think that in our little protective environment here, I'd ever run into that kind of ruthlessness before.

Howard Weiner, the Metro Center's Chairman, put it more bluntly: "If you look at General Growth, they [sic] had the wealth and staying power, the patience—while we ran out of money." Then in response to a question he added:

RFB: Did [General Growth] play pretty straight?

HW: Well, I have no reason to believe that they didn't. I was on a debate with [a General Growth official] on TV and he—I don't think that he was honest with the people. But the difference between honesty and good business is . . . he would not face any of my arguments about the number of square feet, about the economics and the city's ability to pay, and so on. All he would say is, gee, I think we can live nicely together. People in Sioux City, let's have both. Mr. Weiner can get his project done and we'll sure do ours. We'll do all we can. Very slow, soft-pedal, low-profile kind of thing.

RFB: And he whipped you.

HW: I had him from the fact standpoint in every way and I wasn't smart enough to turn that attitude of his into something—a weakness, instead of a strength.

Litigation

Sioux City stonewalled during the balance of 1974 and eventually rejected General Growth's application. So, in February 1975, General Growth filed its lawsuit against Sioux City in the Iowa District Court. In the complaint, General Growth alleged, among other things, that:

> the adoption of said Resolution (Interim Development Ordinance) was for the purpose of denying Plaintiff its right to use and develop its nineteen (19) acres Younkers Center for retail, commercial uses, with the direct intent of prohibiting competition by the Plaintiff as a retail shopping area with the downtown merchants of Sioux City and to prohibit competition with the Defendant for tenants in the sale and development by the Defendant of its Urban Renewal Project area, commonly referred to as CBD West.[5]

General Growth asked $294,000 in compensatory damages and $500,000 in punitive damages in addition to an injunction. Not once did the plaintiff make reference in its complaint to either Section 1 or Section 2 of the Sherman Antitrust Act. This is not surprising, however, because in 1975 few if any developers had expressly raised this issue.

At this point our law firm, Ross and Hardies, was brought into the case on behalf of Sioux City. We were retained to represent the City on the litigation as well as to draft a new zoning ordinance.

At that time (in 1975) the U.S. Supreme Court had not yet decided *City of Lafayette* v. *Louisiana Power and Light,* 433 U.S. 355 (1977), in which a plurality held that cities did not enjoy the antitrust immunity of states articulated earlier in *Parker* v. *Brown,* 317 U.S. 341 (1943).

There were, however, a number of opinions by state courts on the use of zoning power to restrain competition. The cases were mixed but there was a strong thread of judicial opposition to the idea. A common remark was that "use of the zoning power to prevent competition is clearly an abuse of that power."[6] Many of these cases involved efforts to restrain the number of gas stations and in a number of these cases the city's action was upheld. In one relatively obscure case, *Forte* v. *Borough of Tenafly,* 106 N.J. Super. 346, 255 A.2d 804 (App. Div., 1969), the Court asked: "May a municipality which wishes to preserve, rehabilitate and improve an established business area devoted chiefly to retail stores, zone the rest of the municipality against retail sales? We hold that it may."[7]

Later, the decision in *Lafayette* would highlight the competition issue, and the issues of the Sherman Act and municipal regulation would

---

[5] *General Growth Properties* v. *City of Sioux City,* No. 75.20913, February 14, 1975.
[6] *Herman Glick Realty Co.* v. *St. Louis County,* 545 S.W.2d 320, 325 (Mo. App., 1976).
[7] A discussion of these cases can be found in Ben Gailey, ed., *Zoning and Planning Law Handbook* (New York: Clark Boardman, 1983), p. 123.

become popular magnets at conferences of lawyers, planners, and public officials.

The crisis was not so much the potential liability (although the threat of triple damages and attorney's fees were frightening), but the prospects of defending one of these lawsuits, which gave those responsible for municipal budgets the shakes. Some states have tried to grant "state action" immunity to cities by statute, and bills were introduced into both houses of Congress to grant immunity from damages, one of which passed both houses and was signed by President Reagan in 1984.

Preliminary motions and depositions in the lawsuit occupied Sioux City until the fall of 1975, when there was an election for two seats on the Council. The strong proponents of the General Growth plan, Loren Calendar and Donald Lawrenson, were elected, but the Council still stood three to two against the proposal and in favor particularly of protecting the CBD. Calendar was closely associated with support for General Growth through local labor unions, which viewed the proposed shopping center as a source of jobs in construction and permanent employment; his election suggested which way public sentiment truly was going.

General Growth issued a statement that it would proceed to build Phase I of its mall, a Younkers store, on the county property. In a press release dated December 16, 1975, Stanley Richards announced:

> The decision to commence the development in the County portion of the site has been prompted by the frustrations and delays which we have encountered in our dealings with the Sioux City officials. . . . Our proceeding with the development in the County will have no effect on our continuing the lawsuit.
>
> We appreciate the support we have received from the Sioux City community in general. We look to the results of your recent election as further indication that the majority of the people want the free enterprise system to take its own course without interference from special interest groups. There are few, if any, major communities the size of Sioux City that are not served by a major shopping center.

As though in response, the Plan Commission finally issued thirty-two policy statements, one of which strongly reaffirmed the City's policy against outlying shopping centers. One such statement read: "The strength of the entire city is directly related to the vitality and health of its central business district, and . . . all proposals for commercial and residential development . . . must be examined for their effect upon the central business district." Things then began to happen rapidly. One resident, Richard Sturgeon, delivered to the Council petitions allegedly signed by 4,387 people calling for a referendum on the Council's policy against shopping centers. Then Brandeis described its plans for its development downtown: 323,000 square feet including 130,000 square feet of other stores and 50,000 square feet of office space. The planning staff completed its work on a new zoning ordinance and submitted it for public hearings early in 1976.

Impact of the Lincolnshire Parcel

In the summer of 1976, the Council made what was undoubtedly its most serious mistake.

A parcel in the southern part of the city, known as Lincolnshire, had been zoned "general commercial" under the old ordinance. The staff, aware that the classification did not agree with the policy of restricting major commercial growth to the CBD, had recommended (and the Plan Commission had concurred) that a substantial portion of the site be changed to "community business," a more restrictive designation. The Council, in an incredible decision, voted four to one to reject the Plan Commission proposal and change the zoning back to "general commercial." In a straightforward line, the *Sioux City Journal* reported that "the zoning ordinance which is to be given final passage in about two weeks, would not permit development of the city portion of the present General Growth site off U.S. 75 but would permit development of an equivalent center on the Lincolnshire site."[8]

This action was not without charges of bad faith and scandal. Apparently the Lincolnshire owners had contacted three members of the Council to tell them of negotiations with — of course — General Growth. The *Journal* reported:

> The mayor said he would not have voted for the change had he known of the General Growth connection. . . .
>
> James Johnson [son of the owner of the Lincolnshire property] said he had been with his father when they visited with council members. He admitted to "political bungling" but indicated there was no intent of doing anything devious.[9]

The game was up even if the City Council did not realize it.

General Growth, facing a protracted lawsuit and problems with sewer and water at its old site, did not hesitate to negotiate with the owners of the seventy-five-acre Lincolnshire site to trade properties. Part of the deal was to drop the lawsuit against the City.

Margaret Prahl made one more effort. She moved to reverse the zon-

---

[8]*Sioux City Journal,* July 24, 1976.
[9]Ibid.

ing on the Lincolnshire site, but that motion lost three to two. Only the Mayor voted with her. In the meantime, the Iowa District Court had rejected the City's motion to dismiss General Growth's suit.

City Council Election: "Dirty Tricks"

Simultaneously, Metro was going ahead with its plan for the Brandeis block. Excavation was completed. A year passed. Another election was held for the City Council. During the campaign, General Growth ran full-page ads in the *Journal*. One ad asked: "Has the Twentieth Century Passed Sioux City by?" Another one read: "84% . . . *That* is a majority! From 4,256 petitions presented to Sioux City citizens, 84% gave approval to build a shopping mall in the Lincolnshire section of this city." And Younkers, the first prospect for General Growth, ran an ad which concluded with: "WE BELIEVE SIOUX CITY CAN MAINTAIN A VIABLE RETAIL CENTER DOWNTOWN AND HAVE A SUCCESSFUL REGIONAL SHOPPING CENTER AS WELL." A headline in the *Des Moines Register* proclaimed: "Ad during Sioux City primary brought 'dirty tricks' charge." The story went on:

> General Growth, for example, said last week it may abandon its plan to develop a shopping center here and build one across the Missouri River in South Sioux City, Neb., where it would be welcomed with open arms.
>
> Such a move would mean that a large shopping center would be built in the Sioux City metropolitan area but that Sioux City would not benefit from the tax base it would create.
>
> That statement raised the ire of many persons. Grueskin, who previously had stayed out of the controversy, called a news conference Friday to denounce the General Growth statement as a bluff.
>
> Others say Brandeis has tried the same tactic in an attempt to gain support for the three candidates who favor the downtown redevelopment project.
>
> Brandeis is scheduled to be one of the major department stores in the downtown area, but company officials said recently they may reconsider their commitment after the election here. . . .
>
> The "dirty tricks" charge grew out of a series of newspaper and television advertisements that appeared during the primary election campaign.
>
> Those ads included a picture of a deserted street, and they implied that it was taken in downtown Sioux Falls, S.D. The ads said that no one went to downtown Sioux Falls since General Growth built a shopping center in that city.
>
> But the ads were suddenly stopped when the mayor of Sioux Falls, Richard Knobe, complained that the picture was not taken in the downtown area and probably was taken early on a Sunday morning.[10]

---

[10] *Des Moines Register*, November 6, 1977.

As the campaign approached the November election, tempers elevated, and meetings of the Council and the Plan Commission became shouting matches. At a meeting of the Plan Commission, City Attorney James Abshier ruled that a portion of the Lincolnshire site was not available for use as a regional shopping center because no site plan had been filed. An attorney for General Growth shouted at Abshier: "Let's face it, we're playing a game and someone is trying to find a way out of the zoning that has been properly given the property." At that meeting, the Plan Commission voted eight to four in opposition to having a regional center at Lincolnshire.

Lincolnshire Approved

By October the Council had stalled for four months on approving Lincolnshire. The landowners (transferors) became fed up and filed a lawsuit on October 12 against the City, asking the Court to enjoin the City from interfering with construction of a shopping center. Metro intervened in that lawsuit.

In the councilmanic election, three candidates were in favor of the shopping center and three supported the CBD. Voters selected Larry Clausen, a shopping center proponent, and William Skinner and George Cole, who favored downtown. But the election of Clausen meant that a majority of Council members supported an outlying shopping center. In January the Council, by three to two, approved the Lincolnshire site plan.

Brandeis had already backed out. It told Howard Weiner that if Lincolnshire was approved, its commitment to build downtown was revoked. The huge hole covering most of a block remained full of water and was generally dubbed "Lake Brandeis." Someone dumped live fish in the hole.

Meanwhile things were hairy for Howard Weiner and his Metro group. The truth was, nothing had happened since the group entered into its contract with the City in 1974. A great deal of money had been spent, and they had only a flooded hole in the ground to show for it. Five mechanics' liens totaling $550,000 had been filed against Metro. Investigations were underway by federal agencies. In June 1978, a group of thirty-six Sioux City businessmen formed a company known as West End Development, Inc., and the Council approved transfer of some of the CBD property from Metro to the new group.

It was the end of the line for Weiner. Looking back, he said:

> One of the things that you have to remember is the impatience that people began to feel. I already had been in business for four years and not produced

Aerial view of shopping center at Lincolnshire, Sioux City.

anything. I produced a lease with Brandeis but the financing was slow in coming. It was a very difficult thing to do. So, four years is not a long time. The average urban renewal project took five to seven but they wouldn't accept that. . . . They were impatient for success to come. They wanted to see something going up. We, maybe, dug too many holes before we got ready to build because they saw that and it became discouraging. The other side used that right to the hilt, calling it the Brandeis Pond, and the fishing place and the hole, and things like that. And that's what people take up on rather than the effort that was there.

On December 20, 1977, the following headline appeared in the *Journal:* "BRANDEIS SAYS NOTHING DOING IF LINCOLNSHIRE IS APPROVED." General Growth obtained all the necessary permits to build. It dropped its suit against the City. The Mall was built, all 716,135 square feet of it, with a Sears; a Target (a subsidiary of Dayton-Hudson); and a Younkers; about fifty other boutiques, shoe stores, and restaurants; and a minimum of 800 employees. It opened on Tuesday, March 4, 1980. From all signs, it is a huge success.

Arlo Herbold, former Planning Director of the City, noting that 70,000 square feet of commercial development had just been approved across from the shopping center, said:

I don't think we've felt the total impact yet of this mall as far as its effect on the development and growth of the city simply because we haven't had the construction. . . . If this city starts to turn around and we start to have a growth rate, residential growth rate, if that's going to happen and a lot of commercial is going to happen spinning off of that center. . . . We just haven't seen it yet because we're in a period of slow or no growth.

. . . And that could very well have a very serious effect yet on downtown because as this community grows and the growth tends to move in that direction, which I think it will, that market then is not going to be a downtown market. It's going to be a mall market. And it'll be the growth available to population growth, purchasing power will be available to the mall and not as available to downtown.

Downtown? There is the J. C. Penney store built in the mid-1970s. Terra Chemicals International has erected a fourteen-story high-rise, Terra Tower, on the Brandeis block, with 40,000 square feet of retail space on the first and second floors. A savings and loan built a new office building. The Hilton survives—barely. The mall is there. Iowa Public Service has built a new headquarters. In addition to some empty storefronts and an underused parking ramp, a new hospital has opened and Younkers, in concert with the Minneapolis developer, made an attractive deal with the City to construct a small store (60,000 square feet) with 30,000 square feet for specialty stores. With the unleased retail space in Terra Tower, this venture will be quite a gamble. More enclosed skyways are being erected. The central businss district has clearly begun to move toward an institutional, governmental, lawyer-, and accountant-type place not so different from many other medium-size cities of the upper midwest, but the effort continues to encourage retailing.

Conclusion

Could things have turned out differently? (After all, about $12 million of federal funds and $10 million of local funds were invested downtown.) Surely, if the Plan Commission and the Council had articulated an up-to-date plan for the CBD long before the Commission issued its guidelines in 1977. If the Council had in 1973 removed the commercial uses from the industrial zone—well before General Growth let it be known that it was interested in Sioux City. Certainly, if the Council had not rejected the recommendation of staff and the Commission to change the zoning of Lincolnshire so as to effectively prevent a regional center at that location. Perhaps if the Council had been wiser than most and rejected the proposal of Metro—six local men with no renewal experience—and insisted on a developer with knowledge and experience in redevelopment. But that may have been asking a bit much. John Curfman, former Director of Planning, suggested:

There are two things we should have done differently and neither had anything to do with the legal side of the question, in my opinion. First, our development package was not offered in a fashion that made it attractive to those who were successful and experienced developers. What I am referencing here is CBD East–CBD West split in our downtown package. CBD East was too small. It was only three blocks. Two of those three blocks were to be occupied in part by a parking ramp. That didn't leave much left for the developer to work with. The developers recognized that far sooner than we here. . . . That left us then with inexperienced developers working with small packages that left the marketplace's key people, the majors, doubtful of our chance to succeed in this small market.

There was the other problem: The new mall was planned to be built in a cornfield. But downtown redevelopment had to deal with existing stores. The following exchange took place between Curfman and Herbold:

JC: If you offer the package to the developer that he needs, you have to appear to ignore the interests of all those who are already present. You can't do that if you're sitting on a city staff in a small city like Sioux City. You can't do that. You must deal with them weekly in meetings and respond to the question, "What's going to happen to my business and my property?" And as a staff you don't know.

AH: Any failure, any adversity, is immediately public record. We don't know of all the false starts that happen in the private development in the shopping center. It doesn't make any difference. It doesn't bother anyone. But here if we have a false start everyone is after you, after your hide.

JC: We're in that old fishbowl. We can't make deals.

AH: It's not a job for the faint-hearted.

JC: I think it takes a great deal of luck and skill to make something like this happen. We came close, very close, I think.

At heart, it was ultimately a political decision. The people of Sioux City simply became bored and fed up with all the hassle and inaction downtown. They expressed their feelings in the election of 1978. True, the unions were a powerful influence and they saw jobs in the shopping center. But basically, most people did not understand—or if they did, they did not care about downtown. Downtown really did not belong to anyone. Few voters owned property in the CBD. No one lived there.

This was not Tuxedo (see chapter 2), where people perceived a threat to their "way of life." Quite the contrary. Many were ready and willing to accept regional shopping centers and malls as *their* way of life.

8

The Pinelands: A Radical Experiment Works

> *"Good heavens, how big are these woods?"*
>
> *This is always a heady moment if you happen to have been born, as I was, somewhere between metropolitan Trenton and the Bayway Refinery. The answer is "Well, about the same size as Grand Canyon National Park."*
>
> John McPhee, *National Geographic* (1974).

In South Jersey, midway between beautiful downtown Camden and Atlantic City with its South American–style juxtapostion of glittering casinos and urban blight, lies an environmental wonderland, its location as unlikely as its character is remarkable. The New Jersey Pinelands — or "Pine Barrens," as they are popularly known — is a 1 million-acre forest that is environmentally intact despite hundreds of years of human use and misuse. (The word *Barrens* refers to the sandy soils of the pines that were bypassed by row-crop farmers in the 1700s and 1800s.)

To the scientist, the Pinelands constitute an ecological treasure.

> Bog iron accumulating in tea-colored streams, a tiny Pine Barrens tree frog announcing its domain, fires sweeping briskly between streams, ships laden with cedar gliding out of rivers, dwarf forests reaching to shoulder height, silent cries of wolves long gone, nutrients flowing out to oysters and fish, spruce forests thriving during colder periods, a gargantuan lake resting in the sands, and a wilderness absorbing quiet reaction in the shadow of American cities.[1]

Authors' note: Ross, Hardies served as land management consultants to the Pinelands Commission.

[1] Richard R. T. Forman, ed., *Pine Barrens: Ecosystem and Landscape* (New York: Academic Press, 1979).

To the nonscientist, the Pines are quite simply a world unto themselves. As John McPhee describes the area:

> People . . . lead self-sufficient backwoods lives, and while the rest of the State of New Jersey developed toward its twentieth-century aspect, the Pine Barrens all but returned to their pre-Colonial desolation, becoming, as they have remained, a distinct and separate world. The people of the pines came to be known as "pineys"—a term that is as current today as it was at the turn of the century. After a generation or two had lived in isolation, the "pineys" began to fear people from the outside, and travelers often reported that when they approached a cabin in the pines the people scattered and hid behind trees. This was interpreted by some as a mark of lunacy. It was simply fear of the unknown.[2]

Indeed, the Pines are an important resource to all kinds of people, a region for all seasons "so to speak," as reported by the *Asbury Park Press:*

> To the mob . . . the Pinelands is a place to dump bodies of "done-in" enemies because the isolated, swampy land leaves few traces. . . .
> Just out of respect they'd have to bury the guy in the Pine Barrens. That's the Arlington National Cemetery of the mob.[3]

Background and Description

Indians hunted and fished the Pines' teeming lands and waters at least 10,000 years ago, and early settlers made good use of its vast resources. Cannon shot for the Revolutionary War was forged from "bog iron" taken from the Pinelands' streams, and lumber from seemingly endless stands of Atlantic white cedar and pitch pine provided raw materials for boat building, charcoal, and other industries. Sand and gravel deposits attracted the china and glass industries—industries that survive today as "thumbprint" glass from the area is a prized collector's item and high-quality china continues to be laid down with Pinelands sand. Traditional row-crop farming was limited to the edges of the forest; however, cranberry and blueberry cultivation became major industries in the Pines. New Jersey ranks number three in the nation for cranberry production and first in blueberries, and most of the state's berries are produced in the Pinelands area. Both the cranberry and the blueberry are native to the Pines, and careful cultivation and hybridization by "piney" pioneers has produced a major Pines industry.

---

[2]John McPhee, *The Pine Barrens* (New York: Farrar, Straus & Giroux, 1968), p. 42.
[3]June 9, 1980, p. B10.

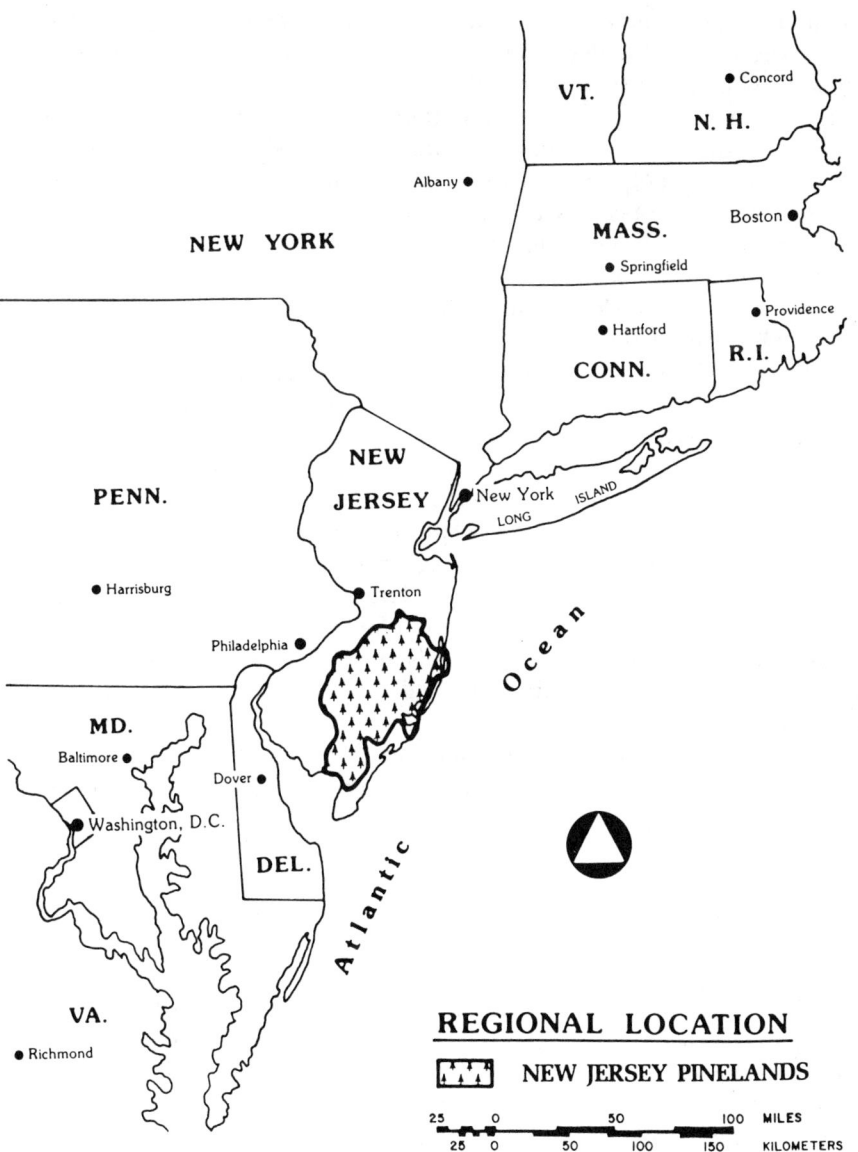

Map showing wide expanse of the New Jersey Pinelands. (Courtesy of the New Jersey Pinelands Commission)

Human perturbations, because of their low intensity or short-lived character, have not (at least until the late 1950s) destroyed the geological, hydrological, and biotic systems of the forest. Berry farming, although it involves the use of wetlands and bogs, is nevertheless considered environmentally good because it "protects" water quality. Cranberries, as it turns out, are extremely sensitive to polluted water, and cranberry farmers maintain from five to ten acres of land for water-quality management for each acre of bog under actual cultivation. Forestry, despite itself, has also proved to be "environmentally" sound in the Pines, as forests have regenerated themselves after logging. Scientists believe that the Pinelands may have been completely logged as many as six times in modern history; yet travelers from Camden to Atlantic City, particularly if they venture off the Atlantic City Expressway, will find themselves in a forest of both expanse and beauty in the most densely populated state in the union.

The Pine Barrens are remarkable in a variety of ways. Numerous species of plants and animals are found there, including a number of threatened and endangered species, not the least of which is the "poster perfect" Pine Barrens frog. The northern and southern limits of dozens of plants overlap in the Pines, helping create an ecological mosaic that is fascinating to the ordinary citizen and irresistible to natural scientists. The soil and water of the Pines are extremely acidic, yielding a unique distribution of water-dependent animals in streams and lakes. Even more distinctive are the pygmy pines, bonsai-like trees that are only six feet tall even though they are forty years old. The reason for the pygmy pines' size is not well understood, although most experts believe fire ecology is responsible. (Some "experts" claim that they are distant subgenus of *Pinus rigida*.)

Protection of the Pines

Not surprisingly, the Pine Barrens area has been the subject of extensive scientific study and innumerable efforts to conserve its unique and valuable character. In the early 1960s, thoughtful work was directed toward a regional approach to management of the area's unique natural resources. Nevertheless, little change occurred except that the efforts seemed to dispel discussion of a "jetport in the Pines." John McPhee's classic, *The Pine Barrens* (1967), portrayed the area in a moving and beautiful way and contributed greatly to environmental awareness of the Pines. In the early 1970s, however, there was precious little visible movement toward the management and protection of the Pines; McPhee closed his excellent article on the Pines in the *National Geographic* with a call for action:

> Unless the state—"state" in the larger or smaller sense—does something

effective and comprehensive quite soon, a great deal more than lightning is going to be tearing up the ground in the Pine Barrens, and over a breadth of not 50 but 50,000 yards.[4]

Shortly thereafter, Governor Brendan T. Byrne set in motion a series of events that would eventually lead to "a brave new world" in southern New Jersey. He formed a review committee composed of the heads of state agencies to prepare a plan to guide state activities in the area and $10 million of the state's "green acres" funding (a sensitive land-acquisition program) was earmarked for use in the Pinelands.

National Parks and Recreation Act

The Governor's initiatives were not the only response to McPhee's call for action. Environmental groups, with the support of Senators Clifford P. Case and Harrison A. Williams, Jr., intensified their efforts for protection of the Pines at the national level. In 1977, a number of bills were introduced in Congress that proposed federal and state management approaches for the protection of the Pines. One bill proposed the concept of a "National Reserve"—what Congressman James Florio would later describe as a second generation of National Parks:

> In 1977 Senators Case and Williams of New Jersey introduced a bill to protect American landscapes "of outstanding ecological, scenic, cultural, historic and recreational importance" that were too populated, complex and costly to protect through National Park designation.

Ultimately an act was passed as the "National Parks and Recreation Act of 1978" and was signed into law in 1978. One section declared the Pinelands to be the nation's first national reserve.

The National Parks and Recreation Act declared that since the Pinelands "provide significant ecological, natural, cultural, recreational, educational, and public health benefits," there is a national interest in protecting and preserving the area. The act contemplated that state and local governments have the primary responsibility for the protection of land and water resources, but that the land and water resources of the Pinelands should be protected by a new program that combined the capabilities of local, state, and federal governments with the private sector.

The Act directed the Secretary of the Interior to request the Governor of New Jersey to establish a fifteen-member planning entity to prepare a "comprehensive management plan for the Pinelands National Reserve."

---

[4]"The People of New Jersey's Pine Barrens," *National Geographic* (January 1974), p. 77.

It also authorized a $26 million appropriation, with up to $3 million available for planning, and the balance for the acquisition of ecologically sensitive lands.

Governor Byrne responded by urging the Legislature to enact implementing legislation. If the legislature failed to react, he threatened an executive order declaring a moratorium on development in the Pines until a management plan could be developed. When the Legislature did not respond, an executive order was issued on February 8, 1979. Byrne's position was absolutely clear:

> The moratorium is needed until comprehensive legislation outlining protection of the area is approved. Meantime we will not let developers run rough shod over this unique resource.

The executive order established the required fifteen-member commission and implemented a moratorium on development in the Pines during the planning period, unless development was approved by the new commission. The political response to the Governor's action was vocal and pointed.

> You're just taking people's property and you are asking people in Philadelphia and New York, "Do you want the Pinelands preserved?" And the people who don't live there, who have nothing to do with it say, "Yes, preserve the Pinelands!" You just can't slam the door on developers.

Pinelands Protection Act

But slam the door the Governor did, and the development community raced to court challenging his authority to declare a moratorium. The issue was resolved, however, not in the courts but in the legislative arena. On June 28, 1979, months of litigation, debate, and controversy came to an end when the Pinelands Protection Act was passed after what the press referred to as "stormy hearings and debate." (Several legislators would later claim that the Governor crammed the legislation down "their throats.") The act, as ultimately enacted, was a crazy-quilt patchwork of compromise and amendment; nevertheless, it created the required regional commission and, importantly, empowered them to implement the Act.

Comprehensive Management Plan (CMP)

When the dust settled, Governor Byrne's signature put the finishing touches on an astonishing legislative feat—a regional commission with overriding land use control over fifty-two municipalities, seven counties, and the state itself. Significantly, the commission was established as an independent state agency, immunizing its tasks from direct political influence. Governor Byrne himself characterized the act as "the thing they will remember me for 100 years from now." For the conservationists, there was but one small catch: the act declared that a Comprehensive Management Plan (CMP) was to be completed on or before August 8, 1980. This was eighteen months after the Protection Act was enacted. Critics complained that opponents of the bill, who recognized the strength of the Governor's position, had sabotaged the effort by exacting a schedule that was impossible to meet.

In July, the Pinelands Commission selected Terrence D. Moore as Executive Director of the Pinelands Commission and wished him well on his "mission impossible." Moore, who was described as a "self-styled flaming liberal" in one paper and was a veteran of Newark's urban and environmental problems, immediately began to put together a staff. Assembling a team of dedicated planners, lawyers, and scientists (largely expropriated from various New Jersey environmental agencies), he (the "E.D.," as he was to become known) set out to prepare and have adopted a comprehensive plan for 1 million acres of land in less than thirteen months.

The Commission's work program called for a team of consultants to prepare background reports on the natural and built environment of the Pinelands and to analyze the legal framework that would control adoption and implementation of the Plan. We were among the consultants (delineated as land-management consultants) and were responsible for the preparation of a five-volume survey of the land-management tools employed by agencies around the country and the world; this survey was ultimately to be the base for the implementing element of the Plan. The comprehensiveness of the survey formed a solid background for the many debates that developed about the form and substance of the draft Plan.

Initially, the Commission's staff worked out of a small group of offices at the Department of Environmental Protection's offices in Trenton. In early 1979, however, the Commission moved its official offices to New Lisbon in the Pines. Ensconced in a large white farmhouse that had most recently served as a work-release facility, the Commission's staff began the difficult process of implementing the work program while, at the same time, processing applications for development under a set of interim rules and regulations.

The Plan, according to the Commission's work program, should include a scheme to manage lands that are to be protected and examine an array of less costly and more flexible land-management techniques. The

View of the New Jersey Pinelands, within the Pinelands Preservation Area. (Photo by Ray Fisk)

Pinelands Plan should also include a natural resource assessment; a detailed boundary map; a land use capability map and a comprehensive statement of land use management policies; a study of appropriate public uses of the land; a financial analysis; a program to ensure local government and public participation in land use decisions; and a program to put the Plan into effect.

History has recorded that the Comprehensive Management Plan for the 400,000-acre "Preservation Area" core of the Pinelands was duly enacted on August 8, 1980, and that the entire Plan was adopted on November 21, 1980. The effort was completed largely due to the dedication of the people involved and their willingness to work together toward a common end. The participants did not necessarily agree with everything they worked on. However, very few participants in the process denied the value of the environmental resource to which the effort was directed.

The Commissioners

Perhaps most significant among the many principals responsible for the planning program were the commissioners themselves. Appointed by diverse authorities, seven by the Governor, one from each of the counties in the Pinelands area, and one representative of the U.S. Department of Interior, the commissioners carried out their duties with patience, dedication, and care. That is not to say that they acted as one; but their personal integrity carried them and the Commission through what was by any measure a very difficult process.

The Chairman, Frank Parker, a successful New York attorney who resided in a northern New Jersey suburb and a long-time conservationist, distinguished himself with infinite patience and a discreet sense of dignity and control. Candace Ashman, a veteran environmental and planning advocate with hands-on experience as the Executive Director of New Jersey's Association of Environmental Commissions, provided unswerving support for the staff and the environment. This position was reinforced by Gary Patterson, a professor of environmental sciences in a local college. Budd Chavooshian, a Rutgers professor and a former director of the state planning agency for New Jersey, brought a wealth of experience and technical skill to the Commission. Joan Batory, who was appointed by Camden County and was Director of that County's environmental agency, contributed technical and practical skills to the effort. Another important contributor was Robert Shinn, a freeholder of Burlington County whose appointment to the Pinelands Commission brought to the deliberations years of experience in political activism on behalf of the Pines. Shinn's Burlington County had itself initiated a preservation program that involved $1 million in conservation easements—a program that would be modified after the Plan's adoption to encourage use of the Plan's transferable development rights (TDR) element.

Not every member of the Commission represented the environmental movement, however; developers and local government enthusiasts provided the needed balance for a forum for the complex issues the Commission faced. The Commission, in the ten months between February and November 1980, held dozens of hearings and listened to hundreds of hours of testimony and workshop discussions. One newspaper suggested in an editorial that "the Pinelands Plan has had more public airings than Bing Crosby's 'White Christmas.'"

The Planning Process

The issues confronting the Commission ranged from environmental protection to mandatory low- and moderate-income housing, from the esoteric to the practical. Typical of the complexity of the Commission's challenge was the question of how to maintain the ecological integrity of a pine forest that depends on, among other things, periodic wildfire. How do you design with nature where nature will periodically burn down the design? Difficult to grasp on its own terms, resolution of this issue was made even more difficult when word reached New Lisbon that a "controlled burn" in Michigan had gotten out of control and burned 35,000 acres of land. The issues engendered protracted debate and discussion, and the Commission met at least two days a week every week from March until November during the planning program. The Commission's durability surprised even the most seasoned observers of the zoning game: "If the Pinelands Commissioners learned one thing this year, it was that you can't please all of the people all of the time, and you can't please some of the people at all."

In April, the Commission proposed land use categories for the approximately 1 million acres covered by the Act. Then, they spent the rest of the year fielding suggestions, proposals, and an occasional legal threat from farmers, environmentalists, builders, government officials, and just plain folks. All wanted modifications in the Plan that would alternately allow for more or less development of the Pinelands.

The planning process involved the preparation of scientific studies on particular subjects by some of the best available experts. Each of the scientific papers examined the character of the resource under study and recommended policies or standards that were necessary to maintain its functional integrity. The policies and standards were then assembled by the staff and their land use consultants, and a management approach was selected.

To a large degree, the approach to be employed during the planning effort was prescribed in the Pinelands Protection Act. The Commission, according to the Act, was to develop a land-capability map that would indicate where projected population growth could be accommodated without adversely affecting the ecological character of the Pinelands. The program focused on how much development environmentally sensitive areas could stand and where growth should be directed. The answer to the latter question proved to be far more controversial than the former. Indeed, the most vocal opponents to the Comprehensive Management Plan turned out to be local authorities who had their own growth-management programs, which permitted only limited development, notwithstanding proximity to job centers or the availability of public services.

Draft CMP

The first draft of the Comprehensive Management Plan was made public on June 8, 1980. Given that the entire Preservation Area was slated for *no* development at all and was reserved for forestry and berry agriculture, it was predictable that some interest groups or individuals would be unhappy. Their concerns were heightened (mostly vocally) by the fact that the draft Plan called for only limited development (one dwelling unit per thirty-nine acres) for an additional 400,000 acres of land in the Protection Area. Public response ranged from irate ("it's obscene") to highly technical dissertations. Typical of the landowner's view was the following observation:

> What right does [sic] the state and federal governments have to tell us that our land, which was purchased for future development, cannot be developed? Who will compensate us for our loss present and future? What's even more incredible is not only are we being told we own a worthless piece of property, but we must still pay taxes on it. Even communist and dictatorial countries who confiscate private property do not demand yearly taxes.

Role of the Commissioners

Undaunted, the Commission moved forward with the Plan. A key question was the role the Pinelands Commission would play under the Management Plan. Would it be an active participant in the permitting or development review process, or did it see itself as a "planning agency" with regional oversight and supervision duties? The Pinelands Protection Act clearly implied the latter role; however, the extent to which local governments were to be trusted to "permit" development proved to be one of the longest-lived issues in the planning process. The Commission ultimately defined the role it felt it should play and set out to adopt a four-part plan. Parts 1 and 2 constituted the factual and policy bases for the Management Plan. Part 3 established the procedural framework for local government certification and development review, while Part 4 set down substantive standards for all new development in the Pinelands.

Elements of the Plan

The Comprehensive Management Plan was quite straightforward in its approach. First, the Commission conceded that the Plan had to accommodate the shelter needs of the regional population projected for the South Jersey region. Second, they agreed that the core of the forest was very sensitive to growth and development and that new development should be directed to the periphery of the forest, where public services were more readily available. Third, the Commission accepted that the ecological integrity of the Pinelands was directly linked to ground- and surface-water quality in the Pines. Fourth, it recognized a distinction between the shelter needs of employees of Pinelands resource-related industries and successful physicians and lawyers in Philadelphia who were looking for second homes. Fifth, the Pinelands Commission understood that the implementation of the Comprehensive Management Plan would catch ongoing projects in the middle and therefore set out to deal affirmatively with the issue of so-called vested rights. Finally, the Commission recognized that the growth-pattern shift that would result from implementation of the Comprehensive Management Plan would produce windfalls to some landowners and wipeouts to others; therefore, a mitigation strategy was needed to equalize the economic impact of the Plan.

The draft Plan responded to these issues by planning for the full measure of regional growth and directing that growth to designated "regional growth areas." One means of achieving this redirection of growth was an ambitious transferable development rights (TDR) program. Pinelands Development Credits (PDCs) were allocated to lands in the Preservation Area and to prime agricultural lands. The PDCs were transferable to any of the designated regional growth areas, which unexpectedly was the source of opposition to the Plan: local authorities objected to the Plan because it provided for more development than their own local plan indicated.

The Plan contained a few other notable elements. One element, popularly known as the "piney exemption," provided density relief for long-term residents and employees of local resource-related industries. The theory was that limited development directed to the shelter needs of the endemic population and the employee needs of forestry and berry agriculture could be accommodated, even in the Preservation Area. Another element directed at the shelter needs of the region stated that all residential developments involving more than twenty-five dwelling units were required to provide 25 percent of the dwelling units for low-, moderate-, and middle-income households (at least 10 percent had to qualify as low-income households and 10 percent had to be moderate).

The draft Plan, released in June 1980, generated a storm of controversy as reported in the press:

> With the release of the proposed Pinelands Master Plan last week, chapter two began in the political battle over control of the South Jersey Wilderness.
>
> It is a tug of war between factions concerned with time, money and control.

Opposition to the Plan

The private sector (developers, farmers, and sand and gravel miners, among others) responded predictably and aggressively. The Coalition for Sensible Protection, one of the many euphemistically named groups formed in opposition to the planning effort, presented an extensive counterplan that called for the protection or acquisition of the Preservation Area and suburban development of the balance of the Pines.

Agricultural interests were particularly agitated by the Plan. According to their "spokesman" (one of the many Trenton lawyers to cash in on the "Lawyers Welfare Reform Act of 1979"), the Plan—which contained a detailed agricultural conservation element—would in fact destroy agriculture!

> In summary, we find that the Plan's provisions are massively and unnecessarily over-restrictive in reference to the Commission's legislative mandate and the likely environmental consequences of farming activities and development in both the Protection and Preservation Areas. In particular, the continued viability of farming, a long term stable and valuable activity in the region, is threatened by the environmental quality standards proposed and the loss of land value resulting from adoption of the Plan.

This was so, he said, because the diminution in the value of farmlands from the implementation of the Plan (by eliminating the future development potential of the land) would destroy the farmers' capability to operate. The only way a farmer could secure operating credit, according to the spokesman, was by pledging the development capacity of his land as collateral. In other words, agricultural interests argued that it was necessary to continue suburban development potential in order to preserve agriculture. Of course, future development potential was valuable as collateral only if development was reasonably iminent — a fact that "foretold" the end of agriculture and its replacement by suburban sprawl.

There were, of course, many other opponents of the Plan, including large-scale corporate developers, who stayed carefully out of the spotlight and let individual lot owners and small farmers carry the public torch of opposition. Literally hundreds of people slowly walked to the microphones in hearing rooms all over the Pines to invoke a common message:

> I bought my land. I paid good money for my land and I have been paying taxes for years. What right do you have to come in here and tell me I can't build on my land? What right do you have to tell me I have to preserve a bunch of trees? I thought communism was in Russia, not in my own back yard.

The Commission was not unsympathetic with the plight of the individual landowners, and yet the Commission's mandate was to preserve the Pines; that responsibility was expressed by Commissioner Tom Darlington, one of the largest landowners in the Pines and a major berry farmer:

> I'm a farmer, as I guess you know. I certainly share your sympathies in trying to get a fair share for not only farmers but the landowners, the people who have preserved this land. All the same, to preserve this by walking roughshod over them is not the way to go.

The tension, of course, was between property rights and environmental integrity, as presented by Commissioner Patterson:

> The track record of local government land use decisions has been disastrous. Five-year-old homes in my area have their wells polluted by their own septic systems, and the lake they are near to is so polluted, that children were getting sore throats and ear infections from swimming there.

In the meantime, political maneuvering in Trenton had produced a change in the schedule. When the draft Plan was published in early June, opponents realized that the Commission was intent on meeting the August 8 deadline and the 500-page draft Plan looked imposing. Their responsive tactic was to try to delay the effort in the hope of exercising more political pressure on the final Plan. Bills were filed in the legislature to postpone the deadline; however Governor Byrne made it known that he would veto any broad attack on the Pinelands Protection Act. An accommodation was finally reached whereby the Plan for the Preservation Area would be adopted on August 8, with the Protection Area Plan deadline set back to December 31, 1980. The primary concern was that any delay in adopting the CMP might jeopardize federal funding, which was expressly contingent on adopting the Plan eighteen months after disbursement of initial funds.

Slowly, then almost defiantly, the Plan began to take shape, and by midsummer, the Pinelands Commission staff began to believe the CMP actually might be adopted. Indeed, if opponents' attempts to extend the moratorium is any indication, the August 8, 1980, deadline for the Preservation Area had become a reality. What originally had been seen by many as the Achilles' heel of the effort—an impossible deadline—had become an unmistakable mandate for indefatigable work and devotion from staff, Commission members, and their consultants. The question of whether anyone would spend the night on the couch at New Lisbon had been disposed of long ago, and the only remaining question was who got the couch. Dinner at the diner at 2:30 A.M. was the rule for both staff and commissioners, as the determination to get the Plan adopted became self-sustaining.

August 8, 1980

Friday morning, August 8, 1980, dawned as every morning seems to dawn across the bogs and forests of the Pines, beautiful and misty. The focus of attention, however, was not the delicate calls of birds; rather, it was the theater of the Burlington County Community College in New Lisbon, where the Pinelands Commission was scheduled to take up the Preservation Area Plan.

Chairman Frank Parker opened the meeting and invited the public to submit comments. The speeches were short, impassioned, and equally divided between proponents and opponents. The Commission discussion was slightly less balanced since the hard work on the Plan made the commissioners tense and edgy; indeed, just before the vote, one of the commissioners attacked the character of another commissioner by accusing him of "profiteering." In what can only be described as a tribute to the integrity of the process and the people, there was unanimous condemnation of this attack followed by several sincere speeches of support for the incorruptibility of the process—one by a developer openly opposed to the substance of the Plan.

When this emotional crisis passed, the roll was called and the Preservation Area Plan was adopted. The goal of regional management for the Pinelands had become a reality. Tom Darlington, the commissioner, landowner, and berry farmer whose integrity had been attacked, summed up the feeling of the moment:

I've had a lot of pressure from my friends, they even suggested I resign. We hired a professional staff and what they have done makes sense. I believe the Plan is right, it's what the Pines needs. I went to my children last night and said what do you think I should do? The Plan will significantly reduce the value of our lands and if you think I am doing wrong then I would like to know that is how you feel. They told me "We're behind you 100%, you do what you think is right and we'll back you up."

Opposition to the Designated Growth Areas

Plan opponents, now certain that the Commission would meet its deadlines, shifted their strategy from opposition to compromise and amendment. One major area of debate was the designation of growth areas — communities that were earmarked for growth but that did not want to grow. During the planning process, the staff and its consultants had understood that Plan opponents would be dissatisfied with the reduced amount of development allocated to their property. Consequently, an extensive report had been prepared delineating the legal principles controlling the anticipated downzoning. What the staff and counsultants had not fully foreseen, however, was the inevitable conflict of the management plan with no-growth attitudes of communities that were in the vicinity of Atlantic City and Camden.

Galloway Township was typical of this kind of Plan opponent. (Not coincidentally, the Coalition for Preservation's expert planner was the planner for Galloway Township.) A small, relatively undeveloped community of large suburban lots, the Township had previously completed a planning program to protect its rural ambiance from the onslaught of the less elegant development spawned by the Atlantic City casinos. The Township met all the CMP criteria for a growth area, as the Plan called for the deflection of residential development away from the forest core to areas that were close to job centers and major public-service systems. Galloway Township, a planned community, now found itself replanned as a distinctly different type of community — at least as its officials saw it.

Pinelands Development Credit (PDC)

Galloway Township's frustration with the Plan was heightened by the CMP's proposed Pinelands Development Credit (PDC) program. PDCs are an economic-mitigation strategy developed to compensate for the windfalls and wipeouts created by the Plan. They are a transferable

Cranberry harvesting within the Pinelands Preservation Area. (Photo by Ray Fisk)

development right that can be freely traded on the private market and used by landowners in designated growth areas to secure a density bonus. To ensure that PDC owners would have a real opportunity to mitigate wipeouts and to recapture at least a portion of the windfall created by the Plan, the CMP required that all residentially zoned land in "growth areas" be eligible for PDC bonus densities. Townships saw the PDC program as a direct assault on the integrity of their neighborhoods.

The PDC program attracted much more attention than that of the disgruntled growth-area townships. The allocation methodology—who got how many PDCs—came under attack, not surprisingly, by owners of land slated for PDC allocations. One much-discussed element of the PDC program revolved around the issue of farm credit for row-crop farmers.

The outer edges of the Pines had always been among the state's most productive agricultural lands; however, labor and transportation costs, plus the reward of selling to developers, had created a serious threat to the continued viability of agriculture in South Jersey. The Pinelands Protection Act clearly stated that agriculture was part of the Pinelands and that it was to be preserved and enhanced. Of course, the preservation of farmlands involves the deflection of development expectations that make up the bulk of the value of the farmers' land. Deprived of the speculative value of their land for development purposes, the farmers were faced with a shortage of farm credit, which constituted a serious threat to the viability of farming. If PDCs were allocated to designated agricultural lands, it would be possible for farmers to sell their credits as a means of raising working capital — that is, to take advantage of the development value of the land without destroying its usefulness for farming.

Environmental Opposition

In late October, the Commission was holding almost continuous hearings; the vote of the Protection Area portion of the Plan was scheduled for November 21, 1980. The Plan had undergone extensive change during the public hearing process as the Commission sought to strike a balance among the various interests affected by the CMP. Now the environmentalists, always staunch supporters of the program, began to question whether the CMP had been compromised to satisfy local governments and developer interests. They doubted that the revised CMP could protect the Pinelands.

> The Commission has gone overboard in grandfathering in subdivisions, environmentalists' objections "were given very rude, short shrift" and the weakened plan "was ramrodded down our throats. . . .
> It was supposed to have been a protection plan, not a development plan.

At one hearing, a representative of one of the national environmental groups went so far as to accuse the Pinelands Commission staff of "carrying water for the developers." Few statements were less well received during the entire public hearing process, and another environmentalist rose to defend the staff that had labored day and night to prepare a comprehensive management plan for the 1 million acres, 52 municipalities, and 7 counties in less than ten months. The development community found the environmentalist's remarks to be ironic: "It's one tough cookie of a plan. It's the toughest environmental plan in the United States, and . . . environmentalists are calling it too weak."

Adoption of the Plan

Final adoption of the Plan was almost anticlimatic. The hearing was unexpectedly brief and the Commission voted eleven to four to adopt the CMP. Congratulations were shared among all in attendance, including development interests, who begrudgingly admitted that the program had been carried out professionally, fairly, and openly.

The Commission and its staff and consultants retired to a nearby restaurant for a scheduled celebration. The warmness of the autumn afternoon was enhanced by the taste of champagne and the sense of accomplishment. Not everyone was satisfied by the CMP as it was adopted, however; and the dissatisfaction was amusingly recalled to the revelers by the arrival of a singing-telegram messenger who sang the following ballad to the tune of "Dixie":

Ode to the Pinelands Plan

Verse 1

Way down south in a land forgotten
Is a plan so misbegotten
(To) take away, take away, take away southern land

In a state well-known for over-regulation
They plan under guise of conservation
(To) take away, take away, take away southern land

Oh they wish to save the Pinelands
They say, they say.
But the Pinelands Plan is just a scam
To extend old Brendan's power
Away, away, away, down south in Jersey —
Away, away, away, down south in Jersey

Verse 2

Oh how dare we question Brendan's motivation
On this noble legislation
(To) take away, take away, take away southern land

They say the tree frog's an important creature
Who deserves to be a major feature
Of the plan to take away, take away southern land

Oh I wish that all God's people
What say, what say
Who live down here were just as dear
To Brendan as those tree frogs
Away, away, away down south in Jersey—
Away, away, away down south in Jersey

Verse 3

You should know the vote in support of secession
Was a vote against repression
Take away, take away, take away southern rule.

You say the plan's a move to save our water
We say for the northern border!!
Pipe away, pipe away, pipe away our sole source

Oh we wish your vote today would
Please heed our call
To save our land from Brendan's hand
And leave a land that's fair to all
Away, away, away down south in Jersey
Away, away, away down south in Jersey

Other Protection Act Requirements

For the staff, the planning effort was not over; it was just beginning. The Protection Act commanded that local governments be given a full opportunity to participate in the implementation of the Plan, and the CMP set forth detailed procedures and standards for the certification of local plans and regulations. Throughout the planning process leading to the adoption of the CMP, much concern had been expressed because other regional programs—a plan for the Adirondacks, Oregon's statewide plan, and Florida's Area of Critical Concern—had experienced very little success in inducing local authorities to submit acceptable programs for certification. In response, the Plan included an incentive for rapid certification. The incentive was the solution to another sticky issue faced by the planners and the Commission: how to deal with the myriad claims for vested rights to platted lots, second phases, secret plans and dreams, and others. Great pressure was brought to bear to include a grandfather clause that would protect the development rights of all individual lotowners; however, the Plan limited grandfather rights to areas with certified local plans.

Parks and Recreation Act Requirements

The adoption of the Comprehensive Plan was not the end of the Pinelands saga. Under the Parks and Recreation Act, the Plan had to be approved by the Governor and then the Secretary of the Department of the Interior. Moreover, the Heritage Conservation and Recreation Service (HCRS) was required to prepare an Environmental Impact Statement (EIS) for the Secretary's action, all against a backdrop of the new, incoming Reagan administration. Once again, the Governor was assailed about the Plan. ("Under the restrictions of the Pinelands Act, this property is practically useless; there can be no development.") On December 2, 1980, nonetheless, he approved the Plan and forwarded it to the Secretary of the Interior.

More Opposition

In the meantime, HCRS's draft EIS has been circulated for review and comment and, to no one's surprise, the opponents kept up their attacks. The Coalition for the Sensible Preservation of the Pinelands, for example, said, "We are profoundly disturbed by several statements and conclusions contained therein." Among the outspoken was Congressman William J. Hughes, whose objections were quoted in the EIS:

> The State of New Jersey has created an entire new bureaucracy to plan for and regulate all activities in the Pinelands. This contravenes the intention of the federal law, which was to emphasize home rule and existing laws and regulations to help meet regional conservation goals.

Hughes, joined by Congressman Edwin Forsyth, even went so far as to advise the Secretary of the Interior that they "would oppose the use of federal funds for the Pinelands Plan if approved in its present form."

Secretary Cecil Andrus, already a lame duck, approved the Plan on January 16, 1981. His action was not just an act of political courage. The Plan was widely supported in the EIS. For example, the much-debated impact on agriculture was cogently analyzed by the Farmer's Home Administration in the Department of Agriculture, which, although they foresaw changes, endorsed the CMP as adopted.

> We have determined, based upon the program review, that . . . the Pinelands Comprehensive Management Plan should not have any adverse effects on the management of our programs. . . .
> Implementation of the Plan will have an effect in reducing land values due to the proposed restriction to land uses. This reduction in land value may effect the borrowing capacity of land owners and farmers. The over-

all effect of this program, however, is considered to be minimal and should adjust itself with the passing of time.

One agency that did not relent was the Department of the Army. The CMP required that federal actions comply with the Plan unless compliance "would prevent achievement of the installation's national defense mission." The Commission had recognized the unique character of federal facilities and had created the "Military and Federal Installation Area" (MAFIA) as a special mangement area. The Army was nevertheless confident of its independent integrity and, oblivious to any idea that it "could do wrong," objected to the CMP. The Army was convinced it was able to judge whether its actions were good or bad for the Pinelands, and by its own definition, whatever it did would be good. Ultimately the Army and the Pinelands Commission reached an accommodation; however, there were numerous occasions when Pogo's lament was recalled: "We have met the enemy and he is us."

Observations

The CMP has been by all accounts a great success. There are, of course, detractors, most of whom reside in Atlantic County. The Commission nevertheless endures, and thirty-six municipalities and four counties have amended their local plans and regulations and been certified as conforming with the Plan. Ninety-six percent of all development subsequent to the Plan's adoption has been located in areas designated for growth.

One aspect of the planning program that is remarkable is the dearth of litigation. Notwithstanding the virulent threats announced during the public hearing process, there have been very few challenges to this Plan. An initial challenge that contested particular procedural aspects of the Plan and the so-called piney exemption was admirably and successfully defended by Rich Hluchan, a Deputy Attorney General who had been assigned to the Commission throughout the planning process.

Observers suggest that absence of litigation is attributable to several considerations. The first is the Pinelands Commission and its staff. While the results of their efforts may not always have been satisfying, almost everyone agrees that they were fair and responsive. When someone had a legitimate complaint he or she got action, and the Commission exuded an attitude of service quite distinct from the bureaucratic annoyance that generally tends to characterize resource-mangement efforts. The second is the state and federal commitment to the Pines. Recognizing the inevitability of the Pinelands Commission as a long-term proposition encourages cooperation as the preferred alternative to conflict. Third, the CMP National Reserve and the CMP contain an acquisition element that calls for purchase of critical areas. Litigation is generally the result of extreme examples, and the acquisition of critical areas eliminates many of the most difficult situations. Finally, the CMP was done correctly. The research on which it was based was sound and the public was given a full and unconstrained opportunity to participate in the process. Where there were "gaps," the Plan called for more research. The Plan was forthright: it admitted that there would be differing viewpoints and it tried to be responsive and flexible. It is human nature to appreciate the "effort" even if the effort does not always succeed. The Pinelands Commission and its staff have made an effort second to none in the Comprehensive Management Plan for the New Jersey Pinelands.

9

Gautreaux: Chicago's Tragedy

> *There have been occasions in the past when chief executives have stood at the schoolhouse and statehouse doors with their faces livid and with wattles flapping have defied the federal government to enforce its laws and decrees.*
> *It is an anomaly that the "law and order" chief executive of this City should challenge and defy federal law.*
>
> Federal Judge Richard Austin
> October 1, 1971

> *Let's face it. This is a racist society and Judge Austin ought to deal with things as they are and not as they should be.*
>
> Dempsey Travis, *Chicago Defender*
> April 11, 1972

This is not a zoning tale, at least not directly. In one sense it is a land use story, but in another real sense it is a tragic account of thousands of people suggesting the dubious attempts by courts to correct blatant political and social injustices. In that regard it resembles the Mount Laurel story (see Chapter 11).

Chicago has long been labeled as the country's most racially segregated city. In 1969 a federal judge, Richard Austin, tried to take action to correct that condition. This is the story of his decision and the ensuing — and still ongoing — struggle between Alex Polikoff, attorney for the American Civil Liberties Union (ACLU), representing the residents of Chicago's public housing, and on the other side Charles Swibel, Chairman of the Chicago Housing Authority (CHA) and close friend of former

---

Authors' note: In this case, Richard Babcock was appointed a special consultant to the federal district court.

Mayor Richard Daley (also a protagonist) and the U.S. Department of Housing and Urban Development (HUD).

The author of the decision, the late Judge Richard Austin, was far from being a flaming liberal. For many years he had been a loyal member of the "Daley Machine." He served as state's attorney and carved a reputation as a tough law-and-order prosecutor. In 1956, Daley asked him to run for Governor when a silly "flower fund" scandal had forced the Democratic candidate to step down. He barely lost when Dwight Eisenhower swept the state.

This is not a happy narrative. Among all the cross name calling and skillful efforts to dodge the consequences of the order, the poor continued to suffer in the high-rise jungles with almost daily murders, rapes, and muggings. The situation *before* the decision was bleak, as well.

Background of the ACLU Lawsuit

For many years, public housing had been a silent scandal in Chicago. In the early days of public housing, under Executive Director Elizabeth Wood, the CHA had built low-rise units such as "Ida B. Wells" and "Julia Lathrop." By 1969, however, there were 36,000 units housing 148,000 people, including 90,000 minors (41 percent of the children had one parent). Many units were in twelve- to sixteen-story buildings. Since 1950, the CHA had built 19,011 units; all but 300 were in black ghettos. There were 23 projects, 16 of which were in census tracts that were 95 percent black and six others in tracts that were over 84 percent black. Prior to 1950, 36 percent of the occupants in public housing were white; in 1969 the figure was 8 percent. Applicants for units were 94 percent black, although in Chicago whites made up 70 percent of those eligible. So we had notorious places like "Cabrini Green" on the Near North Side and the "Robert Taylor Homes" on the South Side, the latter housing 28,000 persons in nine 16-story buildings and looking like fortresses to keep the bad guys in. Oscar Newman, in his provocative book, *Defensible Space,* observes:

> The high-rise prototype, with its myriad of resident janitorial and security staff, worked well for upper-middle-income families with few children but cannot be simplistically transplanted, minus the accompanying staff and accoutrements, for the use of large, low-income families. . . .
>
> High-rise apartment developments are a new genre. . . . As a means for housing low- and middle-income American families, most date back to the early fifties. . . . Their form evolved in response to pressures for higher densities, with no reference to previous traditions and no attempt at understanding the range of need to be answered in human habitat. . . .

Gautreaux: Chicago's Tragedy • 161

Cabrini Green. (©1985 Marc PoKempner: CLICK/Chicago)

Robert Taylor homes. (©1985 Joseph Sterling: CLICK/Chicago)

In this period of high crime rates, they have become containers for the victimization of their inhabitants.[1]

These conditions were probably inevitable in a city with a notorious history of racism, but they were underwritten and in effect guaranteed by a state law, passed in 1949, giving the City Council the right to approve or reject a proposal by the CHA to acquire real estate. This, of course, led to "preclearance" by the CHA with the alderman of the ward where the public housing project was to be located. Hence, except for a few units for the elderly, all units after 1950 were located in black wards.

The ACLU filed its suit on August 9, 1966, to challenge the practice of locating public housing exclusively in black areas. Mrs. Dorothy Gautreaux was the first named plaintiff. Ten years later she died, still residing in a high-rise ghetto unit.

Austin Order

ACLU attorney Alex Polikoff presented an impressive and convincing case, but all by affidavit. In February 1969, Judge Austin found the CHA guilty and invited the ACLU to submit a proposed decree. The basic provision in that decision as signed by Austin in July 1969 was that the CHA must build four units in the white ("General") area to every one unit built in a black ("Limited") area. What was a "black" area? It was a census tract that had 30 percent black residents; that, it was said, was the "tipping" point. It was Professor Philip Hauser, a social demographer from the University of Chicago, whose affidavit provided that concept. The decree went further: the Limited Area also was to include a one-mile "buffer zone," beyond its edge. In 1969, this Limited Area included almost all of the South Side and the West Side of the city. The Far North and Northwest sides, some of the Southwest Side, and a small slice of the Southeast Side were in the General Area.

The order went further: it limited the number of persons in any one project to about 120, and under special conditions, 240 persons; and families with children were to be housed in the first three stories. Finally, in Article X the Court provided:

> This Court retains jurisdiction of this matter for all purposes, including enforcement and the issuance, upon proper notice and motion, of orders modifying or supplementing the terms of this order upon the presentation of relevant information with respect to proposed developments designed

---

[1]Oscar Newman, *Defensible Space: Crime Prevention through Urban Design* (New York: Macmillan, 1973).

by CHA alone or in combination with other private or public agencies to achieve results consistent with this order, material changes in conditions existing at the time of this order or any other matter.[2]

Reaction and Response

Chicago leaders' initial reaction to the decision was, not surprisingly, mixed. The CHA Chairman, Charles R. Swibel, said in a prepared statement that "the provisions of the order are severely restrictive and doubtless will pose problems and complications in the operations of the authority." Cecil Butler, a black leader on the West Side, responded: "I am in favor of the results which this ruling seeks to obtain. It will bring about the destruction of the double housing standard in Chicago." And Richard Newhouse, a black state senator, and Jesse Jackson, head of PUSH (People United to Serve Humanity), a black South Side organization, echoed those views. Black attitudes would change, however. Then U.S. Representative (now Alderman) Roman Pucinski, whose predominantly white Northwest Side district would get much of the public housing under Judge Austin's decision, said Austin "probably has dealt the death knell to public housing here." How true! Mayor Daley hinted at his later position: "Some experts," he observed, "say that there also should be public housing in the suburbs as well as in Chicago."

The general sentiment reflected Rep. Pucinski's belief: it was the end of public housing in Chicago. But three days after Austin's opinion, Swibel announced that the CHA would build 2,000 low-rise units a year throughout the city. This was the first of many unkept promises; it became a broken record for the next fifteen years.

The CHA announced that it would not appeal the decision. In August 1970, Swibel called a press conference to announce "plans" for scattered low-rise, family-type housing throughout the City. As the Lerner newspapers, a local chain, observed, "One still gets the feeling that Charles Swibel's plans for scattered, low-rise family-type public housing were little more than a first anniversary remembrance of Judge Austin's landmark decision." Finally, early in 1970 Polikoff filed a petition before Judge Austin asking the Court to direct the CHA to submit sites to the City Council. Patrick O'Brien, CHA counsel, told the judge that the CHA was not contesting his order "but everyone must bear in mind the realities."

Judge Austin interjected, asking if it were "not a good time politically to do it." He suggested that the CHA might prefer to wait until

[2]*Gautreaux* v. *Chicago Housing Authority,* 304 F.Supp. 736 (1969).

after April 15, 1971, when a mayoral and aldermanic election would be held. He denied the CHA request for more time, threatened to hold officials in contempt, and set the following timetable: August 20—CHA to submit sites to Chicago Plan Commission; September 20—CHA to submit sites to City Council.

In the meantime Polikoff had filed a suit against HUD, as well as the CHA, asking that the suburbs be opened for public housing. Austin turned this suit down. Naturally, there were a lot of sly smiles because the judge lived in Flossmoor, one of the "lily-white" suburbs. Polikoff appealed to the 7th Circuit Court of Appeals.

The changing attitude of blacks began to emerge when six black aldermen, joined by the chairmen of four Model Cities Citizens Councils and a number of black clergymen, petitioned Austin to exempt three Model Cities areas from his order. Austin rejected the petition at Polikoff's strong urging. One black accused Polikoff of "playing God." Chicago was continuing to tear down slum units, about 3,000 a year, mostly in black neighborhoods, but blacks needed housing wherever it might be. Dempsey Travis, a very successful black Chicago realtor and author of numerous books, recalled that he contacted the Metropolitan Leadership Council, which had a contract with HUD to locate CHA residents in suburbia.

> We had three apartments available and we called the Chicago Leadership Council and we said we've got these apartments available and we'd like to have some CHA certificate people in here. We understand you've got some people. They said, "Yes. And where are the apartments located?" And as soon as we gave them the addresses that was the end of that. "There's too many black folks in there.". . . I think the *Gautreaux* decision in its heart was right. In its heart. But in its practicality and living within the philosophy of this City, most urban cities, it's wrong in that it cannot be implemented.

One black interviewed by the *Daily News* (March 15, 1971) three weeks before the election was quoted as saying:

> Daley made a politically motivated statement [in saying public housing would go where the people wanted it]. Now, he knows if public housing projects go up in white areas, he's in trouble. . . . It would cost him votes and he knows it. He knows he can get away with it. He's got his flunky aldermen. . . . This increases the concentration of black people and black people are afraid they're going to get thrown out of the CHA building if they don't vote Democratic.

The election was approaching. Daley made more speeches, condemning the Austin order: "The court order prohibits the construction of any substantial number of low-rise public housing units in the communities where this kind of housing is most needed and accepted." And he played on this "metropolitan" need:

> Although the city has no statutory requirement, it has voluntarily assumed a responsibility to provide housing for poor, low and moderate income families. Part of this responsibility for poor and low income families has been met by the provision of 38,000 units of public housing now in our city. Today fewer than 2,500 units of public housing are located in the Chicago metropolitan area outside of the city.

Polikoff doubts — and we agree — that Daley really meant his remarks about the "metropolitan area":

> RFB: Do you think he was sincere when he began talking all that time about how we ought to make this public housing metropolitan area wide?
>
> AP: So long as you were doing nothing in the city, as long as your position was to do nothing in the city until you had a metropolitan plan, de facto you'd be doing nothing in the city for the foreseeable future. So I have to conclude that even if in principle Daley and Swibel believed that the metropolitan plan was desirable, as a practical matter they knew this was the way to kill public housing going forward in the city.

Daley thundered that the City would build housing without federal aid rather than submit to Austin's order. The CHA submitted 275 sites to the City Council but on March 10, 1971, the Council buried the proposal by a thirty-three-to-five vote, sending it to a graveyard committee. Daley was reelected overwhelmingly to a fifth term.

In May, Pierre deVise, an urbanologist at the University of Illinois at Chicago Circle, reported to the South Side Planning Board that the noose was tightening:

> A close reading of the 1960–1970 census changes in suburban black population should disabuse anyone of the notion that social barriers are breaking down in the suburbs.
>
> What little relative change has occurred suggests a tightening rather than a loosening of the white suburban noose around the black inner city.
>
> Ninety per cent of the blacks continue to live in the four central cities of Chicago, Gary, Hammond and East Chicago, according to the study.
>
> Of the 130,000 blacks living outside those central cities, 80 per cent live in segregated neighborhoods in a dozen of the metropolitan area's 263 suburban municipalities.

One September 10, 1971, the U.S. Court of Appeals reversed Austin's opinion that the federal courts could not order HUD to provide public housing in the suburbs: "We are unable to avoid the conclusion," wrote Judge Ryan Duffy, "that [HUD Secretary George W. Romney's] past actions constituted racially discriminatory conduct." HUD told the City it would withhold $20 million in federal funds if it did not proceed, although earlier HUD had released $26 million in Model Cities funds on the City's promise to provide 500 units in white neighborhoods by September 15.

September 15 came and went, and Daley conceded that the City had again missed a deadline. At a hearing before Judge Austin, George Vavoulis, HUD Regional Administrator, confronted Polikoff in the hallway outside Austin's courtroom and said, "If you want to be the Regional Administrator, file for the job." And Daley attacked the media: "How can the people of the communications media talk out of both sides of their mouths? They talk about the blighted condition in Woodlawn [a black area] and then they won't let you build there."

On October 1, Austin issued an order enjoining the City from using the $26 million already released by HUD for Model Cities. His anger was obvious as he spoke of chief executives with "wattles flapping." And he added:

> You're telling me it's better for a child to have breakfast than to have the opportunity to move out of the ghetto. Let them have cake, but don't let them move to the Northwest side or the Southwest side. . . .
>
> It is perfectly clear that the conditions [of the site selection timetable] have not been met, and it is becoming obvious that they never will be.

The City and HUD announced that they would appeal. This was beginning to sound like Charles Dickens's *Bleak House*:

> [S]ome score of members of the High Court of Chancery bar ought to be — as here they are — mistily engaged in one of the ten thousand stages of an endless cause, tripping one another up on slippery precedents, groping knee-deep in technicalities, running their goat-hair and horse-hair warded heads against walls of words, and making a pretense of equity with serious faces, as players might. On such an afternoon, the various solicitors in the cause . . . ought to be — as are they not? — ranged in a line, in a long matted well between the register's red table and silk gowns, with bills, cross-bills, answers, rejoinders, injunctions, affidavits, issues, references to masters, masters' reports, mountains of costly nonsense, piled before them.

Daley had an abundance of outspoken support. Coalitions of whites of the Northwest and Southwest Side groups organized to resist the Austin order. One of the most vocal was Neighbors Opposing the Chicago Housing Authority (NO-CHA). One of the groups' organizers, William Mulligan, was quoted in the *Chicago Tribune:*

Those residents feel that if the suburbs were included in the order residents would have no place to run but as long as the suburbs are exempted, the communities will not be stabilized. Others are opposed to public housing being forced into their community, period. They fear it will bring poor blacks into their community.

So 1971 came to a close. The City had approved only 288 of the 700 sites selected by the CHA. It had badly reneged on its agreement to provide 1,700 units throughout the City. Nothing would change in 1972 and later years.

On January 7, Austin ordered the CHA to bypass seeking approval of the City Council in spite of the Illinois law that required such approval, and, worse yet, HUD announced that $20 million originally held for Chicago would be redistributed to other midwestern cities. On March 9, the 7th Circuit Court of Appeals reversed Austin's ruling freezing Model City funds:

> We think it was improper for the District Court to threaten the termination of a program which was not tainted with discriminatory action, in order to bring about a cure of a separate program which was found to have been so tainted.[3]

The pressure was, at least temporarily, off the City.

The City was not successful in getting HUD to go along with the few sites it did propose. HUD rejected 450 units on the Far South Side at 116th and Torrence Avenue, declaring the site unsuitable for housing because it lacked transportation, had no public schools, and was close to three steel plants, an auto plant, and a sanitary landfill.

Again five black aldermen asked Austin to allow housing to be built in black neighborhoods. And Dempsey Travis added, "If the judge persists in this direction, the white middle class will all flee and we'll have a city made up entirely of poor blacks and rich whites." But the *Chicago Defender,* a black newspaper, said:

> The black aldermen who are pressing for housing units to be built in black neighborhoods under the plea of a desperate shortage, are in truth more concerned with preserving their political prestige and power than they are with the more intrinsic and fundamental prerogatives of their constituents to live wherever they choose.

Meanwhile the Nixon administration had phased out nearly all money for building public housing anywhere. And the U.S. Supreme Court appeared to put the kibosh on any metropolitan solution to low-income

---

[3]*Gautreaux* v. *Romney,* 547, F.2d 124 (1972).

housing by its five-to-four decision in the *Milliken* case, which struck down a Detroit plan to bus school children across district borders to bring racial balance to city schools. Alex Polikoff, who did not see school busing as the best solution to segregation, had appealed Judge Austin's adverse ruling: "Even if you got black and white kids together in the classrooms the black children would still go home every night to the same dingy ghetto projects." He was successful in the appeal (although HUD did take the case up to the Supreme Court). The Circuit Court held that Austin was wrong. It ruled that HUD had the authority to deal with city-suburban housing issues.

Polikoff went back to Austin with a proposal that Austin appoint a master to hold hearings to determine whether the CHA and HUD had used their best efforts to provide more housing for poor families. Austin withheld an opinion on the request but did observe:

> I think it's time I started thinking about contempt citations for the Chairman of the Chicago Housing Authority [Swibel] and for HUD. I think 63 units after five years and three months is not a hell of a lot of progress.

Patrick O'Brien, attorney for the CHA, attacked Polikoff as a "grandiose commissar of housing schemes." He then told the judge: "Your honor, we're going off on a snipe hunt and the bag will be just as empty in the morning as it has been." Austin appointed Magistrate Olga Jurco a master.

In the meantime, HUD proposed that the CHA take over the approximately 2,000 units HUD had repossessed under the 236 and 235 programs. Unfortunately, most of these units were in the black Limited Area. Magistrate Jurco recommended to the judge that the ratio of building in white and black areas—for Section 8 housing only—be reduced from 75/25 to 60/40, and Austin agreed. Later the ratio for Section 8 between white and black areas was reduced to 50/50.

Public Housing in the Suburbs

On April 20, 1976, on HUD's appeal, the U.S. Supreme Court handed down its decision in *Hills* v. *Gautreaux,* 425 U.S. 285. The Court distinguished *Milliken,* the Detroit school case:

> Here, unlike the desegregation remedy found erroneous in *Milliken,* a judicial order directing relief beyond the boundary lines of Chicago will not necessarily entail coercion of uninvolved governmental units, because both CHA and HUD have the authority to operate outside the Chicago city limits. [Footnote omitted.]

But if it did appear to allow public housing, it carefully noted:

The more substantial question under *Milliken* is whether an order against HUD affecting its conduct beyond Chicago's boundaries would impermissibly interfere with local governments and suburban housing authorities that have not been implicated in HUD's unconstitutional conduct.

Use of the §8 program to expand low-income housing opportunities outside areas of minority concentration would not have a coercive effect on suburban municipalities. For under the program, the local governmental units retain the right to comment on specific assistance proposals, to reject certain proposals that are inconsistent with their approved housing-assistance plans, *and to require that zoning and other land-use restrictions be adhered to by builders.* [Emphasis added.]

So much for public housing in the suburbs! One CHA official noted that if zoning could control the location of public housing, it was probably hopeless:

> Working in cooperation with the Cook County Housing Authority in 1972, we sent letters to 103 municipalities in the country to determine if there was an interest in placing public housing in the suburbs.
>
> Only two suburbs — Flossmoor and Northbrook — agreed to talk about it, but nothing came of it.

In February 1976, Mrs. Dorothy Gautreaux died in a South Side ghetto. Mayor Daley died in December. And Judge Austin also passed away. None of these events put a stop to the game playing.

To forestall a trial court hearing on metropolitan-wide relief pursuant to the Supreme Court's remand, HUD entered into agreement with an organization known as Leadership Council for Metropolitan Open Communities, for HUD to fund the relocation of 400 CHA families in the suburbs and in the white areas of Chicago. (There were now 10,000 families on the CHA waiting list.) The agreement provided for the use of Section 8 funds and also gave priority to developers who were willing to take a few Section 8 families.

By the end of 1977, the Leadership Council had placed 255 families in apartments in the suburbs. The largest number, 74, were placed in Du Page County (the wealthiest county in Illinois), 68 in Cook County suburbs, 24 in Kane County, 23 in Will County, 8 in Lake County, and 28 in white areas of Chicago. Usually, the residents of these apartments were one-parent families, and initially they were required to have a car — which was not easy for someone on welfare. There are a number of anecdotal stories about successful moves. One such story is about "Mary" (a pseudonym):

> When she moved to the suburbs she was receiving welfare payments while finishing her degree in sociology at a Loop College, a degree it took her seven years to get.

Subsequently she got a job and went off welfare. When she gets her next raise, her income will be too high for her to continue on the program.

Mary said she was surprised to find other black families living in the suburbs, and the racial prejudice she encountered was much less than she had anticipated.

Her 12-year-old son hit a white boy in school after a name-calling incident, but when the boys were taken to the principal's office the principal said her son was justified because the other boy had a reputation for bullying both white and black children, she said.

While her children are doing well in school and have immersed themselves in extracurricular activities there, Mary said her life in the suburbs is lonely.

"White single women can find a social life in the suburbs, but there are no black men here. Black men feel threatened in the suburbs, so they stay in the city unless they are married," she said.

But her quiet, three-bedroom apartment and the change she's seen in her children make the move worthwhile to her, and she says she's in the suburbs to stay.

Carol Hendricks of the Leadership Council reports that the program is still progressing. As of July 1984, they had located about 2,300 families, about two-thirds of whom have stayed. Mrs. Hendricks would not divulge the breakdown among suburbs. "It makes some officials nervous." Ninety-one percent are one-parent families. We asked her if the male returned when the female made the move:

> CH: I think you'll find in many cases the male does come back. He comes back or he appears or a new one comes or something. That's one of the things that we have a problem with is the isolation, moving to the suburbs sometimes that female who is by herself with her children, she needs the companionship of someone else. That's very normal and so many times [she] will either get married or have a boyfriend that comes to visit her very often and that can cause a problem because the system does not recognize that.
>
> RFB: You don't try to moralize.
>
> CH: Well, no, that's not our role. And yet some people tend to feel we should.

HUD and Polikoff even allowed them for a while to relocate in the Limited Area. But HUD forbade the Council to require a car. It was too "parental."

In January 1984, when the Leadership Council announced it was going to open up its registration for 1,000 persons, 200 people spent the night in the building and a mob of 3,000 had gathered by the time the offices opened. There was a near riot.

In spite of the few happy stories, the pace of resettlement has been glacial — perhaps thirty to thirty-five families a month, which, considering the incredible number on waiting lists (10,000), has been minuscule. We have heard the experiment described as "sort of a chic liberal 'one black in every block' kind of slogan."

Criticism of the Ruling

And people were getting even more restless. Black developers and members of Operation PUSH went to Polikoff, who agreed to get the original decision modified to exempt rehabilitated buildings from *Gautreaux*. This, at least, gave some relief to the limited prohibition against Section 8 financing. Cardiss Collins, Democratic Congresswoman for the predominantly black 7th Congressional District on Chicago's West Side, mounted a campaign against the 1969 decision and held hearings in April 1978. Black developers lashed out against *Gautreaux*. One black builder told Rep. Collins's subcommittee:

> I must point out that the most devastating effect that has caused a substantial delay in the production of housing and in meeting the goal as set forth by Congress of a decent home and a suitable living environment for every American family has been in the *Gautreaux* decision.

Mr. Laurent, a black mortgage banker, joined in:

> The *Gautreaux* decision as handed down is directly responsible for the lack of decent and affordable housing in the city of Chicago. It has prevented the construction of new units in black areas with few or rare exceptions. . . .
> Blacks become the victims of a policy invoked by local and Federal policy. *Gautreaux,* in form, espouses housing opportunities for blacks but in substance prevents freedom of choice to reside in or develop privately owned and financed housing, which is subsidized by section 8.
> *Gautreaux* then has become an "inverted restrictive covenant," strangling the mortal remains of a large segment of black Chicago neighborhoods.

There is merit in their protests. White liberals may feel strongly about integration, but the blacks feel strongly about adequate housing and the hell with "Whitey." As noted in *Billboards, Glass Houses and the Law,*

> Recently, courts have begun to listen to the protests that these local laws infringe on constitutional rights, and the white liberal has begun to take pride in his contribution to the cause. But, just as he dares hope for success, he is met head-on by indifference or outrage of black leaders. His problem, he learns, is that he is an integrationist — which, of course, is what he thought he was supposed to be. The charge is that his aim is either to dabble with meaningless problems in the suburbs while ignoring the agonizing problems in the black ghetto or to scatter the black population into the suburbs —

"disperse" is the fighting word—just as the blacks are gaining real power in the city.[4]

A white professor of Urban Affairs at Loyola University, J. F. Feurst, testified before Rep. Collins:

> So it has been with the *Gautreaux* case. As a direct result of the ruling, the opportunities for public housing are smaller than they were 10 years ago; prospects for new public housing in Chicago are now virtually nonexistent. Since the case started, not one substantial multifamily public-housing development has been built in Chicago (apart from a few that had already been started by 1966). And no new public housing or even privately-owned subsidized housing for the poor is likely to be built for many years to come, unless the short-sighted court rulings and the administrative measures that followed them are reversed.
>
> This wretched situation came about largely because United States District Court Judge Richard Austin, after justifiably finding that CHA was guilty of discriminatory practices, left it up to the plaintiff's attorneys, led by Polikoff (an American Civil Liberties Union lawyer and currently executive director of Businessmen for the Public Interest), to draw up Procrustean remedies for Chicago's complex housing problems. But Polikoff, who had a fine record of energetically supporting minority causes, was beguiled by the wider aspects of the case. He designed a program to tie the hands of CHA, without considering what the side effects would be on his own clients. The remedy was unenforceable, and later efforts to improve it only made matters worse.

Polikoff appeared at the hearing and testified eloquently, placing the blame where it belonged: on the City Council and the CHA. The NAACP also supported his position. Polikoff said later that he did not hear from Rep. Collins again. Clearly, black contractors and developers had put pressure on her.

Babcock Investigation and Report

In the fall of 1978, Richard Babcock was appointed by the Magistrate as a special urban consultant to make an investigation. His charge was to determine:

1. Whether defendant Chicago Housing Authority (CHA) has taken all practicable steps to identify all residentially-zoned land suitable for the development of remedial housing for the plaintiff class in the General Public Housing Area of the City of Chicago;

[4]Richard Babcock, *Billboards, Glass Houses and the Law* (Colorado Springs: Shepards, 1977), p. 108.

2. Whether CHA has taken all practicable steps to acquire such identified land;
3. Whether CHA has taken all practicable steps in "packaging" projects, soliciting construction bids, and proposing sufficiently large projects to maximize the possibilities of complying with construction cost limitations of the U.S. Department of Housing and Urban Development and to increase the pace of providing remedial housing;
4. Whether CHA has taken all practicable steps to submit proposals under Article X of the Court's order of July 1, 1969 (304 F. Supp. 236, 741) to increase the pace of providing remedial housing;
5. Whether CHA is taking all practicable steps to implement as rapidly as possible the Master's direction to proceed with an acquisition program; and
6. Whether CHA can and should take other actions to increase the pace of providing remedial housing, either in connection with the matters referred to in paragraphs (1) through (5) preceding or otherwise.

The CHA bitterly opposed the appointment, but Judge John Crowley, Austin's successor to the case, authorized it. For six months Babcock and two associates pursued the investigation.

On March 15, 1979, they filed their report. It uniformly found against the CHA. It concluded that the CHA had not used good faith and had not employed all practicable steps (a) to identify all residentially zoned land suitable for the plaintiff class, (b) to acquire all such land, (c) to package projects, (d) to submit proposals under Article X of the July 1, 1969, order, and (e) to implement "as rapidly as possible" an acquisition program. Those conclusions were:

1. Site identification had been carried on with notable reluctance. There was a survey of available housing in 1971 but no one in the CHA was familiar with the methodology of the 1971 survey. Another survey was carried out in 1975, but it had not been updated or reviewed in four years although the CHA acknowledged that the Chicago market is volatile and dynamic. In 1978, the City of Chicago produced about 1,372 sites and buildings suitable for residential development and rehabilitation. The CHA was still reviewing these sites.

2. The CHA did not employ the type of aggressive search for sites that a prudent and reasonable real estate investor would employ. One man, part time, in the Engineering Department was all that was available. No use of nominees or brokers, no use of multiple listings, no use of trade papers or newspaper advertisements had been made. The CHA, in short, acted as reluctant suitor rather than as an aggressive seeker of sites.

3. The CHA's recordkeeping of available or potential sites was so haphazard and confusing that the Authority itself did not appear to have

adequate information. It had not updated the status list used for site acquisition in over two years. As a result, the CHA did not have an accurate picture of the availability of various sites in the General Public Housing Area.

4. The CHA had made no effort to seek Article X exceptions other than on a broad basis that would modify the decree. At no time had it sought an exception for a particular project, nor had it sought at any time to test Alex Polikoff's willingness to accept an Article X exception.

5. The CHA response to the recommendations of Commissioner of Planning Martin Murphy on rezoning of parcels reflected a reluctance to take any chances on a public hearing for rezoning. First, the CHA said that if it were not the owner it could not apply; then, correcting itself later, it offered no excuse except the response that it would be politically impracticable. The CHA also had failed to use the type of purchase contracts contingent upon rezoning used every day in the marketplace.

6. With one exception (of a six-flat family development) the CHA did not submit to HUD any proposal for mixed elderly and family housing in separate buildings although HUD had indicated that it would react favorably to such a proposal, and although the combination of family and elderly housing in the same development program can result in economies of scale that could overcome HUD's prototype cost limitations.

7. CHA officials made it clear that they were philosophically opposed to developing any single project with more than six units. There is no basis in the 1969 decree for such a policy. In light of the well- and long-known HUD prototype policy, this suggests an easy way to avoid any significant development of public housing.

8. At the same time, the CHA had been extremely reluctant to seek out one- or two-bedroom units for acquisition, even though there appeared to be families on the waiting list that would qualify for smaller units.

9. Finally, the report recommended that a receiver should be appointed to assume complete responsibility for new or rehabilitated housing.

The original 1969 order had allowed the CHA to go to 120 persons — or to 240 persons in special situations — in any one project. The CHA had never done so. The prevalent attitude of the CHA, represented by Charles Swibel, appears in the following exchange:

> RFB: Why don't you go for some larger units? . . . Why not go 18–20 units?
>
> CS: . . . You would have approximately 60 children, minors, from a practical, pragmatic management point. It would just not be feasible and livable.
>
> RFB: So philosophically you just don't think that would be a good management decision?

CS: That's correct. I don't think it would be a healthy decision. I could see—and the social services that would be needed; I don't know where they would come from.

So the CHA followed a policy that called for far fewer units in a single development than permitted by Judge Austin.

The record of CHA mangement since 1969 has been dismal. In spite of the number of recommendations Babcock made, he had serious reservations whether the CHA could carry them out with the aggressiveness that was required. Almost every person interviewed—even those who regarded the 1969 decree as a major impediment to development—believed that the CHA could not carry forward new acquisition and development. Babcock likewise questioned whether the CHA was capable of developing new housing for the plaintiff class or Chicago's housing poor. The development of housing is a complex matter. Participants in a fast-moving housing market such as Chicago must be aggressive and thoroughly professional to succeed. The CHA's performance had fallen short of that of a reasonably prudent real estate developer in the private sector, and there was no indication that this would change in the future.

The relationship between the CHA and the counsel for the plaintiffs had, over ten years, developed into one of confrontation and suspicion. This is not an atmosphere conducive to an effective housing strategy. The bitterness that was evident on both sides may be appropriate for one-shot litigation but not for an ongoing, court-supervised housing program. Babcock did not assess blame for this state of affairs. Indeed, it would be remarkable if conditions had been otherwise after more than ten years of litigation. But in his opinion, some change in personnel was essential. It was unlikely that the recommendations could be implemented under existing CHA management.

Further, the CHA sensed that the order was politically unpopular; "public housing" is a dirty term. It was fearful of the consequences if it proposed significant housing in the white neighborhoods, and it had not undertaken the kind of educational program that could help defuse the opposition. In short, CHA management was unwilling or unable to stick its neck out. Babcock was not without sympathy with the CHA in this respect. Yet in equally difficult situations, courts have acted and agencies have responded in spite of the vocal and unpleasant confrontations.

Admittedly, the idea of appointing a receiver was drastic. There may have been alternatives, but Babcock did not believe any of them would be effective. Contempt citations would not get housing built. Nor did it seem probable that detailed court orders to the present CHA management for specific tasks would produce results. What was required was someone with (a) a working knowledge of the real estate market and (b) a commitment to providing low-rent housing in both the General and Limited Areas as rapidly as possible. The CHA board and its staff could have been permitted to remain in full charge of the operation and management of CHA's existing structures. However, a court-appointed receiver could have been given all the necessary authority and all the necessary CHA resources to develop conventional and turnkey public housing, public housing through the acquisition for rehabilitation, and Section 8 new construction. While the receiver would conduct and supervise all these operations and function under the Court's direction, his work, financing, and borrowing authority would be derived from the CHA. The CHA's Board of Commissioners could have been directed to comply with all the receiver's requests with respect to the development of new units of public housing, including but not limited to requests for assistance in authorizing and signing CHA bonds, CHA contracts with the state and federal governments, and CHA contracts with private parties. All dwelling units constructed after the efforts of the court-appointed receiver would be turned over to CHA management upon completion.

There was little precedent at that time for such a step. Later a receiver was appointed by Massachusetts Housing Court Justice Paul G. Garrity in the Boston public housing case and upheld on appeal (*Perez* v. *Boston Housing Authority*, 400 N.E.2d 1231 [1980]. See also *Morgan* v. *McDonough*, 548 F.2d 28 [1977]). A seven-member committee was appointed for the Alabama prison system by Federal District Judge Frank M. Johnson (*Wyatt* v. *Stickney*, 344 F. Supp. 373 [1973]), although he declined to appoint a receiver.

Clearly, a detailed proposal would have to be prepared. The availability of HUD funds would have to be established. The arrangements for transfer of completed housing to the CHA for management would have to be spelled out. In new housing the question of the issuance of bonds to finance the construction would have to be established. HUD funds were available for development, and interim loans were available for planning. Whether the receiver would work with and through CHA personnel and use CHA offices, or whether he would operate entirely independently of the CHA, were questions that could be settled once the concept was authorized. The receiver would certainly be accountable to the court and would report regularly on his work, including the degree of cooperation he received from the CHA. But the CHA clearly was not interested in an aggressive attitude. The Article X provision in the original order of July 1969 permitted the CHA to apply to the federal judge for an exception on the order. The CHA, however, never did apply. Babcock asked Charles Master, Executive Director of the CHA:

RFB: But have you ever gone in with a specific parcel in mind as some others have, I think, and asked for an exception?

CM: No, no, we've never gone in. . . .

RFB: Here's a parcel on, you know, down here.

CM: Well, nobody's gone in just on one—what they would call one development.

And Charles Swibel put it more candidly:

RFB: Right. Well, let me rephrase the question. Have you ever come in for an exception where CHA was going to do the developing—CHA, not TWO, not. . . .

CS: Not to my knowledge.

RFB: Why not?

CS: I think that the atmosphere in the—Mr. Polikoff, being in an adversary position, after so many years of litigation, and private discussions, would not look kindly on any recommendations or suggestions of . . . Cal Hall, our general counsel, to any proposal, because he was gung ho that he was going to adhere to the course we have to build 700 units before he would listen.

While the appointment of a receiver might have appeared to be a dramatic step, it bears repeating that Babcock had spent six months reviewing ten years of CHA activities, which have resulted in the manufacture of only 117 family dwelling units and an almost inexhaustible supply of excuses for poor performance. It seemed obvious that another person or party would be better equipped to provide public housing for the people of Chicago. Babcock did not believe that the federal court could permit public housing authority to ignore a long-standing federal court injunction.

Aftermath of the Babcock Report

The Court did not accept this gratuitous recommendation. After ten years, it believed the suggestion too severe. Yet four years later, when the CHA continued to temporize, Judge Crowley threatened to appoint a receiver.

Events moved along much the same way in 1980 and 1981. Michael Bilandic had replaced Mayor Daley and, in the midst of ferocious snow storms, Jane Byrne replaced Bilandic. Nothing much happened other than Byrne's highly publicized move for a week or ten days into an apartment in Cabrini Green.

In 1983, Judge Marvin Aspen (Judge Crowley's successor on the case) did enter an order appointing a receiver but stayed the order for six months to give the CHA a chance to acquire more scattered housing sites in the white area. Because the CHA partially achieved that goal, a receiver was never named. Alex Polikoff believes that was a mistake:

> And that is one of the great disappointments, I think, in the case. The courts were reluctant, the judges were so reluctant to take that step of appointing a receiver that they failed to do what at least in my judgment would have been a good thing, even for CHA. It would have taken all the politics out of the hot issue of site selection. We would have had a technocrat making the decisions as to where those sites should go.

The Newman Report and Aftermath

But HUD was becoming restless. All public housing authorities were having financial problems. And the CHA was the worst of the bunch. As of December 31, 1980, it had run up an operating deficit of $33,597,055. Although it would receive approximately $60 million in an operating subsidy from HUD in 1982, a deficiency in residual receipts of about $50 million was expected in that year. Quite simply, HUD became fed up and commissioned Oscar Newman and his Institute for Community Design Analysis to do one more study (the latest in a half-dozen such analyses in three years). The CHA flunked this study. Typical of the countless findings were the statement in the report that

> in every area we examined, from finance to maintenance, from administration to outside contracting, from staffing to project management, from purchasing to accounting, the CHA was found to be operating in a state of profound confusion and disarray. No one seems to be minding the store; what's more, no one seems to genuinely care. It is almost as if the CHA exists for a purpose other than the management and maintenance of good quality public housing, and that the pursuit of this other, more primary, purpose has determined what the CHA is today: its physical deterioration, its high debt, its management malaise.

The Newman report recommended that Charles Swibel be fired. *Chicago Magazine* (July 1982) reported that while Swibel was head of the CHA, he frequently entered into private real estate deals with the people with whom he did business as a public official. Following is an account of his activities, entitled "Stalking Charlie Swibel":

> In 1961, for example, Swibel built Marina City with funds from the Flat Janitors Union, whose members were custodians in CHA buildings. A 1975 joint investigation by the Better Government Association (BGA) and the

Sun-Times revealed that, when the much-heralded project fell into financial trouble in 1967, Swibel turned to Continental Bank for aid. The bank took over Marina City, covered Swibel's debts, and paid him $79,000 a year to manage the complex. Just a few weeks later, the CHA shifted its multimillion-dollar main development fund to Continental, which was already holding millions of CHA dollars in a non-interest-yielding account. The BGA-*Sun-Times* probe also revealed that three months after a security firm outfitted Swibel's Winnetka home with a $6,000 burglar alarm system in 1968, the firm received a CHA contract to provide guards for the projects for a fee in excess of $700,000 a year. Swibel didn't pay the bill for his home alarm system until he learned — six years later — that a Federal grand jury was investigating the CHA's contract with the firm. From 1970 to 1974, the CHA granted lucrative electrical contracts to a politically connected firm that failed to perform the work.

So HUD laid down its demand: fire Swibel and the entire CHA Board or lose further subsidies. Mayor Byrne stalled for months, trying to shift public attention from CHA to Reagan and his antipoverty policies. Eventually, a face-saving solution was worked through the Illinois Legislature: make the chairmanship job a full-time salaried position, allowing Swibel to resign, alleging the press of his private affairs. This he finally did in the summer of 1982.

Then came the political revolution of 1983, during which Harold Washington was elected Mayor after one of the dirtiest, overtly racist campaigns in Chicago's history.

The situation has improved under Mayor Washington. Alex Polikoff believes more progress has been made in the last year under a fresh CHA administration than has taken place since the beginning of the dispute. Some 800 to 1,000 scattered site units have been built, rehabilitated, or are in the pipeline. Of course, under the new agreement half of these are in black areas. One of the new ideas being tried out is to subcontract 132 of these units to a subsidiary of Hull House, thereby removing the vast bureaucracy in the CHA's downtown offices. Polikoff also believes there is less fear of the program now that units are in place:

> I believe that the scattered site program, because so many units are now in place, is no longer the great unknown fear it was in the past. There have been some places where in good neighborhoods the scattered site story has been a success. In bad neighborhoods it's been a failure in terms of the social objectives that you hope to be achieved.

Not that there are not protests. According to Polikoff, "Northwest and Southwest neighborhood federation groups have been the most extreme. They picketed my house once last year." But he is optimistic — and a bit defensive—which is understandable when he acknowledges that he held up any public housing for almost ten years:

> So I believe that CHA is shaping itself to act in a more effective way than has been the case before now. I think Irwin France started that and I hope Zirl Smith will finish it. I realize when I say this that I've said like things before and have always been disappointed and if you rely on historical patterns I'm going to be disappointed again.

Whether this will continue beyond Mayor Washington is doubtful. If one remembers how the Republican candidate against Washington appealed to the white bigots and how the City Council is divided into black and white factions, any prognosis cannot be encouraging.

Kurland Tests

Professor Phillip Kurland, formerly of the University of Chicago Law School, has an intriguing theory of how judicial opinions will fare when they trespass into sacred social issues. Simply stated, the proposition is that a judicial opinion must pass two of the following three tests if it is to work:

1. Does it have a simple constitutional formula? Such as one man, one vote? (Even this decree by the U.S. Supreme Court encountered some difficulties and occasionally courts had to step in and reapportion when the legislatures failed to act.)
2. Does the order involve an issue that is within the direct control of the courts (such as the judgment that indigent convicted persons must be furnished with a copy of the trial record for purposes of appeal)?
3. Is there general public acquiescence? (Not approval, just acceptance.) Clearly, the abolition of the poll tax was such a case.[5]

By these Kurland tests, it is hard to see how Judge Austin's decree passes. Certainly, there was no public acquiescence, and it was a matter hardly within the direct control of the court, as attested by the failures of the 1969-1982 period and the Court's unwillingness to hold in contempt or appoint a receiver. A court order holding a city's practices unconstitutional is one thing; but throwing Mayor Daley in jail and disrupting the business of the CHA are highly personal acts. And it is hard to find

---

[5]See 35 *University of Chicago Law Review* 583 (1968).

a simple constitutional formula; even the four-to-one ratio was invented, unlike the simple equity of one man, one vote.

When we pointed out the Kurland tests to Polikoff, he bristled and referred to the school desegration case *Brown* v. *Board of Education:*

AP: I think that the scattered site program is generally speaking receiving public acceptance. There are resisters, of course. There are resisters to the school desegregation orders that continue to be issued, but you don't have the body politic formally or informally en masse resisting any more. And you actually have a scattered site of modest scope going forward, including the most resisting neighborhoods.

RFB: But the scattered site housing is a drop in the bucket compared to the need.

AP: Of course, but the public housing that was being built when the case started was a drop in the bucket compared to the need. . . . It's not like welfare. We don't have an entitlement program, do we, in housing? Any program, or all programs taken together throughout the whole country do not come anywhere near satisfying need.

It seems that Polikoff's question is more to the point: "Well, are you suggesting that Austin should *not* have ruled as he did or that the U.S. Supreme Court should have allowed black and white kids to be separately educated?"

There is no possible way to respond except to concur in Austin's opinion.

In spite of the exciting effort by the Leadership Council in the suburbs and the ongoing scattered-site housing during the Washington interregnum and the infectious optimism of Polikoff, the last chapter in this tragic story is not yet written. With such highly emotive cases, it is necessary to take the long, long view and expect changes to occur over decades.

10

Hernandez v. *City of Lafayette:* Longfellow Replayed

> *"You are convened this day," he said, "by his Majesty's orders. Clement and kind has he been, but how you have answered his kindness, Let your own hearts reply! To my natural make and my temper. Painful the task is I do, which to you I know must be grievous. Yet must I bow and obey, and deliver the will of our monarch; Namely that all your lands, and dwellings and cattle of all kinds Forfeited be to the crown; and that you yourselves from this province Be transported to other lands. . . . God grant you may dwell there Ever as faithful subjects, a happy and peaceable people!*
>
> Colonel John Winslow's speech to the Acadians upon their expulsion from Nova Scotia, as presented in Longfellow's *Evangeline*

> *I'm going to get you.*
>
> Hon. Kenneth A. Bowen (1975)

When the Acadians were expelled from Nova Scotia, they suffered horribly as they searched for new homes along the Atlantic coast, Haiti, and near the mouth of the Mississippi River. More than half the expellees died of smallpox, malnutrition, or exposure within one year of their expulsion, but many of the survivors ultimately settled in southwestern Louisiana, where the life is "happy and peaceable." Indeed the "Cajuns" (a corruption of *Acadians*) dominate the so-called French Triangle of Louisiana and live a genuine and robust life in a land abundant with harvestable natural resources.

Authors' note: Ross and Hardies were attorneys for the City of Lafayette.

There are times in southwestern Louisiana, however, when life is *not* happy and peaceable, and the following is such a story. Take a blind, crippled music teacher, a Louisiana politician, and a horde of neighborhood preservationists; add a dash of "young zoning lawyer"; stir them all together; and what do you have? Zoning jambalaya.

Lafayette

Lafayette, Louisiana, extolled by its faithful as the "Heart of Acadiana" and the home of the University of Southwestern Louisiana's "Ragin' Cajuns," is a classically beautiful southern city, dominated by enormous live-oak trees, unforgettable food, and a distinctive and remarkable architectural style known simply as "Cajun." The City, which lies west of the wilderness of the Atchafalaya Swamp (across which Interstate 10 is elevated on concrete pilings in silent tribute to the power of southern politics) and upriver from Jefferson Island, the home of Tabasco sauce, is known far and wide for its cultural traditions in music, food, and politics. Crawfish, the quintessential southwestern Louisiana delicacy, is fried, stuffed, boiled, etoufféed, and baked in backyards, kitchens and restaurants throughout the City. The real cause célèbre, however, is oil and gas — lots and lots of oil and gas. Indeed, Lafayette is the home of more oil companies and oil-related companies than any city in the world.

The City's reputation has spread, but not just because of its character and oil. (It has more than ample character, not to mention restaurants, millionaires, and what is surely the largest private air force in the world. Petroleum Helicopters operates an offshore oil-rig service from the Lafayette Municipal Airport that rivals the size of the air forces of many small countries.) The City's reputation has also spread because it does everything in extremes. For example, when the City got into a little dispute with a competitor in the electric utility business, the battle raged all the way to the U.S. Supreme Court, where the Court ruled against the City in a landmark case holding cities subject to the federal antitrust statutes.

Lafayette is also the home of James E. Hernandez and Kenneth F. Bowen, opponents in what became a zoning battle of titanic proportions.

The Effect of Growth

Lafayette, along with every other community with an oil-based economy, experienced explosive growth in the 1960s and 1970s; its population more than doubled in less than twenty years. By 1970, the traditional character of the City was beginning to change as nonresidential development began to spread to areas other than the City's traditional downtown. This new pattern of growth raised concern about the future character of the City and the long-term integrity of established neighborhoods. One proposal—to link the downtown with a developing southeast area by way of a bypass road through one of the City's most prestigious and stable neighborhoods—was particularly disturbing to its residents. Another major concern of neighborhood groups was the development of nonresidential uses along newly widened thoroughfares in what had always been residential neighborhoods.

One of the activists who opposed such "commercialization" and the downtown-neighborhood bypass (which was to be constructed along the route of an existing roadway—West Bayou Parkway) was Mrs. James Hernandez, a native of the City:

> As many of you gentlemen know, I appeared before this Board a number of times in the past few years. I have become vitally concerned with the manner in which all the zoning decisions are discussed and carried out.
>
> I am speaking as the President of the South College Road Civic Association tonight. I am representing the people who live in that area that is residential in nature at the present time. We are most upset about the recent attempt to rezone this area into commercial enterprise.

The area in question was the South College neighborhood in the vicinity of the intersection of South College Road with West Bayou Parkway. Mrs. Hernandez's house was located on West Bayou Parkway near the intersection. South College Road had been improved as a major arterial roadway, and Mrs. Hernandez's group was concerned about commercial rezonings along the road. They feared that a "domino effect" would drive residential uses out of the area and that the residential character of the area could be destroyed. The City fathers did not listen to Mrs. Hernandez's warning and granted a number of nonresidential zoning requests along South College during the late 1960s and early 1970s. By 1974, many parcels of land along South College Road had been rezoned to office or medical office and a trend was clearly evident along the once-residential roadway.

The Hernandez Petition to Rezone (B-1-M)

In 1975, Mrs. Hernandez and her husband, James, a blind and crippled music teacher, apparently decided to "switch rather than fight," and filed an application to have their 16.7-acre parcel of land at the intersection of West Bayou Parkway and South College rezoned to a business classification. To many neighbors and fellow civic association members, the Hernandez petition for rezoning represented a shocking betrayal of neighborhood solidarity. Moreover, the prospect of a new line of dominoes falling along West Bayou Parkway, the route of the often-proposed and much-maligned bypass, engendered substantial neighborhood opposition.

The Hernandez property, inherited from Mr. Hernandez's father, was strategically located between the most affluent neighborhood in town and the "Oil Center," a low-rise office park that housed much of Lafayette's oil industry. With the exception of Mr. Hernandez's home—custom designed to accommodate both his disability and his talents—and a small tenant home that had been his father's residence, the property was unimproved and was used, somewhat incongruously, as pasture for a small herd of cattle kept by Mrs. Hernandez.

The property was irregularly shaped along the contours of a large improved drainage way, the Coulee Mine, and West Bayou Parkway. A small neck of the property, fifty feet wide, fronted on South College Road; however, there was no direct access to South College from the Hernandez property because of a bridge ramp on South College leading across the Coulee Mine.

To the south of the property was a large municipal waste water treatment plant on land sold to the City by Mr. Hernandez's father. To the southwest across West Bayou Parkway was a subdivision of detached single-family dwellings bordered by vacant land and a low-rise townhouse project. To the west was another townhouse project at the corner of the intersection of West Bayou Parkway and South College Road. Along the north and northeast were expensive single-family dwellings on the other side of the Coulee Mine in a subdivision named "Bendel Gardens."

Mr. Hernandez consulted with an architect friend (whose children happened to take piano lessons from him), who recommended a modest medical office complex of 80,000 square feet as an appropriate use for the property. A site plan was prepared, and on August 12, 1975, Mr. Hernandez filed a petition for a zoning change from R-1-A (single-family residential on 8,000-square-foot lots) to B-1-M (medical office). The City of Lafayette, which had previously relied on a regional planning commission for its planning effort, directed the Hernandezes to its new "in-house" Planning Department and its Director, a professor on a leave of absence from the University of Southwestern Louisiana. The Director's response and recommendations encouraged the Hernandezes. In his recommendation, he wrote:

> A B-1-M zoning classification would provide the least traffic congestion at peak hours. A B-1-M zoning classification would provide for clustering

Aerial view of sewage treatment plant. Hernandez property is north of plant.

of like activities because of the close proximity of the Surgical Center, the South College Medical Center, and dental offices. The property is not desirable for R-1-A development because of the proximity of the sewerage treatment plant.

The Planning Commission did not agree with the Planning Director's assessment, however; and on September 25, 1975, after hearing extensive testimony and receiving petitions in opposition to the rezoning, the Commission, by unanimous vote, recommended denial.

The Chairman of the Planning Commission, who did not vote, was an outspoken home builder, and was apparently unimpressed with the concerns of the neighbors. He forwarded a "minority report" recommending the rezoning to the City Council "so that the individual property owner, whomsoever he may be, would have the right to the best equitable use of his property."

West Bayou/Girard Park Realignment

Coincidentally, the City of Lafayette, concerned about the impacts of growth on the area and attendant traffic congestion, had initiated a study of traffic improvements at the intersection of West Bayou Parkway and South College Road. The result of the study was a proposal to straighten out two "T" intersections (one at West Bayou and South College and another at Girard Park Drive and South College) and to connect the two roads with a bridge structure across the Coulee Mine, an alignment that would run right through the center of the Hernandez house.

The announcement of the realignment proposal was greeted by a hail of opposition by area homeowners, and Mr. and Mrs. Hernandez were among the most outspoken critics. The Hernandezes took the proposal personally because they believed it represented a change of position by the Mayor, who they claimed had long ago promised them that the traffic study would not affect their home. Responding to pressure from the neighborhood, the Mayor issued a press release (November 21, 1975) stating that he would not recommend the realignment to the City Council:

> The people of the area have spoken against the improvement and I personally feel that if those people who traffic [sic] the intersection do not want the improvements, then it should not be forced upon them.
>
> Therefore, I shall recommend to the Council that in keeping with the wishes of the people, the project should be abandoned.

Later events would reveal, however, that the Mayor had only intended to abandon the realignment temporarily.

The Hernandezes continued to oppose the realignment, and when the Mayor eventually admitted that the realignment was still under consideration, they openly accused him of reneging on his word to the people of the neighborhood. The Mayor, not one to shy from confrontation and apparently irritated by the Hernandezes' persistence, told Mrs. Hernandez, "I don't owe you anything"; "I'm not married to you, honey"; and, most memorably, "I'm going to get you."

On February 16, 1976, the Hernandezes' requested rezoning came before the City Council, and predictably, the zoning matter became entangled with the realignment issue: "If we change the zoning to another classification, we're going to have to pay more money when we create the right of way." The City Council promptly tabled the requested rezoning until the roadway issue could be resolved. The petition languished for more than a year, as little or no progress was made on the realignment issue.

Second Hearing on the Hernandez Petition (B-1-M)

In early January 1977, the Planning Commission, at the request of the City Council, held a second hearing on the Hernandez rezoning petition. This time, a new staff recommended denial and the Commission agreed, although the difficulties of the City's position are obvious from the minutes of the meeting:

> Mr. McWilliams [the City's new planning director] said all these zoning reclassification requests are examples of poor or no land and transportation and traffic planning by the previous planning staffs, Commissions, and other City Officials. . . .
> Mr. McWilliams felt we must resort to the best honest judgment of which recommendation would contribute least to the already heavy damage to the public interest. Damage may have also already been done to the petitioner through this lack of planning and lawsuits against the City may result.

On May 3, 1977, the City Council itself adopted a resolution rejecting the Hernandez request for rezoning from R-1-A to B-1-M.

New Petition to Rezone (R-2)

Several months later, a new petition for rezoning the Hernandez land was filed with the City. The new petition sought an R-2 classification, the City's highest-density residential zoning district, and was filed on behalf of Mr. Hernandez by a lawyer known as the "best zoning lawyer in the parish." In late September, the Planning Commission considered the staff's recommendation of approval and voted to recommend a zoning change from R-1-A to R-2. The action, although described by the Hernandezes' lawyer as no more than "half-a-loaf," was nevertheless threatening to the neighbors who saw the rezoning as nothing more than a first step toward creating a development corridor along West Bayou Parkway. Initially, the City Council tabled the petition for ninety days of further study and then, in response to public pressure, voted not to hear the petition for rezoning until the plans for the proposed realignment were complete.

Not too surprisingly, Mr. Hernandez took offense at these events, and on February 8, 1978, his lawyer filed a lawsuit in state court. The City responded by scheduling the rezoning petition for a Council hearing, and after a few starts and stops (including an unexpected direction from the Council to the staff to reconsider the issue of B-1-M zoning for the property), the City Council voted to rezone the Hernandez property to R-2. At last, it seemed that the Hernandezes' plans for development of their property were falling into place. But as they say, appearances can be more misleading.

Mayor Bowen (proponent of the by-now notorious West Bayou/Girard Park Drive realignment and, according to Mrs. Hernandez, their archenemy) vetoed the ordinance:

> I am vetoing this ordinance because I feel that the retention of the present R-1-A classification will protect, preserve and provide continuing compatible use of this property with the adjacent and contiguous R-1-A properties. Further, it will maintain and perpetuate the single family dwelling characteristic of this neighborhood.

When the Mayor's veto failed to be overridden by the required supermajority of the City Council, Mr. Hernandez's counsel escalated the intensity of the already-pending litigation and filed the first of what were to be many supplemental and amending petitions for relief.

Settlement and B-1-O Zoning

Between March 1978 and January 1979, the litigation lurched along the usual path of land use litigation with little apparent activity by the City until the very eve of the trial. When a trial date was set for February 7, 1979, the City's counsel for zoning matters confronted the matter square-on in a memorandum to the administration:

> Plaintiff's attorneys have filed a motion in the referenced case to have the matter set for trial. You will recall this is the Hernandez suit which attacks the action on the zoning request.

Aerial view of Hernandez property, showing proposed realignment.

It was hoped that we could avoid having to try this case by way of an early resolution of the right-of-way requirements on the West Bayou Parkway/Girard Park realignment. When may I expect to receive the plans?

The City's attorney, quite clearly unenthusiastic about trying the case, initiated settlement discussions during early January 1979 and just days before the scheduled trial, advised the City Council, in a letter captioned "In re: *City of Lafayette* v. *James Hernandez* (Acquisition of Rights of Way Necessary to Construction of West Bayou Parkway/Girard Park Drive Realignment)," that a settlement had been negotiated for "many of the numerous issues faced by the City." The terms of the settlement provided that the City would rezone the Hernandez property to B-1-O, an intensive professional office classification ("the Mayor will, in fact, sign the Ordinance") and that the Hernandezes would waive "severance damages" to the newly zoned property and would be compensated for the realignment portion at the fair market value of the B-1-O zoned land only if and when their land was expropriated for the realignment.

The attorney's letter outlining the details of the proposed settlement contained spaces for the signatures of all members of the City Council and the Mayor. All six signed the document under the caption "APPROVED." Depositions would subsequently reveal that the Mayor took the position that his signature was to be understood as conditional and that he was signing only so that the process of considering the B-1-O rezoning could be initiated.

On February 1, 1979, the City Council, to further the settlement agreement, directed the Planning Commission to hold a public hearing on rezoning the Hernandez property to B-1-O. On the same day, the City Council introduced an ordinance declaring the West Bayou Parkway/Girard Park Drive realignment to be a matter of "public necessity," a required predicate to condemnation of the right-of-way across the Hernandez property. Twelve days later, the Council formally declared the right-of-way to be a matter of public necessity. Once again, the Hernandez zoning matter seemed to be on its way to a final resolution.

The B-1-O zoning classification that had been negotiated by the City Attorney did not rest well with the planning staff or the Planning Commission, who suggested that their deliberations were a sham because the Council had already made up its mind. The City Attorney, however, carefully placed the matter in context for the Planning Director in a classic "cover your backside" letter, dated February 5, 1979:

> B-1-O as applied to this particular property reflects the proximity of this property to the adjacent sewer plant. One should note that the two parcels remaining after the proposed improvement are odd shaped, and much of the land area involved is suited only for use in computation of open-space

areas. Flood plain areas and the banks of the coulee must be considered in development potential.

The configuration of the properties reflect both natural and critical buffer areas separating them from other properties, including the large Coulee Mine Channel, the sewer plant, the new and the old West Bayou Parkway.

The only adjacent landowner is Mr. Hernandez himself, and even the adjacent property is separated from the subject property by West Bayou Parkway itself.

The traffic which might be generated by a B-1-O utilization should be no problem to any other segment of the public. The proposed realignment project is designed such as to provide safe access to local traffic utilizing the property itself.

In light of these circumstances, if one were to deny the B-1-O request, how would such denial bear a substantial relation to the promotion of public health, safety, morals, or general welfare?

All of the foregoing duly considered, it was my opinion that a lengthy and costly trial of the zoning litigation would probably have resulted in a decision adverse to the City of Lafayette with respect to the propriety of continued R-1-A zoning. The court could have alternatively either left the property unrestricted or mandated the Council to rezone the property to one of the alternate classifications suggested by the landowner.

It was, therefore, my advice to the Council that it review the changed circumstances and consider favorably, the zoning change to B-1-O.

The City Attorney's perspective was objectionable to the neighbors, and the local paper editorialized that the attorney "crammed the settlement down the Council's throat." Particularly galling to the neighborhoods was the attorney's refusal to make the proposed settlement agreement public, a refusal the City Council agreed to support.

It was bad enough to have the City Council consider B-1-O zoning, but it was outright offensive to the public to have the agreement kept a secret. Eventually, after four months of conflict, a citizen published the following letter in the *Lafayette Daily Advertiser,* addressed to the councilman in whose district the Hernandez property was located:

Dear Mr. Cantrelle:

Your statement in the *Lafayette Advertiser* of Sunday, June 3, 1979 deserves a reply independent of any that Mr. Hudson and his beleaguered citizens group may make.

Accordingly, please be advised that:
1. When you hold public office there will be criticism, and if your motives are suspect, they will be challenged. Office holders are the servants of the people and not their masters.
2. There is a legitimate difference of opinion as to whether the realignment of West Bayou Parkway with Girard Park Drive will solve any traffic people feel that it will merely shift the problem a few hundred yards

down the road at considerable expense for the taxpayers.
3. The agreement between the City Council and Hernandez was not executed after public deliberation. The Council signed it in secret and the document remains secret to this date, your comments notwithstanding. HOWEVER, IT NEED NOT REMAIN SO. I HEREBY OFFER TO PUBLISH THE ENTIRE TEXT IN THE LAFAYETTE DAILY ADVERTISER AT MY SOLE EXPENSE. Just deliver a copy to my office.

Mr. Cantrelle, the people are speaking out on this issue and you are not hearing them. Why isn't there a citizens group in favor of the interchange and in favor of the commercialization of West Bayou Parkway? The answer is obvious — the people don't want it.[1]

In response, Councilman Billy Cantrelle complained bitterly about the abuse he was receiving from the public and the press, but provided his antagonist with a copy of the agreement, which was dutifully published in the paper at the critic's personal cost.

B-1-O Agreement Not Signed

When Mr. Hernandez's attorney presented a formal "Agreement" for execution by the Mayor, the Mayor would not sign it, citing the pending Planning Commission's consideration of the rezoning, and advised the City's attorney of his reasons (March 6, 1979):

1. There is to be, under the law, another Hearing by the authorized body of the Lafayette City Planning Commission for the purpose of determining the proper zoning classification.
2. Upon receipt of their recommendations and due process having been made available to all parties concerned, I will advise you as to my intentions on the above mentioned subject.

Federal Court

Complicating the situation was a new legal attack launched by Mr. Hernandez. Apparently unsatisfied with the "threatening" character of his state court suit, Mr. Hernandez filed a $1 million federal court action under the Civil Rights Act of 1871, invoking the U.S. Supreme Court's open door policy which had recently been established in *Monell* v. *New York City Dept. of Social Services*, 436 U.S. 658 (1978). The two events

---

[1]*Lafayette Daily Advertiser,* June 10, 1979, p. 5.

were unsettling to the City Attorney, who hastened to further cover himself in a letter, dated March 7, 1979, to Mayor Bowen with a copy to the Hernandezes' counsel. He was personally concerned, he said, because he had secured approval for the settlement and then was placed in the position of in fact not having the Mayor's approval. He pointed out:

> On January 29 I met with Mayor Bowen explaining the final settlement proposal and secured his oral agreement to the proposal, including the commitment to, in fact, zone the property to B-1-O. The Mayor expressed reservations concerning the principle of including a specific zoning change as a condition to such as agreement; however, he concurred that in the best interest of the City of Lafayette, and especially in the interest of going forward with the realignment project, the settlement would be concurred in.
>
> As you know, the Federal civil rights violation suit which had been previously threatened has now been filed as reported to you at the Council briefing last evening.

RUDAT Report

In the meantime, Lafayette's land use consciousness had been upgraded by the visit of a Regional Urban Design Assistance Team (RUDAT), an American Institute of Architect program in which a team of professionals visit a locality and perform an intensive analysis of a designated land development issue. Critical of the City's unplanned growth and politicized land use decision making, the RUDAT report recommended a variety of procedural and substantive changes. The neighbors who were opposed to the Hernandez rezoning and the realignment saw the RUDAT report as a confirmation of their criticisms and vigorously opposed the B-1-O zoning. The Mayor, both chastised and intrigued by the RUDAT report, retained us to consult with the City to restructure the City's land use decision-making processes. We were attracted by both the dynamic character of the City and the intensity of the Mayor, and promptly walked innocently into the middle of the Hernandez dispute.

Another Veto

In April, the City's Planning Commission, after extensive public testimony (almost all of it opposed B-1-O) and a staff recommendation that the property be rezoned to R-2, voted to recommend that the property remain R-1-A. Notwithstanding the Planning Commission's recommendation, the City Council went on to rezone the Hernandez property from the R-1-A classification to B-1-O. We attended the meeting because the Mayor had suggested, "You may get a little flavor for how we do things here" by going to the meeting. The vote was three to two and was described by two councilmen as regrettable but a matter of "living up to the bargain we made."

The opponents were obviously unhappy, but once again it appeared that the end of the matter was in sight. A week later, after a great deal of thought and pressure, the Mayor notified the City Clerk that he planned to veto the ordinance rezoning the Hernandez property:

> I veto this Ordinance because I support the people of the neighborhood who would be affected by this action to commercialize this property at this time. Also, I continue to applaud and publicly support the actions of the City Planning Commission who have labored with this problem in this area for years.
>
> I support the right of the people because I honestly believe what has been proposed is wrong.

After a number of delays and attempts to negotiate a new settlement, the City Council voted three to two to override the Mayor's veto; however, the veto stood because the City's Charter required a four-fifths majority to override. The litigation in state and federal court was immediately reactivated as a flurry of supplemental and amended pleadings were filed recounting the recent events in the now four-year-old dispute.

Federal District Court

The City's defensive strategy was simple—hire new counsel and "go to the mats." (The City's current Director of Planning, frustrated by the caustic nature of the City's planning ethic, chose another course and returned to military service.) We were retained to defend the City in the litigation, in what Babcock suggested would be "a piece of cake." Our tactic was simple and followed the old adage: "The best defense is a good offense." Immediately, we moved for summary judgment on the grounds that the Mayor and the City, both named as defendants in the federal court, were immune from suit for money damages for acts taken in their legislative capacity. The argument was, that while the Supreme Court had held that a municipality was a person for purposes of the Civil Rights Act, the Court had expressly reserved the question as to whether defendants could invoke pre-existing common-law immunities. The City claimed that even though the Mayor and the City were persons, they were nevertheless immune from damage suits because their actions were legislative in character. Our objective was to achieve a small victory of a summary judgment in favor of the Mayor, and then to work out a practical compromise because virtually everyone agreed that some relief from the City's R-1-A zoning was justified. In a stunning turn of events, however, the Federal District Court, after oral argument on the motion, entered summary judgment in favor of both the Mayor and the City, holding that an absolute legislative immunity applied to both because the proximate cause of the alleged claims were legislative acts. The District Court's decision was immediately appealed to the Fifth Circuit Court of Appeals in New Orleans by Mr. Hernandez.

Preparation for Appeal: Defense of R-1-A

The federal court's decision in favor of the City was not our only big surprise. Faced with defending the merits of the R-2 zoning, we set out to assemble a team of expert witnesses to defend the City's position. The reputation of the planning staff had been battered during the proceedings and most local experts were either convinced that Mayor Bowen "had done the Hernandezes wrong" or were unwilling to step into the middle of one of the City's most intense political disputes. Initially a number of state experts were approached; however, their preliminary assessments were critical of the Mayor's veto and gave the defense team little comfort. Eventually, national-level experts were employed. Because traffic was a major issue, Richard Gern, a well-known traffic planner and engineer, was selected and met with us in Lafayette to look over the situation.

New Traffic Study

On the first morning of his visit, Gern and his associate stationed themselves at the intersection of the West Bayou Parkway and South College so that they could observe first-hand the traffic congestion that was to be relieved by the realignment and was the basis for the Hernandez claim of more intense zoning. The problem was that there was no congestion. Traffic moved quickly and efficiently through the intersection and no car waited in the queue for more than a single signal change. Mystified, they spent the balance of the day reviewing engineering reports and then returned to the intersection to observe the afternoon rush hour. Again congestion was minimal and when the defense team assembled to discuss the traffic problem, they concluded that the problem had already been solved. When the original traffic study (justifying the realignment) had been prepared in 1975, the intersection had had no turning lanes and no traffic signal. During the ensuing four years, while the debate over realignment and spreading commercialization raged through the corridors of City Hall, the public works department had solved the traffic problem.

The situation, were it not for the intensity of the plaintiff's increasingly bitter attacks on the City, was almost amusing. The City, in response to a rezoning request based on traffic conditions that did not exist, had refused to rezone the property to avoid paying more money for a road right-of-way that was unnecessary. The realignment, which previously had been declared a matter of public necessity, badly complicated the impending zoning issue and therefore had to be reconsidered immediately.

Realignment Reconsidered

The dispute over the proposed realignment represented an underlying community concern about where growth was taking the City. Traffic was already an obvious problem in the City, particularly to the south of the downtown area, and citizens and city employees wondered aloud if there were any City values that would survive the City's growth. A landscape architect, who had joined the City's Planning Commission because of the "tremendous potential" of the City, quit after less than a year on the job because "the people in power" were not sensitive to the quality of life in the community. An example was the plan to improve Girard Park Drive with the infamous realignment. He felt that although it is all right to be cost-conscious, sometimes "a straight line" can cost a community far more than just money. He said:

> Girard Park is unbelievably well situated. It has everything that a good city park should have. It has urbanity and background of Civil War history; it is almost rural in appearance; it is enclosed with mature trees and it has water for beauty, comfort and variety. It is a genuine area for people to relax in. It is surrounded by a meandering road to slow traffic. There are controlled vistas and a feeling of "separateness." It is appropriately situated in an area near a hospital, a university, and commerce as well as homes.
>
> If re-alignment occurs, it will be in direct lines between those two streets which will be four-laned to the freeway. When traffic starts using the wider streets drivers will become frustrated with the bottleneck at the park. Area people will get tired of fighting the city, and there goes your park as well as an important part of the charm and quality of your community's life.

On September 28, 1979, the Mayor, after consultation with the new defense team, announced that he was going to ask the City Council to repeal the Ordinance declaring the West Bayou Parkway/Girard Park Drive realignment to be a matter of public necessity. He explained:

> I was advised, last Wednesday, by the City's special legal counsel for the

> Hernandez cases; that the two Hernandez suits, plus expropriation suits, could take two to four years to resolve in the courts. That delay [in construction] raises serious questions in my mind about the feasibility and the utility of the proposed realignment at this time. . . .
>
> The City's Traffic Engineering Department has already made some changes at the intersection which have improved the flow of traffic.
>
> The cost of the project has tripled.

One month later, the Council followed the Mayor's recommendation and unanimously abandoned the project until a comprehensive reassessment of its need could be completed. The Hernandezes took a different view of this turn of events as described in a pleading filed on behalf of Mr. Hernandez.

> When an expert retained by the City indicated that defendants would probably lose the zoning litigation if the re-alignment project were maintained, the City "re-assessed" the re-alignment project literally on a moment's notice . . . to win the zoning lawsuit.[2]

State Court Litigation

The trial of the state court matter commenced in January 1980 and was completed, after a one-month intermission, in the second week of February. The plaintiff hammered home on the Mayor's role in the matter and reiterated, at every opportunity, that *but for* the Mayor, the City would have zoned the property B-1-O.

Witnesses

According to the Hernandezes' witnesses, the entire zoning dispute was nothing more than a subterfuge directed at extracting the right-of-way for the proposed realignment at a cheap price, or an alleged personal vendetta against Mrs. Hernandez. Mr. Hernandez, who testified by referring to notes in Braille, said that the Mayor had threatened his wife over the realignment "issue" and that the Mayor had made a promise—"I'm going to get you"—which Mr. Hernandez would describe in a later brief as the only promise the Mayor ever kept. In addition to Mr. Hernandez's testimony, his counsel called as witnesses the City's first Director of Planning (now returned to academia), a local appraiser, various city officials, and another former City planner. The City countered with a planning consultant, a traffic engineer, the City's current Planning Director, the City's zoning administrator, a civil engineer, and an appraiser.

[2] *James E. Hernandez* v. *City of Lafayette,* Number 78,0381A, Post Trial Memorandum.

The Impact of Neighbors' Testimony

The Hernandezes persistently focused on West Bayou Parkway, nonresidential development, the realignment, and the sewage treatment plant. Repeatedly their counsel asked, "Would you live next to a sewer plant?" The City's response, of course, was yes—a response the opposing neighbors were all too willing to support. At trial, the City called three residents to the stand to describe the impact of the sewer plant on residential use. Their testimony was debilitating to the plaintiffs: "My house, which is valued at from $250,000 to $300,000, is located within several hundred feet of the sewage plant, which is in plain view from my house and yard, and the sewage plant is not a negative factor in the neighborhood."

Decision

The Court took the matter under advisement and after four months ruled in favor of Mr. Hernandez:

> The repeated denial of rezoning the Hernandez property, combined with the City's experts advising the passage of the requested zoning change and the statements made by the Council members themselves clearly show a scheme by which Mr. Hernandez's rights were denied.[3]

Local wags opined that the judge "just wasn't going to let the Mayor get away with it."

A New Mayor

During early 1980, Mayor Bowen (then in his second term) found himself confronted by a serious challenge for reelection by a popular local politician. The challenger made good use of the Hernandez matter in his campaign literature, accusing the incumbent of governing by confrontation and causing unnecessary conflict. The Mayor was defeated and his successor inherited the pending appeal in the federal court case and the state court matter then still under advisement (but which was decided shortly after his installation).

Effect of the Owen Case

The new Mayor wanted very much to heal the wounds of the previous

---

[3] *James E. Hernandez v. City of Lafayette,* Number 78,0381A (5th Judicial Circuit Court, Parish of Lafayette, State of Louisiana).

administration and pursued every opportunity to settle with the Hernandezes. The matter, however, was largely taken out of his hands by the U.S. Supreme Court, which had once again forayed into the area of municipal liability. In *Owen* v. *City of Independence,* 445 U.S. 622, 657 (1980), a case involving a City decision to fire a police chief without a hearing, the Supreme Court in April 1980 rejected the City of Independence's claim of immunity and stated:

> Municipalities have *no immunity* from damages liability flowing from their constitutional violations. . . .
> No longer is individual "blameworthiness" the acid test of liability; the principle of equitable loss-spreading has joined fault as a factor in distributing the costs of official misconduct. [Emphasis added.]

Read literally — as of course the Hernandezes attorney read it — *Owen* foretold bad results for the City of Lafayette's pending appeal in the federal court and required that the City pursue an appeal in the state suit in hope of reversing what was now a determination of liability. Mr. Hernandez's counsel emphasized such a literal reading of *Owen,* and he openly told anyone who would listen that Mr. Hernandez was sure to win a large award. The new Mayor found himself in the anomalous position of defending the prior administration's actions — actions that he had openly criticized during the campaign.

Appeal — Federal Court

We labored in the Fifth Circuit Court of Appeals to distinguish the Supreme Court's opinion in *Owen* and to justify the immunity invoked by the District Court in Lafayette. Focusing on the Fifth Amendment flavor of the landowner's claim, the City argued that the "taking issue" was a myth and that the appropriate remedy for an overly restrictive regulation was invalidation. Although oral argument was contentious, we remained hopeful.

Once again, however, an action of the U.S. Supreme Court intervened in the Hernandez matter when the Court rendered its decision in *San Diego Gas & Electric Co.* v. *City of San Diego,* 450 U.S. 621 (1981). The decision was published after oral argument in *Hernandez* but before the Fifth Circuit's opinion was issued. In his dissent, which a concurring Justice William Rehnquist described as "largely" agreeable, Justice William Brennan concluded that a regulation that is overly restrictive actually effects a "taking" and that just compensation must be paid. Needless to say, Mr. Hernandez's counsel wasted little time in filing a notice of supplemental authority.

The Fifth Circuit's opinion, although sustaining the Mayor's individual immunity, relied heavily on Justice Brennan's dissent in regard to the City and was not good news for local government:

> An action for damages will lie in favor of any person whose property is taken for public use without just compensation by a municipality through a zoning regulation that denies the owner any economically viable use thereof. The measure of damages in such a case will be the amount equal to just compensation for the value of the property during the period of the taking.[4]

In one way, the Hernandez dispute was the direct and proximate result of the U.S. Supreme Court. On three separate occasions, *Monell, Owen,* and *San Diego Gas & Electric,* the Supreme Court had issued an opinion that escalated the ante in what would have otherwise been a simple zoning case. Coincidentally, each of the opinions was authored by Justice Brennan.

Appeal — State Court

On the state court level, the appeal to the Third Circuit Court of Appeals in Lake Charles had gone a lot better. On April 16, 1981, the Appellate Court reversed the trial court's invalidation of the R-1-A zoning:

> In conclusion, our review of the record convinces us that plaintiff has failed to meet his burden of proving that the City's classification of the property was unreasonable, arbitrary, or a denial of due process. Further, we do not find that there has been an abuse of discretion or excessive use of power by the City in refusing to rezone the Hernandez property.[5]

Mr. Hernandez petitioned the Louisiana Supreme Court for review, and then, when the Louisiana Supreme Court denied his writ, appealed to the U.S Supreme Court in what were becoming increasingly embittered terms: "blatant misuse of the massive police power to strongarm this landowner into forfeiting his rights to due process and just compensation.[6]

---

[4]*Hernandez* v. *City of Lafayette,* 643, F.2d 1188 (5th Cir. 1981).
[5]399 So.2d 1179 (3d La. Ct. App. 1980).
[6]*James E. Hernandez* v. *City of Lafayette,* No. 81-600 (Jurisdictional Statement of Appellant).

Remand to Federal District Court

Simultaneously, the City of Lafayette filed a petition for writ of certiorari in the United States Supreme Court, having been rebuffed by the Fifth Circuit Court of Appeals when the City filed a petition for rehearing, urging that no further consideration of the matter was necessary given the state court's decision that the R-1-A classification was valid. When the Supreme Court denied the petition, the matter was remanded to the Federal District Court in Lafayette for further proceedings. Coincidentally, on January 18, 1982, the U.S. Supreme Court dismissed Mr. Hernandez's appeal from the Louisiana Supreme Court for want of a substantial federal question.

Almost immediately, Mr. Hernandez filed a motion in the district court asking for permission to file another supplemental and amending complaint, alleging new facts and claims that had arisen subsequent to the state court trial. The City responded with a motion for summary judgment on the ground that the doctrine of *res judicata* barred relitigation of the zoning issue. At oral argument on the motion, Mr. Hernandez's counsel reviewed the parade of alleged horribles; nevertheless, the District Court ruled that the plaintiff was not entitled to relitigate the issue of the R-1-A zoning, already decided against him by the state courts.

Once again Mr. Hernandez appealed to the Fifth Circuit Court of Appeals; on March 7, 1983, however, the Court, without entertaining oral argument, affirmed the invocation of the doctrine of repose and finally ended the litigation, which had by then been pending for five years in front of six different trial and appellate courts. At long last the zoning of the *Hernandez* property was finally settled—or was it?

Another Petition to Rezone (R-2)

In the late summer of 1983, Mr. Hernandez filed yet another petition for rezoning, seeking to have a portion of his property rezoned from R-1-A to R-2. Incredibly, the asserted justifications for the changes were the very same claims advanced and rejected during the earlier litigation. The City's professional staff, now matured into a full-service Planning Department (headed by the zoning administrator who so successfully testified in the Hernandez trial), recommended denial. The Planning Commission, however, voted six to one to rezone the property and a familiar sequence of events threatened. The zoning reincarnation reached its zenith on January 10, 1984, ten years after the Hernandezes started to "plan for their future" when the City Council took up the Planning Commission's recommendation in front of a large audience of unhappy neighbors.

Mr. Hernandez, now represented by his prior lawyer's former young assistant, urged that the petition should be granted:

> In conclusion, in the past, 2 members of this Council have supported R-2 for this property. One member has expressed support for B-1-M. This Council, in the past, has voted the property R-2 and B-1-O, which was then vetoed by the then Mayor, Mayor Bowen. The Staff recommended R-2 or R-4 on the property in 1979, the Planning Commission has voted 6 to 1 staff recommended R-2 or R-4. The City's land-use plan discourages low intensity residential use, next to utility uses such as the sewage treatment plant. We honestly believe that wisdom and good policy support the R-2 on this property. I'm going to ask each of you to ask yourself — would you buy your home next to the sewage treatment plant? I think you know the answer.

The neighbors, however, were not less adamant in 1984 than they had been in 1975, 1977, and 1979. They challenged the wisdom of the proposed action in light of the court's decisions and urged the Council to respect the integrity of their neighborhood. Their task was substantially easier because the President of the City Council, who presided over the meeting, was a former president of the neighborhood group whose political activism had been initiated by the Hernandez matter. As the time came near for voting, the audience whispered among themselves at how eerie it was to be revisiting this issue so soon; however, the breathholding did not take long, as the Council voted five to zero to deny the petition.

Afterwards, members of the jubilant audience agreed on two general propositions: "I guess the City learned a little something after all" and "Here we go again." No litigation, however, materialized.

The story is still not over — at least not quite. In late 1984 Mr. Hernandez submitted a site plan approval for an R-1-A subdivision, the original zoning; however, ten years after his first meeting with a city official about his development plans, no development has yet commenced on the Hernandez parcel.

Conclusion

The Hernandez story is a classic in many ways. A land use conflict of modest physical proportions escalated into an "all-out war" with nationally known experts called in to deal with the issue. The Mayor who started the fight was defeated at least in part because of his penchant for conflict. Nevertheless, the City had to fight on because of the financial threat posed by Justice Brennan's theories of compensation. In the end the City, of course, won; however, the land has not yet been developed and its future is no more planned today than it was in 1975, when this story began. The litigation resolved the landowner's claim for compensation and the record developed during the litigation clearly demonstrated what land uses are not appropriate for the Hernandez parcel. However, the litigation did nothing to answer the obvious corollary question of what *is* appropriate for the property.

11

Mount Laurel II: Après Nous le Déluge

> *We may not build houses but we do enforce the Constitution.*
>
> Chief Justice Wilentz,
N.J. Supreme Court

> *In Mt. Laurel lawsuits, municipalities are like Canadian baby harp seals; they can slither and bleat but only for a short time.*
>
> Attorney Henry Hill

> *If it means going to jail I'll go to jail. . . . I'll not surrender my community into the hands of the court. . . .*
>
> Mayor Peter Garibaldi,
Monroe Township

This chapter is about an extraordinary land use case, a case unlike any other (if we except its predecessor, *Mount Laurel I*) during the almost eighty years of zoning in any of the fifty states. It has been shattering to the municipalities involved; it has generated a half-dozen bills in the New Jersey Legislature, forced the Governor to call for a moratorium on the decision's implementation, cost municipalities millions of dollars, and threatens to rearrange the smug posture of suburban communities from one end of the state to the other. And it all began because one man—the late Justice Frederick Hall—set out his objections to exclusionary zoning in his famous dissent in *Vickers* v. *Gloucester Township*. (We say "one man" but it must be acknowledged that trial judges such as Felix Martino and David Furman earlier had been handing down decisions increasingly critical of the zoning practices in New Jersey towns.) Before we discuss the details, however, we must first look at origins.

Background

The success of many municipalities—particularly the more well-to-do suburbs—in protecting their communities from change by means of subdivision and zoning controls was noted by the students of planning at least three decades ago. We believe it was Professor Norman Williams, Jr. who first protested this practice in the mid-1950s. Richard Babcock mocked it in *The Zoning Game,* and Professor Larry Sager attacked the consequences in his article "Tight Little Islands."[1] Others since have joined the early critics. Large-lot (five-acre minimum) zoning, minimum house size, the exclusion of apartments and mobile homes, and exorbitant and unnecessary standards for subdivisions are only a few of the techniques employed.

Oddly, the courts and most litigants did not appear to take much interest. Among the thousands of reported zoning cases there was little talk of "exclusion," the buzz word for the economic and occasionally racial impact of these techniques. The Supreme Court of Pennsylvania did, in 1966, hold that a suburb of Philadelphia could not zone for residential lots with a minimum five-acre requirement (a municipality may not "stand in the way of natural forces which send out growing population into hitherto undeveloped areas in search of a comfortable place to live"), but that case appeared to be more a sport than the start of a trend. One justice joined three others for a majority because he simply did not believe in any zoning.

Vickers

Then, in 1962, Justice Frederick Hall of the New Jersey Supreme Court set out his objections to exclusionary zoning in his famous dissent in *Vickers* v. *Gloucester Township Committee,* 181 A.2d 129 (1962). The majority of the New Jersey Supreme Court held that a rural township could validly exclude all trailer parks from its boundaries. At that time New Jersey, the state with the greatest densities per square mile of any jurisdiction, was noted for its exclusionary practices to protect its areas of gracious living, and the courts had already accepted the practice. Morris and Bergen counties in the north were the most egregious examples, but most parts

[1] 21 *Stanford Law Review* 767 (1969).

of the state were caught up in the practice. The courts had sustained the regulations enforcing minimum lot size and minimum house size, as well as other devices.

Hall, in an eloquent dissent, said that this widespread practice was wrong:

> Certainly general welfare does not automatically mean whatever the municipality says it does, regardless of who is hurt and how much. . . . The general welfare transcends the artificial limits of political subdivisions and cannot embrace merely narrow local desires.

Hall could persuade only one other judge, Justice Thomas Shettino, to join him. Five judges adopted the traditional view of municipal power.

Hall once said that he wrote that dissent in the hopes that the U.S. Supreme Court might take the case, but the Court refused to hear *Vickers*. This was at least twelve years before the Supreme Court became interested in local land use practices. It had remained silent on the question of zoning since 1928.

Mount Laurel I

But Hall's words and changes in the personnel of the New Jersey Supreme Court gave ideologues hope. Norman Williams, Jr., then lived in Princeton and taught at Rutgers University. With his help and that of others, the Camden Legal Services brought an action on behalf of the National Association for the Advancement of Colored People (NAACP) against the Township of Mount Laurel — charging that by its restrictive zoning regulations, it excluded the poor, the young, and the old.

Mount Laurel in effect is a suburb of Philadelphia. It is a flat, sprawling township about 14,000 acres in area in central New Jersey. It is a few miles east of the Delaware River, New Jersey's boundary. It is about seven miles from the boundary line of the City of Camden and ten miles from the Benjamin Franklin Bridge over to Philadelphia. In 1950, the Town had a population of 2,817; by 1960, the population had almost doubled to 5,249, and by 1970 it had more than doubled again to 11,221. In 1975, 65 percent of the Town was still vacant or agricultural land.

By the time the case reached the Supreme Court of New Jersey (1975), Justice Hall apparently had persuaded the other justices to come around to his point of view in *Vickers*. The Court handed down what was regarded as a blockbuster opinion. It recited a veritable trunkful of techniques in the Mount Laurel ordinances that effectively excluded low- and moderate-income families. And he held the ordinances to be invalid. Hall, inferentially, acknowledged that in the past the New Jersey courts had gone along with the practices:

> In sum, we are satisfied beyond any doubt that, by reason of the basic importance of appropriate housing and the long-standing pressing need for it, especially in the low and moderate cost category, and of the exclusionary zoning practices of so many municipalities, conditions have changed, and . . . judicial attitudes must be altered from that espoused in . . . other cases cited earlier, to require, as we have just said, a broader view of the general welfare and the presumptive obligation on the part of developing municipalities at least to afford the opportunity by land use regulations for appropriate housing for all.[2]

More dramatically, he made clear that this applied to all New Jersey municipalities. Well, almost all. He said the opinion applied only to "developing" communities. Hall later told us that he had to make this exception to secure, for his unanimous judgment, two justices who were worried about small towns that were not in the path of the outward population explosion from the central cities.

Hall was especially shrewd in his treatment of the constitutional issues. The plaintiffs had challenged the regulations under both the federal and New Jersey constitutions. He expressly based his opinion on the New Jersey Constitution, knowing that the U.S. Supreme Court could not then take the case for review: a state Supreme Court is the final arbiter of that state's constitution. The U.S. Supreme Court did refuse to grant certiorari. Mount Laurel was told to return to the drawing board and rewrite its zoning ordinance.

Perhaps the "developing communities" exception was Hall's mistake. While commentators and many news editorials supported the seminal opinion, New Jersey municipalities were not ready to give in. They found many excuses for delay and fudging the Court's order. Many of the municipalities against whom suits were brought to challenge their regulations under *Mount Laurel* claimed they were not "developing," and in some cases they won. Other municipalities, such as Mount Laurel itself, rewrote their ordinances purporting to comply but in fact only giving the appearance of complying. Still others pleaded that the available land was environmentally sensitive and pointed to Hall's blessing in *Mount Laurel* of efforts to save New Jersey's ecology.

It should be noted as well that a major part of the problem after 1975 was the response of the courts themselves. Not only did the Appellate Division (the intermediate courts) construe *Mount Laurel I* in a progressively narrower and narrower fashion, but the Supreme Court itself—in *Pascack Ass'n. Ltd.* v. *Washington,* 379 A.2d 6 (1977), *Demarest* v. *Mayor and Council of Borough of Hillsdale,* 386 A.2d 875 (1978), and in particular

---

[2]*Southern Burlington County NAACP* v. *Mount Laurel,* 336 A.2d 713,728 (1975).

Oakwood v. *Madison*, 371 A.2d 1192 (1977)—was generally perceived as backing off Justice Hall's language of 1975.

Mount Laurel II

Lawsuits piled up. Finally, six were waiting to be heard by the state Supreme Court. In 1978, the Court consolidated all of them, announcing that they would be heard ensemble (eventually to be known as *Mount Laurel II*). Then in May 1980 the Court issued an unusual request: it sent out a series of written questions to attorneys for all parties and asked that in their oral arguments they focus on answers to those questions. Twenty-four questions dealt with *Mount Laurel* issues, such as "Discuss the wisdom of limiting the reach of *Mount Laurel* to developing municipalities," or "Discuss the wisdom of a per se rule against large lot (e.g., five-acre) zoning," or "Discuss the function of expert planners in exclusionary zoning cases."

These questions suggested that the Court intended to undertake a major review of its earlier *Mount Laurel* decision. But no one really knew what the questions forecast. The case was argued in September 1980, and then it sat and sat, through 1981 and 1982. On January 20, 1983, the New Jersey Supreme Court handed down its 150-page unanimous opinion. To say it was explosive would understate its impact. The Court, in short, reaffirmed *Mount Laurel I* in spades.

The Court acknowledged that *Mount Laurel I* was fast becoming "infamous" because of its failure. Justice Robert Wilentz began the opinion by exposing the facade of Mount Laurel's blatantly exclusionary ordinance. For ten years, since the original trial order, Mount Laurel and other communities have been successful only in excluding the poor. Obviously outraged, he continued:

> To the best of our ability, we shall not allow it to continue. This Court is more firmly committed to the original *Mount Laurel* doctrine than ever, and we are determined, within appropriate judicial bounds, to make it work. The obligation is to provide a realistic opportunity for housing, not litigation. We have learned from experience, however, that unless a strong judicial hand is used, *Mount Laurel* will not result in housing, but in paper, process, witnesses, trials and appeals. We intend by this decision to strengthen it, clarify it, and make it easier for public officials, including judges, to apply it.[3]

---

[3]Southern Burlington County NAACP v. *Mount Laurel,* 456 A.2d 390, 410 (1983).

The Policies

Accordingly, the Court then set out ten major policies. Summarized, they are as follows:

1. *Every* municipality's land use regulations . . . must provide a realistic opportunity for decent housing for its indigenous poor except where they represent a disproportionately large segment of the population as compared with the rest of the region.
2. The existence of a municipal obligation to provide a realistic opportunity for a fair share of the region's present and prospective low and moderate income housing need will no longer be determined by whether or not a municipality is "developing." The obligation extends, instead, to every municipality, any portion of which is designated by the state, through the SDGP [State Development Guide Plan], as a "growth area." The obligation . . . does not extend to those areas where the SDGP discourages growth — namely, open spaces, rural areas, prime farmland, conservation areas, limited growth areas, parts of the Pinelands and certain Coastal areas.[4]
3. *Mount Laurel* litigation will ordinarily include proof of the municipality's fair share of low and moderate income housing in terms of the number of units needed immediately, as well as the number needed for a reasonable period of time in the future. "Numberless" resolution will be insufficient. . . .
4. Any future *Mount Laurel* litigation shall be assigned only to those judges selected by the Chief Justice with the approval of the Supreme Court.
5. The municipal obligation to provide a realistic opportunity for construction of its fair share of low and moderate income housing may require more than the elimination of unnecessary cost-producing requirements and restrictions. Affirmative governmental devices should be used. . . . Mobile homes may not be prohibited.
6. The lower income regional housing need is comprised of both low and moderate income housing. A municipality's fair share should include both in such proportion as reflects consideration of all relevant factors, including the proportion of low and moderate income housing that make up the regional need.
7. Providing a realistic opportunity for the construction of least-cost housing will satisfy a municipality's *Mount Laurel* obligation if, and only if, it cannot otherwise be satisfied.

---

[4]The State Development Guide Plan is crucial to the Court's disposition of the *Mount Laurel* cases. The Plan was prepared by the State Department of Community Affairs, Division of State and Regional Planning, and was originally published in 1977 and revised and republished in 1980. It purports to provide a planning rationale for future development of the state and provides four major divisions of land: (a) "growth areas"; (b) agricultural areas; (c) conservation areas; and (d) limited growth.

8. Builder's remedies [a court order to municipal officials to allow a specific development to be built] will be afforded to plaintiffs . . . on a case by case basis.
9. The judiciary should manage *Mount Laurel* litigation to dispose of a case in all of its aspects with one trial and one appeal, unless substantial considerations indicate some other course.
10. The *Mount Laurel* obligation to meet the prospective lower income housing need of the region is, by definition, one that is met year after year in the future throughout the years of the particular projection used in calculating prospective need. Trial courts shall have the discretion to moderate the impact of such housing by allowing even the present need to be phased in over a period of years.

Moreover, in a long footnote the Court suggested that 20 percent of any development for low- and moderate-income housing would be adequate. The decision called for a family to pay no more than 25 percent of its income for shelter. Under this definition, housing affordable to low-income families cannot be priced at more than 50 percent of an income which is half the median income of the designated area and a moderate-income unit cannot be priced higher than 80 percent of the median income of the area. To demonstrate how low these prices actually have to be, consider these examples. Assume that the median income for the area is $30,000. Fifty percent of that is $15,000; 25 percent of that is $3,750; $3,750 number divided by 12 is $312.50, which would be the monthly income set aside to cover principal, interest, taxes, and insurance — or, if the unit is within a condominium development, the Homeowner's Association dues.

Assume further, for a moment, that taxes would be $30 per month, and that the Homeowner's Association dues could be $40 per month. This would leave $242.50 per month to support principal and interest. If the interest rate is 13 percent, the mortgage term is thirty years, and a 10 percent down payment is assumed, the units would have to cost no more than $24,500. If one varies the interest rate, the unit can be priced higher or lower, depending on the variation.

If the median income is *lower* than $30,000 for the area, or if the interest rate is higher, the impact is dramatic. For example, assume that the median income is $25,000 and the mortgage rate is 15 percent. Then, with the *same* assumption as to taxes, Homeowner's Association fees, and term, the unit could be priced at $17,000. (Fifty percent of $25,000 is $12,500; 25 percent of that is $3,125, which is $260 a month. After taxes and homeowner's dues, this leaves $190 per month to support a mortgage, which at 15 percent would support a home costing less than $17,000.)[5]

[5] Alan Mallach, a sociologist who has been deeply involved in the *Mount Laurel*

The Court did, as indicated in policy item 10, recognize the impact this could have on some communities. If we take a municipality that has a lower-income obligation of some 2,000 units (which is not an unusual number) and multiply that by a factor of four or five (i.e., the *market* units to be built with a 20 percent set-aside requirement), we find that the requirement to build, by 1990, is approximately 8,000 to 10,000 units of housing, both low/moderate and market units. It is this builder's remedy of 2,000 units of lower-income housing, with the market multiplier to yield 8,000 to 10,000 units, which is horrifying to municipalities. Of course it should be added that in spite of the four-to-one ratio, no more market-priced units will be built over time than the market demand will support. Individual communities initially may be harder hit, such as Warren Township, which may end up with a disproportionate share of its region's total housing.

There could not, of course, be any appeal to the U.S. Supreme Court because the case was based on the New Jersey Constitution.

Reaction

The initial reaction of municipal attorneys and officials was numbness and shock. After all, not one of the fifty states had ever gone this far. This was the Court acting as a legislature, spelling out detailed procedures. This the Court had readily acknowledged:

> As we said at the outset, while we have always preferred legislative to judicial action in this field, we shall continue — until the Legislature acts — to do our best to uphold the constitutional obligation that underlies the *Mount Laurel* doctrine. That is our duty. We may not build houses, but we do enforce the Constitution.

II litigation, painted an even grimmer picture in a letter to Babcock dated April 11, 1985:

> One point perhaps worth noting, because it has become an issue of some importance in implementing *Mount Laurel II*, is that if you price a unit so that a household earning 80 percent of the area median income can afford it, spending 25 percent of income for shelter, a household earning, say, 70 percent of median can only afford that unit if it pays 28.5 percent of income, and one earning 60 percent of median can only afford the unit by paying 33 percent of income for shelter. Since lenders will not, as a rule, qualify households for a mortgage if the percentage exceeds 28 percent, it becomes apparent that households between 50 and 70 percent of median, roughly, would not be able to qualify for the unit. Clearly, however, if they were to be able to qualify, the units would have to be priced even lower than in your example. This tension, between creating a range of affordability that includes more than a small part of the lower income population on the one hand, and economic feasibility on the other, is a major problem being confronted in terms of implementing the decision, without Federal subsidies to fill the gap.

The initial response of the New Jersey newspapers was cautiously favorable. The *Atlantic City Press* said: "The Mount Laurel ruling must be embraced as an effective tool for ensuring that everyone who works in the region has a chance to have a decent place to live in the region"; the *Hudson Dispatch* on August 14 opined: "We've said it before and it's worth repeating: the Mount Laurel decisions were humane and badly needed"; and the *Bergen Record* early on declared: "It was a proud day for this state." *The Times Journal* of Vineland in the far southern part of the state wrote:

> We would hope that those in leadership positions in the Legislature—like those who serve on the Supreme Court—would have the wisdom to determine what's fair (housing for all), the courage to buck a popular cause (home rule) and the vision to see what's best for Jerseyans in the long run (freedom of mobility).

The Republican Governor, Thomas H. Kean, was less charitable. In a *New York Times* article, he referred to the decision as "communistic." "I don't believe," the Governor said, "that every municipality has got to be a carbon copy of another. That's a socialistic country, a communistic country, a dictatorship."[6] In his State of the State address to the Legislature on January 10, 1984, he declared: "I believe that the wholesale revision of local zoning ordinances by the judiciary is an undesirable intrusion on the home rule principal that has served our state well for many years." Kean also revoked an executive order issued by his predecessor, Governor Brendan Byrne, that had established allocations for all towns because it was "inadequate and ineffective in meeting their stated goal." Kean also, in his first budget, emasculated the Planning Division of the Department of Community Affairs by slashing its budget. In his 1985 State of the State address on January 8, Kean was more specific. He asked the Legislature to enact a moratorium and said, "We simply cannot allow the courts to dictate the population of individual municipalities in the state."

Many mayors were outspoken in their opposition to the decision. Mayor Peter Garibaldi of Monroe not only offered to go to jail, he added:

> I don't think judges who are not elected can dictate such policies. . . . Here we have a decision that can be devastating not only to my community but to the entire state of New Jersey. The court is coming and telling New Jersey that we have to overpopulate. What gives them this insight, this knowledge that they know more than we know?

Garibaldi did not, however, have the support of his City Council. Mon-

---

[6]*New York Times*, February 29, 1984, p. B-5.

roe Township is governed under mayor-council form, with strict executive-legislative separation of powers. The Township Council voted, in spite of Garibaldi's opposition, to comply with *Mount Laurel II*. The Mayor then forbade the township planner to assist the Council in its efforts to come up with a compliance plan, so the Council had to retain its own planning consultant. The Council came up with a plan but the Mayor vetoed it; then, at a Council meeting loaded with screaming partisans of the Mayor's position, the Council could muster only three votes—one short of the required number to override. Garibaldi wrote a letter to all Middlesex County mayors urging them to join together to resist the consequences of *Mount Laurel II*. Most, but not all, sympathized with him. East Brunswick Mayor William Fox said the letter was "one of the most disturbing pieces of mail I have ever received. . . . Perhaps elected officials have a greater responsibility than remaining in office at the expense of the oath they took upon remaining in office." But this attitude was rare. More common was the expression of Mayor Michael English of South Plainfield: "We will spend whatever amount is necessary and hope to get up to 80 communities to join us in our fight against *Mount Laurel II*. . . . No one has the right to run our government."

Jerome Rose, lawyer and professor of planning at Rutgers University, has been the most outspoken critic of the decision. (He says that is because lawyers, as officers of the courts, do not dare to speak out.) He does not see how *Mount Laurel II* is going to solve the problems of the Newarks, Trentons, and Patersons: "It is going to drain off the upwardly mobile middle class and it certainly is not going to help more than an infinitesimal, insignificant proportion of the urban poor." The argument goes that *Mount Laurel II* will help the teachers, firemen and policemen, and security guards who work in Princeton, Warren, or Bedminster. No one really knows yet who will occupy these below-market houses when they are built. State Senator John Dorsey, a Republican who opposes the *Mount Laurel II* doctrine, doubts that local employees—teachers and other public employees—will be the occupants:

> People who would fall into that category of low and moderate income at this moment tend to be very upwardly mobile. They also tend, at least in this generation, to start married life when they'll take a home with a nestegg of one sort or another provided by their parents. . . . And they are not buying a twenty-five or a forty-thousand dollar home; they're buying a hundred, a hundred and fifty thousand dollar home [as] their first home. So, I think you are talking about attracting people other than the teacher, the doctor, or the teacher, the policeman and the fireman, I really do.

Everyone seemed to be a demographer. Stewart Hutt, an attorney who had an unusual case in Branchburg, New Jersey (which we will explain later), explained his theory to Richard Babcock:

> SH: I think there's mostly fear in it that's involved. There's still that fear that, you know, the hordes are gonna come outta the cities and come and pollute the suburbs, which is not going to be the case. No question in my mind. . . . Now you take a guy from Newark; let's say he's making $22,000 a year; let's say he's making $30,000 a year. And he's a Portuguese concrete laborer. He lives in the Portuguese section of Newark; all his pals are there; he's going to go schlep to Branchburg? Now he's got to buy two cars to get back and forth to Newark. It'd cost a fortune. You burn up a car, burn up gas. He's not going to want to do it. The guy that's gonna want to do it is, you know who?
>
> RFB: That guy who has a job up in Branchburg?
>
> SH: The policeman, the teacher, the janitor in the school system.

Jerome Rose, of course, is neither a builder nor a municipal official. Referring to the three judges appointed to hear all post–*Mount Laurel II* cases as "zoning czars" in an article that appeared in many New Jersey newspapers, he wrote:

> The phrase "principles of sound planning" appears to have been used by the court to convey an implication of unerring, precise, rigorous and constant truths that would be associated with the principles of physics or engineering principles of sound bridge construction. . . .
>
> To the extent that the Mount Laurel II decision rests upon the application of "principles of sound planning" it may rest upon little more than a set of undeclared and illusive principles of social, economic and political philosophy of members of the court.
>
> Under these circumstances municipal officials have little choice but to surrender their zoning authority to the judicial zoning czars.[7]

Methodologies

The real trick was to come up with a formula that would determine the number of low- and moderate-income units a town must take, so that it can enjoy an exemption from *Mount Laurel II* for six years. There have been a number of ways suggested for computing quotas. One is the so-called consensus formula devised in the course of litigation against Warren

---

[7] Jerome Rose, "New Additions to the Lexicon of Exclusionary Zoning Litigation," *Seton Hall Law Review* (June 1984).

Township in the northern part of the state. Judge Eugene Serpentelli, one of three judges appointed by the New Jersey Supreme Court to handle *Mount Laurel* cases, told the eight separate homebuilders to get their lawyers and planners to come up with a methodology. Hence the "consensus" formula, which came to be known by the name of the chairman of the ad hoc committee, Carla Lerman. To obtain a "fair share" for a community, it is necessary to define the region of which the town is a part. This can be done by rigid lines (for example, county boundaries), or it can be done by commuting distance. Then the Court has to have some way of determining present and prospective need. Present need covers substandard and overcrowded housing. Prospective need is based on the Department of Labor's projected growth—the number of people who will be entering the region in the next ten years. Judge Serpentelli melded both the rigid-line concept and the commute formula. According to Robert Burchell, author of the Rutgers formula (to be discussed shortly), this was as though the husband wanted to go skiing in Vermont, the wife wanted to go to the beach in Florida, and so they "melded" their wishes and went to New York to see the theater in October. No one as yet has embraced an alternative to either the Rutgers or the consensus formula.

New Jersey Legislature

Politically, New Jersey is an odd state, full of contradictions and anomalies. Apart from its reputation as a state that had crowned home rule and exclusionary tactics, more than its share of municipal officials have been convicted of malfeasance in office. Yet, sometimes the Legislature has shaken free of its stupor and taken imaginative steps in land use policy. About fifteen years ago, it created the Hackensack Meadowlands Commission to regulate that miasma of garbage-dumping across the Hudson from Manhattan. The Commission, charged with superseding all local land use regulations, has performed magnificently and has transformed that dreadful area into a remarkable mix of housing and industry. More recently, the legislature created the Pinelands Commission to regulate that million or so acres between Philadelphia and Atlantic City made famous through John McPhee's book *The Pine Barrens*. (See Chapter 9.) This Commission would take over the drafting of land use regulations from five counties and three dozen municipalities. It drafted the regulations to which the towns and counties had to comply. Over the bitter opposition of cranberry and blueberry farmers, land developers, and local politicians, the Commission has prevailed.

Although the two Commissions, Hackensack and Pinelands, have vastly different responsibilities covering dramatically different environments, the apparent success of these two operations (not to mention their creation in the first place) suggests that when the Legislature decides to act, it can perform admirably. That it did not respond to the need for housing hints at the mind-set of the most reasonably well-to-do citizens of the state.

The Rutgers Formula

One of the strangest events to emerge from the *Mount Laurel II* litigation was the association of two unlikely allies: the New Jersey State League of Municipalities and the New Jersey Builders Association. They hired the Center for Urban Policy Research of Rutgers to develop a method of determining allocations of low- and moderate-income housing among municipalities. Under Professor Robert Burchell and David Listokin the Center did just that. It produced a 425-page report that divided the state into six regions. It did *not* make the actual allocations, but the complex formulas did permit that to be done. It was not an easy job. Burchell was in the middle of the assignment when he recalled trying to deal with the two sponsors:

> And it's tough to keep them in the same room. Almost impossible. Because when you get into these physical and financial dimensions the response on the part of the League of Municipalities is here we are funding a study and one of the ways we're meeting inexpensive housing in the state is to reduce subdivision and zoning requirements and streamline permitting. By that very definition, by the fact that we have supported that study are we not placing our existing subdivision controls, zoning controls and permit requirements in jeopardy? . . . On the other hand, the home builders have said hey look we're not talking about increases in density from 8 to 16 units per acre. This is Mount Laurel. We want 30.

The Rutgers formula was substantially different from the consensus report, and Burchell issued a report on December 10, 1984, that was highly critical of the latter report. Rutgers chose smaller regions than did the consensus; and it chose the center of the residential area rather than the center of the commercial area of a township as the point from which the work–home trip was measured. Rutgers believed its competitor overstated present housing need and believed the "consensus" report would count much good housing as bad by not using sufficient indices.

This quarrel suggests the difficulties courts will have when experts disagree. There are those who feel quite strongly that the so-called Burchell report has had little impact because of his belief that there is a right way and a wrong way to develop a fair-share plan. "The most one can hope for," said one commentator, "is that one's plan is reasonable and not arbitrary. I believe it is unrealistic to expect that there can possibly be a 'right' and 'wrong' way to develop a fair-share plan." In the *Mount Laurel II* case, this is particularly dismaying because the Court is obliged to determine the allocation of low- and moderate-income housing for each town and has to rely on professional demographers and planners.

Builders' and Developers' Attitudes

The Builders Association, surprisingly, is not happy with *Mount Laurel II*. The do not relish more government intrusion. Carl Busher, Executive Vice President of the Association, said bluntly with reference to *Mount Laurel II*: "Builders generally wished to hell it had never come down. . . . A lot of builders have said to me they don't like it. They don't like government, they don't like the courts paneling the entire state with [Chief] Justice Wilentz's way of doing things."

The Association has about 2,100 members, but most of them are smaller builders who construct fewer than 100 homes a year. In a period when government subsidies for housing have all but disappeared, the prospect of providing 20 percent of low- and moderate-income housing—one such unit for every four market-priced houses—is not very appealing for the small builder who would have to take a substantial loss on the subsidized units or add a substantial addition to the sale prices of the market units. (As we shall see, the latter is precisely what is being done by a large developer in Bedminster, a wealthy, horsey community in northern New Jersey.)

For the larger, more financially secure developers, however, *Mount Laurel II* was an opportunity, particularly with its focus on a "developer's remedy" to build on the land he already owned or held under option in the municipality. As of early February 1985, better than 135 lawsuits were in process against municipalities by developers seeking a builder's remedy. Thirty of these suits have been filed in District One against twenty-eight towns (multiple suits against the same municipality); eighty-six suits in District Two against thirty-six municipalities; and eighteen in District Three against eight municipalities. Three towns have been judged to be in compliance with *Mount Laurel II*. Twenty towns have settled and are working out the decree. Of the balance, it is estimated that about half have thrown up their hands and caved in. One source who has been following these cases closely suggested that the lawsuits have been filed in roughly equal proportions by ideological plaintiffs (e.g., the NAACP), by builders, and by speculators. Few towns have not been sued. The same source estimates that, of the 125 to 150 towns in the growth area with high median-valued homes, only 34 towns have not been sued.

Henry Hill, an attorney in Princeton, represents at least fourteen developers in lawsuits. He has a map of New Jersey showing the "growth areas" under the SDGP. Small flags are stuck on the map that show the location of his lawsuits, the location of other suits, those that have been settled, and those that are still in litigation. He employs a staff of six lawyers doing nothing but preparing and trying *Mount Laurel II* lawsuits. Mr. Hill has discussed the strategy:

> Exclusionary zoning litigation is expensive and complex and players who are not ready, willing and able to spend substantial sums of money and wait an indefinite length of time for a resolution of their dispute should not play. Most of the tactics of this game involve ascertaining whether or not your opponent has the staying power and funding to play the game out to its end or whether he can be expected to forfeit at an earlier stage of play. The opening moves in an exclusionary zoning lawsuit consist of propounding the massive quantities of interrogatories and the taking of many depositions in order to fool the opposition by getting him to reveal the strategies he will use during the lawsuit. This gambit, which is called "discovery" by lawyers, is also very expensive because it consumes vast amounts of attorney's time and the time of the various expert witnesses. The function of discovery is to separate out the serious from the non-serious players. Perhaps as many as one-third of exclusionary zoning suits are settled during the discovery process when the teams begin to understand the magnitude of the game they have embarked upon.

Bedminster

Henry Hill has represented a developer in Bedminster since 1973, well before the *Mount Laurel II* decision. He originally represented Johns-Manville, which bought 1,600 acres for its headquarters. Then Johns-Manville decided to move its corporate headquarters to Denver. The corporation sought a buyer (the land was zoned for one housing unit for every five acres) or a co-venturer, and it carried on litigation for ten years to change the large-lot zoning. Before *Mount Laurel II*, Hills Development Company, which acquired the land from Johns-Manville, won its case but obtained the right to build "least-cost" housing under the decision then operative, *Oakwood* v. *Madison*. After *Mount Laurel II*, the case was remanded and the plaintiffs agreed to provide 20 percent low- and moderate-housing. The case is still before Judge Serpentelli. Now the Town is being supported by both Hills Development Company and the Public Advocate, but another buider, Leonard Dobbs, is attack-

Hills Development, Bedminster, New Jersey. (Photos by Richard F. Babcock)

ing the settlement because Dobbs did not get a "builder's remedy." The *Mount Laurel II* disputes abound with such ironies.

Bedminster is a very posh town. It is a one-hour commute from New York City, and in or near the town are the sites of campus-style facilities of major corporations such as Exxon, Chubb Insurance, Ortho Pharmaceutical, and the Long Lines headquarters of AT&T. Cyrus Vance's property adjoins the Johns-Manville tract. Malcolm Forbes lives down the road; Douglas Dillon lived in Bedminster. Nicholas Brady, a former U.S. senator, was a resident. The median income in the Middlesex–Somerset–Hunterdon SMSA where Bedminster is located is about $32,000 for a family of four; it is higher in Bedminster. Thus a low-income family cannot have an income in excess of $16,000.

This was the first effort to build low- and moderate-income (half and half) units in New Jersey — 260 of them — under *Mount Laurel II*. And they are being built. The Hills Development Company, as part of its settlement, was given the right to build 1,287 housing units, of which 20 percent would be set aside for lower-income residents. One-bedroom or studio market units, of townhouse or condominium configurations, are priced from $75,000 to $100,000. Units with more bedrooms range from $125,000 to over a quarter of a million dollars. The market units in the $100,000–$200,000 price range are very "hot," and are snapped up as soon as they are built. The higher-priced units — those over $200,000 — are moving somewhat more slowly, but they are also being sold at a pace that has been more rapid then the company's expectations.

Construction of the lower-income units came about because of a settlement between Hills, the Public Advocate, and Bedminster Township. In the first part of that settlement, 260 units of lower-income housing were proposed, which were to be price-controlled, and deed-restricted to remain "below market" for thirty years. All the parties to the case (which included the Public Advocate and the Township, as well as Hills) agreed to create a corporation, the Bedminster Hills Housing Corporation, to supervise and manage the lower-income housing. Funding for the Bedminster Hills Housing Corporation initially came from the Hills Development Company; over time, it will be funded by a percentage of the appreciation of the lower-income units.

It was more complicated to deal with the low- and moderate-income housing. There are no public subsidies today. The housing corporation set up a very complicated scheme under the Court settlement to deal with selection of applicants, sales price, and the contingencies of default of payment.

The prices of the below-market housing units ranged from $26,500 to $55,000 for one-, two-, and three-bedroom condos. Over 700 families applied, and priority was given to those who worked in Bedminster. Buyers received 11 percent mortgages from the New Jersey Mortgage and Finance Agency. Among those who meet the income guidelines, top priority goes to families who have at least one member working in Bedminster and who are:

1. Township and school district employees living in substandard homes;
2. living more than twenty miles away, or in a nearby urban municipality (e.g., an "urban aid" municipality such as Plainfield and New Brunswick); or
3. Township residents who live in substandard homes.

Second priority goes to families:

1. who live in substandard homes and who have one or more members working within ten miles of Bedminster;
2. who live in substandard homes within ten miles of the Township.

Caroline S. Auger, Director of Sales and Marketing for the developer, said:

> We know we're meeting a need, but it stirs our conscience because we know there's still a gap.
> The ones who fall into that gap are those who cannot afford to live in Mayfield, the least expensive of Hills' market housing, but whose income exceed the requirements for Village Green.
> That is a frustration. Hopefully, in the next go-round there'll be something for those people. But right now, they just feel like there's no hope for them.

The Town officials are not happy about the results of their eleven-year litigation, which cost over $1 million. Mayor Paul Gavin, a retired AT&T executive and Bedminster resident for thirty-one years, said:

> They're going to put 1,287 dwelling units and 350,000 square feet of commercial space on less than 200 acres. . . . We didn't like it, we didn't want it. But we said let's make it the best we can. After all, 10 years from now the developer will be gone, but we'll have to live with it.

But then, the occupants of the moderate-income housing in the Hills are not all that happy about what they have. After a year, they complained that the recreational facilities allegedly promised them have not been delivered, that parking facilities are not adequate and the streets are too narrow for fire trucks to get by parked cars, that the swimming pool for the low- and moderate-income families is just a "postage stamp," and that there are no tot lots. The Hills' President, John Kerwin — who used to drive around Bedminster with a license plate that read "Rezone" —

denies these complaints: "If the [swimming] facilities prove to be inadequate we would have to consider adding another pool. . . . If residents want a lot more parking, they'll have a lot less open space, a lot less trees."

The market and below-market units are built in distinctively different styles—one can spot both easily. The below-market houses, as a saleswomen for the market housing said, "are way over there." Each neighborhood has its own neighborhood association, which provides for the upkeep of the specific units within that association. For example, there is a Fieldstone Neighborhood Association, a Mayfield Neighborhood Association, a Stone-Run Neighborhood Association, a Crestmont Neighborhood Association, and a Knollcrest Neighborhood Association. All are associations for the market units. In addition, there is a Village Green Neighborhood Association for the units for lower-income occupants, and its fees are lower than for the other associations, but not because the amenities are so markedly different; probably these, too, are subsidized. In addition, the residents of Village Green, as is the case with all residents of The Hills Planned Unit Development, are members of the Hills Village Master Association; it is that association which is providing the major recreation facilities. Lower-income homeowners are members of the same recreational facilities as the market-income homeowners.

It is too early to know how well the mix will work in this wealthy community; whether the concept will spread to other New Jersey towns with substantially lower median incomes is even more problematical. The Hills' one-bedroom unit that sold for $27,000 probably had a market value of about $60,000. Because there are no available subsidies, the market units have to be surcharged. Henry Hill suggested some figures:

HH: The Hills' single family—the Hills' one bedroom unit that's going to sell for $27,000—has a fair market value of about $60,000. That's what it would sell for if it were market. It's smaller than what they're selling for $80,000 but on a square foot basis, that's what it would sell for on this market. In fact, it costs, depending on how good a builder you are, between $22.00 a foot and $35.00 a foot for a production builder to build in New Jersey.

RFB: What do you think is the surcharge on each of the market houses?

HH: I think that the moderate-income units don't cost anything and I think that the low probably costs $10,000 to $15,000 apiece to subsidize. . . . These are condominium stock units, stick built, non-union built, as is the building industry in New Jersey largely. . . . To use the Hills as an example, there are a total of 260 lower-income units in that project. 130 of them are moderate-income units, on which the builder probably doesn't lose a thing. The other 130 are low-income units, and I think they're losing probably $10,000 a unit.

This $10,000 a unit is spread on the rest of the PUD [planned unit development], but since there are over 1,000 market units, it looks to me like the per unit surcharge for the low-income units on the remainder of the development, if there is such a thing, is close to $1,300 per unit.

Some interesting preliminary demographic data have come in on the applicants in the low- and moderate-income levels in the Hills development in Bedminster. Seventy-one percent are in their twenties, and 20 percent are in their thirties. Thirty-eight percent are high school graduates, 30 percent have some college education, and 23 percent are college graduates. Of those who did give their occupation, the most prominent job listed was "clerk"; a few listed themselves as "word processors," a few as "bookkeeper," only two as policeman, and one as teacher. Among the more esoteric jobs, two identified themselves as "assistant golf pro" and one was a "tree climber." Incomes ranged from a low of $6,200 to $22,800, although by far the largest number of residents had been employed at their current job for two years or less. There is no information on race, but it is believed there are very few minorities among the applicants. The *Philadelphia Inquirer* quoted John H. Kerwin, President of Hills Development Company, as saying, "I don't want to burst anyone's bubble but these people are not the hard-core poor." In the same issue, the newspaper quoted Peter J. O'Conner, Executive Director of Fair Share Housing Center in Cherry Hills, as charging:

> My contention is that they're getting lower-middle-class people who are upwardly mobile and will eventually become middle-class, anyway. My feeling is that under [*Mount Laurel II*] they should be helped, but they shouldn't be the sole beneficiaries.[8]

Henry Hill says there is real difficulty in qualifying many of these applicants for mortgages while still keeping them within the allowed ceiling on income. "It's a very narrow spectrum," he says. Whether the applicants are thinly veiled "Yuppies" remains to be seen. Certainly sales housing, no matter how low the prices, will have only a limited reach into the poor sector because of the difficulty the poor will have in qualifying for mortgages or coming up with even a 5 percent down payment. As Alan Mallach has said: "While I do not find fault with the Bedminster experience, if *Mount Laurel* does nothing but replicate that experience across other affluent outer suburbs, it will certainly fall far short of both [the decision's] intent and its potential."

---

[8]*Philadelphia Inquirer*, February 25, 1985, p. 4A.

Other Communities

Whether this can work in the absence of subsidies in areas farther south in New Jersey, where the median income is much lower, and where it will be hard to have an add-on to the market units, is problematical. And this raises an interesting equal-protection question. If the doctrine will work only where the median income is very high—the northern counties—is *Mount Laurel II* durable?

Many New Jersey towns are reeling at the idea of the total number of units they imagine they will be expected to accept, figuring four fair-market units for every below-market unit. Judge Serpentelli, the *Mount Laurel* judge for central New Jersey, recently signed an order that will compel Warren Township to allow 946 below-market units, or 4,730 total units. Warren, which has a population of 10,000, is a wealthy township; the average price of a house is about $235,000, with a median income of around $52,000. Except for a few nonconforming units, there are no multiple-family dwellings in the Township. Warren is still fighting the decision, although it seems hopeless. The Township apparently feels that if it acquiesces, it is lost. But, as one knowledgeable participant in the litigation said: "Warren Township feels there will be a change politically in this somewhere and that as long as it keeps the case viable and keeps appealing it has a chance."

If it has to let in low- and moderate-income housing, Warren already owns some land, a large tract on which it will build prefabricated houses, and it believes it can sell the houses for about $44,000.

Cranbury, New Jersey, located near Princeton, is a prime agricultural area. It has a state and federal historic district of nineteenth-century homes, a population of 2,000, and 8,400 acres. The court order in four developers' suits calls for Cranbury to permit 816 below-market units. Multiply this by four—4,080 units—and it would more than quadruple Cranbury's present population. A Cranbury committeeman, Thomas Weiderer, added, "Ten years from now, I don't want our historic district gone, our farm land gone and people say [sic] it's too bad *Mount Laurel* didn't work."

If you multiply the *total* number of units to be built in the growth areas of New Jersey, the figure is somewhere around 1.2 million. Even in the best of building years, the total construction was about 50,000 units and the market may well preclude the likelihood of the 1.2 million projected by frightened town officials. The implications for the infrastructure alone are staggering—the sewers, water, and roads will amount to billions. And New Jersey does not so pervasively enjoy the practice, widespread over many other jurisdictions, of "exactions," that is, demands that the developer contribute off-site improvements to assist the town's fiscal sit-

"Mount Laurel" housing under construction (foreground) adjacent to Village of Pluckemin. (Photo by Ray W. Jones/courtesy of Township of Bedminster)

uation. Indeed, it is hard to see how such a practice could be consistent with *Mount Laurel II*. Exactions would have to be paid by homebuyers, and that means higher-priced houses. The below-market buyers cannot afford this, and the market units are already priced to subsidize the low-

and moderate-income residents.

It may be expected that other towns will provide different solutions—all of them apparently reconciled to the need to accommodate the decision in *Mount Laurel II*. Stewart Hutt, General Counsel for the New Jersey Builders Association, represents Kenneth Pizzo, who wanted to build in Branchburg, a rural, well-to-do community along Route 22 in northern New Jersey. Hutt got a builder's remedy from the judge after months of fruitless negotiations with the Town prior to *Mount Laurel II*. Pizzo agreed to pay the Town $1.4 million cash so the Town could build its own low- and moderate-income housing. In return, he can build 756 market price homes at seven dwelling units to the acre. (The land had been zoned for one unit per acre.) The Town has bought the land off Route 22 and presumably will use Pizzo's money to put in the infrastructure for about 600 mobile homes and the site will be sheltered by a twenty-acre ring of woods "so it won't be a bother to the neighborhood." The vote in the Township Committee was three to two in favor of the settlement; that compromise probably saved the Township $150,000 in legal fees.

Current Status

Justice Wilentz expressed dismay that the New Jersey State Legislature had been unwilling to act since the 1975 *Mount Laurel I* decision. *Mount Laurel II* did get some response. Eight bills were introduced into the Senate and Assembly, both of which are controlled by Democrats. Two bills by Senator Thomas Gagliano, Republican, would establish a State Planning Commission and enact a moratorium for eighteen months on any *Mount Laurel* activity. Senator Gagliano does not expect those bills to go anywhere although, as noted previously, Governor Kean in his 1985 State of the State address did ask the Legislature for a moratorium. Another bill by Senator John Dorsey, Republican, would amend the constitution of the state to prohibit interference with municipal control over zoning. This bill is effectively dead.

Only two bills appear to have much chance of moving through the Legislature. The chief sponsor of one is Senator Wynona Lipman of Newark. It creates a seven-member Council on Affordable Housing in the Department of Community Affairs. The intent is to provide for a mechanism for implementing the *Mount Laurel II* 20 percent solution. The Council would establish guidelines for municipalities that elect to participate in the Council's fair-share program. Municipalities whose plans and ordinances are certified by the Council would be entitled to a presumption of validity in any exclusionary zoning challenge. The bill also established a Low and Moderate Income Housing Trust Fund with revenues derived from an increase in the realty transfer tax from $1.75 to $3.50 per $500. Senator Lipman is the very powerful Chairman of the Senate State Government Committee, but it is doubtful whether Governor Kean will eventually sign the bill.

The only bill that early on appeared to have a chance to be enacted and signed by the Governor was introduced by Senator Gerald Stockman, a Democrat from Trenton, a district that includes downtown Princeton. That bill establishes a twenty-one-member State Planning Commission and an Office of State Planning in the Department of the Treasury. In effect, the bill calls for the Commission to prepare a new growth guide plan for the state. The Court in *Mount Laurel II* acknowledged that that plan was dated and decreed that a new guide plan be prepared by January 1985. Clearly, if the Stockman bill goes through—and today that appears unlikely—this date would not be met, not by at least a year; and no one in the state executive offices is undertaking such a task primarily because Governor Kean effectively abolished planning by heavily cutting the budget of the Planning Division of the Department of Community Affairs.

Senator Stockman is an interesting, rare politician, a throwback to the old FDR liberals. He is a young attorney who specializes in personal injury matters. How did he get involed in land use? He answers:

> When the opinion came out my instincts told me it would be a major battleground of social change and redirection into the 21st century. I have a penchant for the big issue and really a distaste for sentimental or ceremonial resolutions, the balcony kind of stuff, and I just said to myself it's an important unanimous decision, I'm a lawyer, I respect the Court. I sensed that there was nothing being done within the legislature and in effect I sensed that there was a responsibility on the part of the legislature to act. I sensed that there weren't many people in the legislature who were likely to get seriously into the mix. I sensed that I possess the equipment to do a reasonably credible job as an attorney and it was really a civil rights kind of a decision for the poor and the near poor and that's the angle I come from.

A bill finally emerged from the Legislature, approved basically along party lines, forty-two to thirty-four in the Assembly, twenty-two to sixteen in the Senate. In essence, it is the Lipman bill but there are two notable additions. To hold some of their party, the Democrats agreed to a provision that puts a one-year moratorium on builder's remedies. But they added a novel condition, namely, that the Attorney General must go to court within thirty days to determine if such a moratorium—interrupting the judicial process—is valid. If such action is not taken, then the moratorium is to be stricken.

Governor Kean announced that he would veto the legislation, although he held out a willingness to negotiate further. But in April 1985, he conditionally vetoed the bill (something akin to the more familiar line veto), leaving in, of course, the moratorium but removing the required court appearance and the state funding. The Legislature, presumably exhausted by this time, in the spring of 1985 upheld the conditional veto and passed the bill as resubmitted by Governor Kean. There remains the possible challenge to the Governor's effort to interfere with the judicial process.

So none of this hysteria appears likely to reduce the chaos in New Jersey or to stanch the flow of millions of dollars in legal and planning expenses out of strained municipal treasuries. The Republicans are simply trying to reverse the Supreme Court's decision or, after eleven years of suburban stalling, to put it on hold for another eighteen months. The Democrats, with the exception of Senator Lipman, are not addressing the major issue of *Mount Laurel*—how to finance the great number of low- and moderate-income units.

A more bizarre effort was made by some mayors, Senator Gagliano, and others. They sought to raise $3,000 apiece from eighty or more municipalities to go into federal court to overturn the decision. They have thus far attracted at least eighty municipalities. What grounds they had hoped to plead is hard to fathom. They talked about "separation of powers," but there is no such clause in the U.S. Constitution. There was some murmur too about the protection of a republican form of government, which is based on the theory that the Court has effectively taken this away from the municipalities. No reference to municipalities, however, appears in the U.S. Constitution; they are creatures of the state. All their authority comes from the state, and the Supreme Court of New Jersey is an intimate part of the state apparatus. This effort demonstrates the unwillingness of some communities to address the realities of *Mount Laurel II*.[9]

Of course, this story has not yet ended. It is too soon to predict an outcome. Some consequences, however, appear to be emerging.

1. The towns, in spite of their initial panic and the seemingly futile effort to reopen the case in the New Jersey Supreme Court, do appear to be accepting the Court's order—not happily, but they're going along. They are coming up with different systems to work out their obligation and we may expect that the three "zoning czars," the three trial courts, will accept these various techniques.

---

[9]The mayors did raise enough money to hire a prominent New York City law firm. But the case did not go into federal court. Instead, in the Cranbury lawsuit, a direct appeal was filed to the New Jersey Supreme Court, and just as directly the Court threw the case out. So far no further word has been heard from them.

2. The absence of any state or federal subsidies is the most serious problem. Under the Lipman Bill, as conditionally vetoed by the Governor, no state funds will be available. The cost burden will certainly continue to be borne by the buyer of the market housing. While this may work in wealthy communities such as Bedminster and Branchburg, it is doubtful that it can succeed in the poorer areas of the state.

3. It is doubtful whether this decision is going to be of much assistance to the larger cities such as Newark or Trenton, unless the Court accepts Senator Stockman's idea that a suburban town can, in discharge of its duties, pay to, for example, Trenton, monies to build new housing in the decaying urban area. There is no evidence at this time that the Court will accede to this scheme.

4. Perhaps the most intriguing question is whether this judicial adventure in New Jersey will leak to other jurisdictions. New Jersey is engaged in a great experiment that recalls the bold *legislative* action that other states, such as Oregon (maximum hours for women) and New York (workmen's compensation), took decades earlier. These novel concepts do have a way, in our federal system, of being picked up if they seem to be working. No other state at this time is even nibbling at the idea. New York and Pennsylvania courts show some awareness of the serious problems, and California inserts some ambiguous language in its statutes, but there is nothing in those states that even begins to approach the dramatic action in this crowded eastern state. Certainly, this is true in the so-called heartland of Ohio, Indiana, Illinois, Michigan, and Wisconsin. Why this should have occurred in New Jersey, that zoo of municipalities where so many public servants are convicted of abusing their public offices, may seem a mystery. It seems to us that it only can be explained by one accident: Justice Frederick Hall's presence on the state Supreme Court. This suggests how much history is the image of a great man. Without his dissent in *Vickers* there would have been no *Mount Laurel I* and without *Mount Laurel I* and the aftermath of apparent failure, there would have been no *Mount Laurel II*.

5. A small point: the chaos after *Mount Laurel II* was a Lawyers and Planners Endowment Act. Many millions of dollars have been spent by municipalities in futile efforts to fight the inevitable. We observed one trial involving Franklin Township and half a dozen developer-plaintiffs. It looked like a multijurisdictional antitrust case. We counted fourteen lawyers. Perhaps the profligate expenditures, the drain on municipal budgets, more than anything else will bring the most intransigent communities around.

6. Finally, we believe New Jersey should be applauded for this daring step. Without such experiments, our federal system would lose much of its resilience and its capacity to survive. It is hard to imagine Con-

gress or the U.S. Supreme Court daring to venture into such socially and politically treacherous waters. Indeed, the absence of the police power by the federal government in this land use field makes such a step almost unimaginable.

Nor are we particularly worried about this activism by the seven judges. We have through our history always moved forward by such declarations of policy in defiance of strong public disapproval and indifference by the legislature. That's the stuff of great constitutional victories, and as nearly always they usually occur in our courtrooms rather than in our legislatures.

Epilogue

Following Governor Kean's conditional veto, the Senate passed his version of the bill, twenty-one to six, on June 24, 1985, and on June 28 the Assembly also approved the bill, forty-four to thirty.

So now the legislation provides for a one-year moratorium on builder's remedies, but it is not clear to which of the many lawsuits this applies, nor whether such a legislative interference with the Court's jurisdiction will be upheld if it is challenged.

The bill also creates an Affordable Housing Council to which cases are to be referred in lieu of the courts. Again, a challenge may be forthcoming.

Most opponents of *Mount Laurel II* seem pleased with the action. As Professor Jerome Rose said in the *New Brunswick Home News*, "This is the end of judicial terrorism."[10]

[10]June 28, 1985.

12

Sea Ranch, California: The Devil's Due

California, more than any other part of the union, is a country by itself. . . .

Lord Bryce,
The American Commonwealth

I believe that the California Coastal Act as administered by the Commission was truly different in kind. It was a revolution, not a reform.

Attorney Malcolm Misuraca

Sentence first — verdict afterwards.

Queen, *Alice in Wonderland*

Most Americans, when they think of California, recall a visit to Disneylar ', a tour through Tinseltown, the clank-clank of a cable car, or a day on the bland beaches of the south coast. This is a story about a far less languorous area of California: the coast about 110 miles north of San Francisco. It is a rugged, harsh, foggy, and windswept area — a place of dramatic and stark shoreline, a far cry from Malibu or Monterey. The breathtaking panorama of the coast moves inward to the coastal range covered with second-growth Monterey and Bishop pines. Along the coast winds California Highway 1, meandering through meadows with occasional glimpses of the coastline. (Don't travel this coastal highway on Sunday afternoon — you will get behind a recreational vehicle and move about twenty miles per hour.) It is a two-lane road that probably never will be widened; it is a treasure to northern California just as it is.

Background

Originally settled perhaps two thousand years ago by the peaceful, fun-loving Pomo Indians, the land was bountiful and the weather blustery and wet but endurable. The Pomos did no farming.

Although Sir Francis Drake and many Spanish galleons passed this area of coast, no one stopped here until early in the nineteenth century when a Russian, Ivan Kuslov, an official of the Russian American Fur Company, came. He brought 120 Russians and Aleut Indians and built a fort, which they named Fort Ross, an ancient name for Russia. These settlers ravaged the land. Judith and Neal Morgan, in their charming booklet, *Island in the Coast,* recounted how these settlers violated the laws of nature:

> With brutal dispatch, they raped the virgin land and slaughtered the sea otter. . . . Within a decade, the herds were all but exterminated. The soil on this narrow coastal plain could not take the massive assault by crops and cattle. Seasons of heavy rains, along with raids by gophers and rabbits, hastened the end. In 1839, less than 30 years after the triumphant establishment of the outpost, the Russians admitted defeat.[1]

The Mexican Declaration of Independence in 1821 cost Spain its California claims, and for two decades the Republic of Mexico's flag flew over northern California. Then came the revolt of Californians against the Mexicans, and for a short time the Bear Flag of the Republic of California flew over Sonoma County. The republic was accepted as a state of the American Union in 1846.

The parcel that we are concerned with, which came to be known as the Sea Ranch, is on this coast on both sides of Highway 1, at the north end of Sonoma County, separated from Mendocino County by the Gualala River. At the time of its acquisition in 1963 by Castle and Cook, the huge Hawaii-based pineapple and sugar cane company, it was a sheep ranch run by two brothers named Ohlsen, who had taken it over after lumbering and rum running had died out in the late 1920s. Seeing that the sheep had devastated the land, the Ohlsens tried to convey the ten miles of land along the coast to the State of California for $750,000, but the state turned them down. Instead, the brothers sold the 5,200 acres to Oceanic, Inc., Castle and Cook's subsidiary, for $2 million.

Sea Ranch

Oceanic began costly and elaborate plans for a residential community,

[1]Judith and Neal Morgan, *Island in the Coast* (Oceanic California, Inc., 1974), p. 6.

a planned development to consist of 5,000 units, which would have made it the largest coastal development between San Francisco and Eureka, 275 miles up the northern coast. They began a sophisticated analysis of the ecology: they set up anemometers to study wind currents, and marine biologists studied the migration of whales and monitored the sea lions and the abalone. Still other researchers inventoried the wildflowers. Tree specialists, geologists, architects, and planners analyzed and drew plans. The plans called for clustering of the units, most of them single-family detached houses, many on eighty-foot lots with septic fields out in the common areas, which comprised over 70 percent of the land east of Highway 1. Oceanic organized a homeowners' association, known as Sea Ranch Association, one vote for each lot owned, and established very strict convenants and design controls. Oceanic built a small lodge with twenty rooms, a restaurant, and bar, and started to sell lots. A few scattered houses were built, all of them in a brownish gray style that came to be referred to as "stove-pipe" or "mine shaft" modern, and soon architectural and planning awards were thrust upon the developer. Melvin Lane, the publisher of *Sunset Magazine* and former Chairman of the State Coastal Commission, recalls:

> I remember one year we had a big judging here for the American Institute of Architects and the judges were all saying, "This time, by God, we're not gonna pick a whole bunch of houses from Sea Ranch." But they did anyway because under AIA rules they didn't know where they were.

Public Access

During those early days Oceanic, as part of the unincorporated area of Sonoma County, dealt with the county for subdivision and zoning approvals. This was not a very difficult effort—at least not when contrasted with what was to come later. Oceanic obtained approvals of the first lots they subdivided. But there was in the county a group who insisted that accessways be provided from Highway 1 to the mean high-tide line, the point where the public ownership begins. They argued that since Article 15, Section 2, of the California Constitution declared all seaward property to be public, it was outrageous to deny access for a stretch of ten miles. Bill Kortum of Petaluma was one of the organizers of this protest. We met and talked with him. He is a zealot and for the most part a successful one. Elected to the Board of Supervisors of Sonoma County, he was later recalled.

Bill Kortum's group tried to fight for public access at the public hearings. The supervisors, however, had agreed, in a private deal, to take over a park as an alternative to various vertical accessways.

Housing at Sea Ranch. (Courtesy of Mildred Howie)

The "deal" made was for Oceanic to deed 125 acres at the northernmost part of the county for a park at the mouth of the Gualala River. Later, Melvin Lane said that the donation of the park did not "cut any ice" with the State Commission: "We didn't think we could accept that as a matter of principle. The developer shouldn't be able to keep the public out of five miles by giving them a half-mile. . . . That's debatable, but that was our opinion."

Having failed at the public-hearing level, Kortum's group organized a movement to put a voter initiative on the ballot to require public access in Sonoma County. Kortum describes the campaign:

> We got about 12,000 signatures in six weeks . . . and put it on the ballot. And we're so amateur in our political knowledge that we raised about $1,500 to sell the idea and the other side in two weeks spent $40,000. And beat us; nobody thought the people would vote against their own interests.

COAAST and Proposition 20

This defeat mobilized the Kortum group. They organized a group known as COAAST—Californians Organized to Acquire Access to State Tidelands. COAAST was charged by everyone we talked to as a group of abalone hunters who wanted access to the tidelands to seek out their prey. An editorial in the *Independent Coast Observer*, whose publisher, Joanna McLaughlin, lives on Sea Ranch, proclaimed:

> We know what the secret acronym really stood for. COAAST spelled with that offensive extra "A" doesn't spell "coast." It spells "CO-AAST" and that stands for Clan Obsessed with Acquiring the Abalone off Sea Ranch Territory. . . .
> Perhaps we need a new organization called STAFF, for Save The Abalone From Fakes.
> And it could sue CO-AAST for obstructionism, economic destructionism, and possibly for unconstitutional deprivation of property rights of Sea Ranch owners from building on their hard earned lots.

Now COAAST was determined to deal with the entire California coast. The concept of Proposition 20 was born, a statewide initiative to control land use along the coastline. For a number of years, efforts had been made to get such legislation through the Legislature; while the bills went through the Assembly with ease, the more conservative Senate always killed the bills in committee. It may be said that the availability of the initiative acts as a soporific on the Legislature: they feel that the people can always vote the proposition in by initiative if they really want it. In their efforts to get signatures to place the proposition on the ballots, the proponents had a great deal going for them. People were increasingly concerned about overdevelopment and consequent loss of the coastal beauty. Another concern was the lack of public access to the beach (Malibu in the Los Angeles area has a twenty-seven-mile string of houses where there is almost no public access). There was also a notable shortage of public beach and campgrounds. A third concern was the impact of development on wetlands and other wildlife habitats. Later, this was made particularly poignant in California and beyond by pictures of fowl soaked with oil after the spill in the Santa Barbara Channel.

So the leaders turned to the initiative and brought together various groups, including COAAST, the Sierra Club, the American Institute of Architects, Common Cause, the California Medical Association, the United Auto Workers, fifty-seven State Senators and State Assemblymen, and both U.S. Senators, Alan Cranston and John Tunney. Kortum was the first President of the Coastal Alliance. They needed 325,000 signatures to qualify for the November 1972 ballot and they obtained 418,000.

The opposition—chambers of commerce, oil companies, local governments, and developers—were quick to respond. They hired a well-known public relations firm, Whitaker and Baxter, and mounted a strong media and billboard campaign with slogans such as "Conservation YES, Confiscation NO—vote NO on Proposition 20" (shades of the opposition to the New Jersey Pinelands) and "The Beach Belongs to You, Don't Lock It Up—Vote NO on Propo 20"—an allegation about as misleading as it could be.

The proponents won by a strong 55 percent of the vote. The proposition carried in twelve out of the fifteen coastal counties, including Sonoma County, but lost in Mendocino, Del Norte, and Humbolt—the three northernmost coastal counties. This does not mean 55 percent of the voters understood what Proposition 20 meant. Initiative propositions are notably vague, representing only a summary of what is in the full proposition. Moreover, Californians have become satiated with a multiplicity of propositions at every general election. Sabatier and Mazmanian, in their book *Can Regulation Work?*, quote Mervin Field, the well-known California pollster, on initiative propositions:

> Initially, while not many people fully grasp all the details and ramifications, their instinctive reaction is generally favorable. . . . Typically, the public only becomes fully aware of the opposition to the measure relatively late in the campaign, sometimes only a few weeks before Election Day. . . . And more times than not the original instinctive support of the idea is replaced by a negative view.[2]

[2]Paul A. Sabatier and Daniel A. Mazmanian, *Can Regulation Work?* (New York: Plenum Press, 1983).

Basically, the initiative set up one statewide coastal agency or commission and six Regional Commissions. All development within 1,000 yards of the water line was subject to the approval of the respective Regional Commissions with an appeal to the State Commission in San Francisco. In addition, the State Commission was charged with preparing a plan for an area back from the coast to which local governments were to comply, and legislation was to be submitted to the Legislature by 1976 to make the initiative a legislative act.

So one might say Sea Ranch was in part responsible for Proposition 20. It was clearly within the geographic area for which the California Coastal Commission was responsible and was presumably subject to the regulations of the North Central (Regional) Commission. Indeed, some of the original builders of second homes had strongly supported the idea of Proposition 20 and voted for it even though Bill Kortum, their prime antagonist, had helped lead the fight to set up the Commission. The issue, however, that was the subject of dispute for ten years was whether the Sea Ranch should be given a pass because of prior approvals by the county.

By the time the voters brought in Proposition 20, about 1,700 lots had been sold and about 300 had houses on them. Here was to be the source of the division within the Sea Ranch Association that was to embarrass them later. Nor was it surprising that many who owned property at Sea Ranch supported Proposition 20. After all, this was not posh Pebble Beach or exclusive Santa Barbara. It is a rugged, isolated place, a hard two-and-one-half hour drive from San Francisco with only a narrow road after leaving U.S. 101 and only the small hamlet of Gualala across the river. Outside of the Sea Ranch itself, there were no amenities. The owners regarded themselves as true-blue environmentalists, many of whom belonged to the Sierra Club or similar organizations. At first, most if not all of the houses were built as second homes; now perhaps one-third are occupied permanently.

It soon became apparent that the 1,400 people who owned lots but had not built were going to have problems. In 1973 and 1974, Oceanic and the Sea Ranch Association began to negotiate with the North Central Commission, and here they first encountered Michael Fisher, now Executive Director of the Commission.

By all accounts, Fisher was a tough egg. An Oceanic employee commented that Fisher as a planner had a certain commitment, but that he was a young political opportunist with too much unchecked power. Others refer to Fisher as a "bandit" or a "maniac." When not bargaining from across the table, he is a very personable young man with a certain charismatic zeal.

More than one person we talked to referred to a comment that Fisher allegedly made: that "he was going to beat Sea Ranch because it was the best-designed project along the coast. If he could lick Sea Ranch, he could beat any proposal." A former Chairman of the Association, Dr. Donald Hines, theorized why Fisher and his group were so opposed:

> I finally decided that they were acting on two premises: first, that all developers were devils, and that all development was inherently evil; and that the Sea Ranch gave the lie to these religious principles, you see, and consequently, had to be destroyed.

Three Overall Conditions

The North Central Commission demanded three major overall conditions before it would issue any building permits. First, there must be public accessways, the old bugaboo, with no compensation. (The Commission did not have the power of eminent domain.) Presumably, these public accessways would have to go through the common areas and public parking would have to be provided. As we shall see, this condition would prove to be the most intractable of the requirements. Second, Oceanic had to cut down many of the Bishop pines along the coast road. The pines, the Commission said, blocked views along the highway. This seemed particularly ironic—the idea of a conservationist agency insisting that trees be destroyed. It seems Oceanic had planted about 200,000 trees expecting that probably half would die, but most thrived. There is considerable doubt about the usefulness of this requirement: if you drive the coastal road, you do not dare take your eyes off the highway. The odd thing is that between Jenner, about thirty miles south, and Sea Ranch there probably is not more than one public pull-off. The related requirement for views was a control over height, site, and bulk limits of houses on the west side of the highway. The third condition was that the Association must monitor the operation of the septic system.

The Picchi Case

One of the most poignant cases involved Dr. Joseph Picchi, an Oakland physician. He had bought a lot in 1967 on the west side of the highway. He wanted to put up a two-and-one-half story, five-bedroom house for his large family. The Commission said no, for it would block the view from the highway. He kept coming back, but the Commission told him to build a one-bedroom, twelve-foot-high house located as far down the slope as possible from the highway. Michael Fisher commented to Babcock:

MF: And, of course, he'd get out his whole family and trot them up and say how can this family live in that kind of house that you're going to allow us. So we said buy another lot. Being an insensitive regulator, you know, you got the wrong lot, Mr. Picchi. So my understanding is that just pushing Joe's lawsuit through the Superior Court, cost the Homeowners' Association $70,000 or something like that.

RFB: You mean they won that?

MF: No, they didn't. They lost the case, but in losing that case they burned up $75,000 of Homeowners' Association dues.

Reverdy Johnson, a San Francisco attorney who for a time represented both Oceanic and the Sea Ranch Association, recalls that the then-manager of Sea Ranch, Bill Rand, took some snapshots along the highway in front of Dr. Picchi's lot. The five slides represented in sequence the view of the lot, driving at forty or forty-five miles an hour. Bill Rand explained that all one could see was the fence line: "There is no impairment of the view; there is no view to be seen from there. And what's more, you're on a curve at that point, and if you're looking at what I just photographed, you're gonna crash."

This made no difference to the Commission. They told Dr. Picchi, "Well, your house is obviously part of a process of building a whole series of houses there, and if you do so, there will be a wall of houses and they will block the view."

Most of the public who supported Proposition 20 (including the *Oakland Tribune*) thought the law would be carried out prudently in the public interest. The inklings of growing public concern with the Commission's policies with respect to the building permit denials appeared in the *Tribune*:

> There are no state funds to pay Dr. Picchi for this substantial, involuntary loss of equity. Yet the regional commission seems to show little concern that the property owner must let his land stand vacant, all the while paying taxes on it, or sell out at a greatly discounted price. . . .
>
> Whatever the legal obligations of the coastline control agency in this case, there is a basic moral duty to treat fairly and equitably those individuals incapable of standing up to the awesome, unrestrained power of government.[3]

Plight of the Lotowners

Both Oceanic and the Sea Ranch Association rejected the three condi-

[3]*Oakland Tribune,* August 23, 1973.

tions. The North Central Commission also cut back the buildable lots from 5,200 units to 2,329.

Applications kept piling up. Dr. Bradford Lundborg, then Chairman of the Commission, observed: "It really became difficult for me to believe how incredibly hardnosed those people were about not having the rabble going across their common land to those beaches." The Commission brushed aside the cries of the lotowners that they could not agree to these conditions and that compliance was the responsibility of Oceanic or the Association. Tough, fella! A lotowner on the east side of the highway could not do anything about accessways from the highway west to the beach, nor about cutting the trees, nor about monitoring other people's septic systems. Beyond a doubt, the Commission expected the individual lotowners would put pressure on Oceanic and the Association to fulfill these conditions. It was a form of extortion. Dr. Lundborg acknowledges as much:

> Our only feeling was simply that, one way or another, since this was a unified development, access to the public had to be provided. Who did it and how it was done between Oceanic and the Association. . . . Once it became apparent that the individual property owners would not permit the Association to do it then the law simply said that you can't have development without the access being permitted. That argument, that the individual property owner couldn't accomplish it and that therefore it was holding the individual property owner hostage, was repeatedly made and obviously there's some justification in that point of view. . . . It was argued within the Commission, there were several of the Commissioners who were bothered by that — Margaret Azevedo (a Commissioner) among them.

Lundborg, as Chairman, was in a particularly awkward position: his father, an officer of Bank of America, owned a lot at Sea Ranch. He had voted for Proposition 20 — as had his father — and reminisced:

> At about that point the realities of the Act and their own personal feelings that certain classes of people deserve the right to the exclusive use of the beach even if it was public domain and other classes of people did not. It became apparent and we had some very, very bitter arguments — my wife and I and my kids on one side and my mom and dad on the other. Soon thereafter we simply ceased discussing it and literally, but for an occasional very brief apologetic reference that was made essential by some other topic, we never discussed it again to the day he died.

Negotiations

These access demands created understandable panic among lotowners.

The North Central Commission, Oceanic, and the Sea Ranch Association held scores of meetings in an attempt to negotiate. The Commission held a dozen public hearings that were bitter shouting matches. Michael Fisher recalls a hearing in Gualala, in which there was potential danger:

> The place was just jammed. We had the Commissioners up in the front. . . . And as people wanted to testify I would go through the crowd and hand the bullhorn to them so they could then talk and the Commissioners could then hear them. . . . At the end of the thing Bill and I walk outside and here were two highway patrolmen and a couple of Sheriff's cars, some of them with the red lights blinking. . . . He said, "Oh, about an hour and a half ago we got a bomb threat.". . . That was not the only bomb threat or meeting that we ever had that we had to have police protection at.

For almost nine years, during the interminable negotiations and the ensuing lawsuits, not one permit was issued.

Dichotomy in the Association

There was in all this the beginning of a split among members of the Association, between those who already had their houses up and those who owned lots and wanted to build. The former, commonly called "gangplankers" ("Bos'un pull the ladder up, I'm aboard"), did not really care whether the Association ever solved the problem. They had their houses and they loved the openness and tranquility. In addition, the idea of 1,400 additional cars trying to get up Highway 1 scared them. Babcock questioned Reverdy Johnson about the Commission's position against the Association.

> RFB: I would think that the Commission would tell them to go to hell, we have and can beat you guys time and again.
> RJ: They did and they could and they would have, but I think that in winning the battles, they would have lost the war.

He went on to explain that a certain segment of the public was becoming very aware that the Commission was "a bunch of bandits," and that steps needed to be taken to safeguard the people who bought property and were prevented from building on it by the Commission. Compounding the situation were the various involved parties and their specific interests. The Legislature, for example, did not want to confront the problem but had to effect a solution that was satisfactory to the Association. And Oceanic had an economic interest: how were they to complete the project and move on? And then there was the Association. In Johnson's words:

You've got the Association as an uncontrollable beast, because you have some people within it who say, "Get me a way to use my property"; and you've got some other people who may or may not have the gangplank syndrome of having built a house but, in any event, their attitude is, "This is our damn property; don't touch it; don't give away a thing; you're violating my constitutional rights." And that's all they would say. But you had the totally divided constituency within the Association.

In June 1974, the State Commission came up with an idea: each applicant would be allowed to build if he deposited $1,500 to be used by the Association to provide for eventual hookup to a sewer system. Most lotowners did so over the next few years—enough to accumulate a quarter-million dollars. Later, all of this cash, when the final deal was cut, was returned to the depositors. The Regional Commission was never happy with the $1,500 idea. Fisher had explained that the in-lieu fees were a very inequitable burden. People who had their houses already did not need to pay a fee, and those who would eventually come in after the accessways were completed would also have no reason to pay an in-lieu fee.

Litigation

About this time the Association brought in Malcolm Misuraca, a Santa Rosa attorney. Misuraca gained fame some years back beating Petaluma's growth-control plan, but he lost in the U.S. Appeals Court. He filed suit in June, 1974, before a three-judge federal court, on behalf of the Sea Ranch Association and fifteen lotowners challenging the constitutionality of the Coastal Commission's requirements for accessways. He really wanted to settle the case, believing Sea Ranch could live with the conditions called for by the Commission. The rub was that the Commission would not agree that these would be the final conditions. Misuraca explained that a future majority of the Coastal Commission might not feel that the settlement was adequate. He said:

> Because you can't deprive the later majority of the same police power that the early majority had they could change their mind and ask for more. How then, we asked, do we fix it so that we get to give once and never have to give again? You can't do it, said the Attorney General. You may have to give again no matter what you do.

Misuraca argued that the plaintiffs who owned already subdivided lots enjoyed vested rights at the time Proposition 20 became law. He had no better fortune in this case than he or other lawyers for Oceanic or the Association had in subsequent litigation. He lost when the federal court chose to abstain because the issue had not yet been resolved by the state courts. (Two years later, in 1976, a California appellate court held that the issuance of permits with a $1,500 deposit was valid. It also held that the aforesaid conditions were legitimate.)

At about the same time, Oceanic had filed a suit in the California court to challenge in toto the constitutionality of the law because the entire development enjoyed vested rights. Oceanic's attorney by this time was Howard Ellman, a feisty and outspoken litigator. He described the Commission's conditions as "constituting the longest and most verbose extortion note I have ever had the pleasure of reading." Misuraca recalls a nasty exchange during a hearing before the Regional Commission in San Francisco presided over by Bradford Lundborg:

> Howard Ellman, who by then was completely estranged from everybody on the Commission except Mel Owen, who was one of the really thoughtful people, had a way of infuriating the people on the Commission. He would hitch up his pant leg over his cowboy boots, because he always wore cowboy boots, probably still does. He would take off his coat and roll up his sleeves. He would wait to roll up his sleeves until his turn to speak came and then he would show his contempt for them while he was starting to talk by rolling up his sleeve on each arm. Lundborg that night said that it's been recommended to us that we hire outside counsel because there are certain members of this Commission who believe the representation we have gotten from the Attorney General's office is incompetent. Well, I want you to know, said physician, Dr. Lundborg, that I for one will vote no on that proposition, not because I think we've gotten particularly good advice from you, Bill, he said to the AG who was there that night, but because I never want to meet another lawyer. And Howard Ellman, who was standing there at the time, without a moment's hesitation, quoted from the Bible and said, "Physician, heal thyself."

Ellman, however, did not have any better luck. The California Appellate Court held that Sea Ranch had no vested right and the Commission was within its authority to impose the conditions. The California Supreme Court and the U.S. Supreme Court refused to hear the case. In the meantime, Misuraca's appeal to the Ninth Circuit Court of Appeals was thrown out. This was beginning to look more and more like "Casey at the Bat."

Futile Negotiations

More futile efforts were to come.

In 1977 and 1978 Oceanic and the Sea Ranch Association continued their negotiations with the Regional Commission. The State Commission withdrew its demand for a $1,500 deposit and reinstated the conditions. Back to square one.

The overall conditions were adopted and the permit process began again, subject, of course, to the conditions being met. The lotowners, however, who needed the building permits, could not promise on what they could not deliver. The active people on the Board of the Association were the ones whose self-interest was to vote in a way that did not create any more houses or any more access. Michael Fisher did not grant the permits and said:

> Your permit is here. It's going to be waiting for you in the file. Here's your commencement of construction authorization. As soon as you give us the overall conditions you can start building.

Malcolm Misuraca had quit as attorney for the Association. Probably, he says, he would have been fired if he had not departed. For there had been a turnabout on the Board of the Association based on the dichotomy between the "gangplankers" and those who owned vacant lots. Misuraca explained that lotowners were willing to be flexible about access because inflation of construction costs had gone up as much as 40 percent. But the people who had houses would not budge. He continues:

> They would insist that there was virtually unanimous opinion to give the commission nothing. . . . It was easy for those who had houses to say you're depreciating our values if you grant access without one ounce of concern for the values that were being eroded by inflation in those that haven't been built yet.

The Board hired other attorneys, Pillsbury, Madison and Sutro, of San Francisco. They amended Misuraca's old complaint and trundled back into federal court. The answer was the same: too bad, the coastal legislation was valid.

Bane Bill or Judicial Solution?

Misuraca had been telling the Association that they should try to work out a legislative settlement. So the Board went to Sacramento. They hired a former Assemblyman, Leon Ralph, who went to Assemblyman Tom Bane with a draft bill to exempt Sea Ranch. Bane was from Malibu, of all places, hundreds of miles south.

The bill ended up with a provision to pay the Association $500,000 in settlement of the litigation and provided for five accessways that some public agency was prepared to construct and maintain. And it required that the Association deposit deeds in escrow within a few months or else the bill would expire. The homeowners—the ones with houses at Sea Ranch—did not like it. They wanted to carry on the lawsuit. They were reliving that old gypsy curse: "May you have a lawsuit you know you can win." Both sides took large ads in the *Gualala Independent Coast Observer*. The opponents of a legislative solution:

> DO NOT VOTE TO TURN OUR BEAUTIFUL SEA RANCH INTO A PUBLIC PARK. Settlement of the Sea Ranch Federal Suit under terms of the Bane Bill is not "COMPROMISE" but unconditional surrender.

And the supporters of the Bane Bill:

> THANK YOU, TOM BANE. SOME SEA RANCHERS DO NOT UNDERSTAND THE ART OF COMPROMISE OR THE POLITICAL AND ECONOMIC FACTS OF LIFE.

The Board decided to hold a referendum. The members who voted supported taking the judicial course by six to one. The Association had already spent in excess of $180,000 just on their federal case—not counting what Oceanic had spent on their state court litigation. The Directors of the Association were getting advice that they should accept the Bane Bill. The upcoming election for the Board witnessed a multitude of mailings to the membership. John Marchant, former president of the Association, wrote one strong supporter of the Bane Bill:

> If the Board opts for Bane, it is important that those candidates who support this action receive strong support in the upcoming elections so that the gangplank club will not control the next Board and do us all in again.

Senator Bane himself wrote, "I may be wrong but I personally think those who are already living there are happy not having anyone else moving in." Two lotowners, Ruth and Frank Hagie, wrote an officer of the Association:

> Up to the present time, the issue has been debated for Sea Ranch primarily by the homeowners who have little to lose by prolonging the fight, while the lot owners stand by and incidentally contribute their equal share of the assessment as the debate drags on.
> This, we feel, is a no-win situation for TSRA, that should be laid to rest by us all! Let us all accept the Bane Bill.

Outcome of the Bane Bill

But why did the Commission go along? The Bane Bill in effect was paying the Sea Ranch Association $500,000 for accessways. Why didn't the Commission use some of the clout that was so clearly behind it when Proposition 20 won by 55 percent?

The reason seems apparent. The Commission no longer had much clout. As Reverdy Johnson said, people up and down the coast were angry when they realized the power the Commission had and how it was using it. The Sea Ranch may have been the first and biggest but there were many others from San Diego north. Bradford Lundborg admitted that had they had sufficient influence in the legislature, they would have repudiated the Bane Bill. Michael Fisher said, "The money part of it in my view was outrageous and an unconstitutional gift of public funds." COAAST and other environmental groups brought a lawsuit challenging the Bane Bill, but the California trial court threw it out and there was no appeal.

So the Bane Bill went through the Legislature, Governor Jerry Brown allowed it to become law without his signature, the deeds were deposited, and the half million paid to the Association. The staff of the Commission tried to make very clear, for fear of future similar bills, that the payment was for settlement of a lawsuit, *not* in payment of the accessways. And building is going on again, that is, for the people who can afford it. Joanna McLaughlin, publisher of the *Independent Coast Observer*, commented to Richard Babcock:

> RFB: I was told there are some sad stories of people who bought, didn't build, can't afford to build.
>
> JM: Oh, there are lots of those. Yeah. We see the lots go on the market for sale. We have people who are in our own subscription list. During the whole time when the moratorium was on, and prices were rising while nothing was happening, I'd get little letters from people saying that they had really enjoyed the newspaper all these years, but they couldn't stand to get it any more because they were selling their lot and they didn't want to hear more about it.

McLaughlin and her late husband bought a lot and built for $17,500 in 1970. It is a very special lot, and Oceanic gave them back 10 percent because they built within eighteen months. Today there are advertisements in her paper for *lots* selling for $100,000 and houses and lots that go for $250,000. An entirely different breed—younger and richer—is now moving in. An employee of Oceanic, Inc., spoke of the difference:

> But they're smart buyers; they don't buy as most of our original buyers did; they came up and fell in love and said, "I love this place; I must have a lot here." And even if it was very hard to afford they would put their money down and buy it and slowly pay it off. These new people tend to come up four or five times, think about it for a year. And when they buy, they don't want any advice. They can figure it all out themselves, and they're very much more sophisticated buyers. But we still find that most people buy because they intend to use it, but they're still buying environment. After all, it's hardly Jet City.

McLaughlin recalls a man who bought early but never could afford to build. These days he comes out once a year to picnic "and just stares at the sea."

Oceanic still owns about 400 lots. Its parent, Castle and Cook, got into some financial difficulties in 1983. Its agricultural interests in Hawaii lost millions, but it recovered sufficiently to carry on with Sea Ranch. Now it would like to sell off its entire holdings provided it can enlarge its lodge from 20 to 120 rooms. Apparently, it has that permission.

The accessways have not yet been constructed but they are going to be managed by the county with funds provided by the Coastal Conservancy, a state organization that appears to be able to obtain significant funds from the Legislature.

The Due Process Question

It is a sad story. Here was a development hailed as the ultimate in planning and architecture and concern for the environment, stopped for almost ten years. The 1,700 individuals who bought lots were stopped from building even though when they bought they had clearance from the county. And costs probably went up 200 percent in those years and priced many of the lotowners out of building. And then there were the procedural practices of the Commission that outraged many lawyers, as they should have: no cross-examination; a limited time to speak (ten minutes); and commissioners leaving the room or turning their backs when the lotowners' lawyers spoke. But anyone who practices public law in California should know better than to expect the California courts to be sympathetic with procedural due process protests when they challenge governmental practices. The Fourteenth Amendment appears to be nonexistent. As Howard Ellman said:

> For all practical purposes, we have no vested rights doctrine in California, and I think its absence adversely affects the ability to plan, I really do. I think that it also encourages developers to go for small projects. . . . And the net result of it is that in California the competent developers don't make deals here unless the project—the potential profits in the project justify a tremendously enhanced level of political risk. . . . If it's a housing deal they just won't do it and, as a result, housing costs out here are three times as high as they are in most of the midwest and east.

Malcolm Misuraca provided the ultimate, eloquent summations; he contrasted a California Coastal Act, as administered by the Commission, with a reform. According to him, it was more like a revolution:

> If you consider the nature of a revolutionary change, even a bloodless revo-

lution, it has certain characteristics. One is a determination for a complete discontinuity with past law. It's a wholesale casting out of past principles, even those that are relatively supportive of the new regime. It is a determination to rid the new regime of anybody from the old and the more reasonable the remnant people may be the more they are bound to be cast out. A revolution can't tolerate continuity with the past. It is a willingness to let a disproportionate, and usually small close class of people pay an enormously disproportionate price for the outcome. It leaves the intention that they will pay the price rather then leavening the price throughout the public treasury. It is a complete disregard for process and its part in liberty. If process is the essence of liberty, process is the first thing to be thrown overboard in a revolution. Finally, it is the focusing of the power of the revolution in the hands of a few ideologues who are determined that each will be purer than all the others.

Years later, in the *San Francisco Sunday Examiner and Chronicle*, one of the Commissioners, Margaret Azevedo, issued a *mea culpa*. One of the other commissioners said Azevedo did not understand what was going on but voted for the restrictions imposed on the lotowners. Azevedo said in part:

> What was an innocent intention [by the North Central Commission] has become a monument to governmental ineptitude. How could a bunch of well-meaning intelligent public servants have gone so wrong?
>
> I cannot speak for the other members of the North Central Coastal Commission, of course, but I came to believe there is a subtle private kind of dishonesty to which public officials under pressure are susceptible.[4]

To which we can only add "Amen!"

Conclusions

What to make of all this? We suppose it raises some doubts about the efficacy of the initiative process in a democracy. This direct access to legislation always sounds good, but it tends to turn into legislation via television commercials and public agencies, reminiscent of the 98 percent and 99 percent votes for Adolf Hitler or Josef Stalin — with little role for procedural due process. Of course, the initiative had its origins in the days of revolt against the California Legislature when that body was in the pockets of the railroads and mining interests. In spite of all its faults and weaknesses, the representative process seems the best compromise between the Alexander Hamiltons and the Thomas Jeffersons of this country.

[4]February 8, 1981.

Of course, in retrospect the protagonists have widely divergent views. Melvin Lane suggests:

> Developers in California in the 1970s were slow to accept the fact that the rules for development on the California Coast are different from the rest of the state. The fact that the state withdrew police powers from local government and vested control in a state agency in itself was a change. The state constitution guarantee of public access over private lands if no public access exists certainly makes the coast different from other lands. This section was not enforced in earlier years, but it was crucial in many court tests of the Coastal Initiative.

To the contrary, Howard Ellman:

> I could have lost the *Sea Ranch* case on exactly the same grounds without feeling this way about the adversaries. It was as though all of the rules upon which we have been taught to rely had been suspended so that these little people could do their thing. They were not carrying out the will of the people. They were implementing their own extreme interpretation of that will; an interpretation which was repudiated by the legislature. More than once during the *Sea Ranch* proceedings, I had the awful feeling that if these people could do what they were doing in the name of coastal preservation, how could we be sure that the system would effectively deter or derail other people, pursuing other more destructive causes which had temporarily caught the public's fancy? It was frustrating, depressing, and frightening.

The Commission's loss of support indicates that extremists, whatever their political stripe, are sooner or later discovered by the public. The zealousness of the Commission administrators, their indifference to fair play, and their use of what amounted to extortion against lotowners finally caught up with them and the Legislature turned on them.

Finally, there are the unfortunate persons caught in the squeeze for almost ten years, watching interest rates and inflation soar and denied the right to build. It is reminiscent of San Antonio and the absolute moratorium (see Chapter 5). But there's a difference: that was Texas, and this story took place in California. In the former jurisdiction, the courts would have thrown it out with no second thought. In California, the courts have elevated governmental arrogance to a fine art. Of course, we should not forget that originally most, if not all, of the Sea Ranch houses were second homes that most middle-class Americans cannot afford, and hence politically there is little risk in halting their construction. It leads to a paraphrase of an old American slogan: millions for abalone but not a cent for a house.

* * *

Authors' Comments

We sent drafts of this chapter to a number of people on both sides of this dispute. Some were highly critical. Mary Allen, project manager for Oceanic, said, "The article says little"; Melvin Lane wrote, "Your equating the Bane Bill with Coastal Protection and/or Commission popularity is mostly wishful thinking. . . . As a leader specializing in land use law and processes, I am hoping you will review your position." Malcolm Misuraca suggested that "there were crazies on both sides of the Sea Ranch dispute." Finally, according to Howard Ellman, "The account is much too balanced."

If all these contestants could find something to protest, perhaps we were not too far off the mark.

13
The Game Goes On

> *A man knocked at the heavenly gate;*
> *His face was haggard and old.*
> *He stood before the Man of Fate*
> *For admission to the fold.*
>
> *"What have you done," Saint Peter asked,*
> *"To gain admission here?"*
> *"I've been in the zoning business, Sir,*
> *For many and many a year."*
>
> *The pearly gates swung open wide;*
> *Saint Peter touched the bell.*
> *"Come in and choose your harp," he said,*
> *"You've had your share of Hell."*
>
> Wis. A County Code
Administrators' Newsletter, June 1977

> *It is easier to make certain things legal than to make them legitimate.*
>
> Sebastien Chamfort

What can be made of this potpourri, this strange assortment of adventures in confrontation and occasional resolution? Who are the villains? Who the heroes? What lessons are to be drawn? What changes should be made in our unique system for resolving land use disputes? Does professionalism have any place in an area so politically flavored?

We, as practicing lawyers who have become hooked on the jousting in this field over the years, are probably not the ones to answer these questions—but that does not mean we won't try. Successful attorneys vehemently denounce the notion that they purport to be penny-ante philosophers. We experience a good story, we talk to the persons involved in the confrontation, we think about what we've learned, and we do our best to report what we have seen. Professor Charles Haar has suggested that we are "oral troubadors." He probably is right. You may draw your own conclusions; we can only share ours.

The Actors

Clearly neither side—neither members of the government nor developer-landowners—has a monopoly on virtue or evil. This becomes apparent in contrasting, for example, the characters of the people at the heart of the stories in Tuxedo and Sanibel and the Pinelands or in the *Hernandez* case. Unfortunately, people do make a difference. We say "unfortunately" because this human variable is such a chance occurrence—fortuitous to the point of cliché. A Rasputin may appear as well as a Raphael. Yet it must be said: a strong, rational, good-humored person often emerges to push along an unpopular program, and yet he or she persists. Terry Moore in the Pinelands, with the endurance of Job and the skin of an armadillo, is one; Porter Goss of Sanibel is another. Both encountered bitter opposition, but they persevered and won. Alex Polikoff, with his bulldog faith in the right of his cause, as dubious as it might be, represents the lawyer at his best; he did make waves and changes in spite of the relentless evasion by Mayor Daley and Charles Swibel. And surely the late Justice Frederick Hall went from a voice crying in the wilderness in *Vickers* to see before his death a thunderous victory in *Mount Laurel II*. So Leo Durocher was wrong—good guys do not always finish last. How does the gem show up? There is no answer. It is pure luck, which obviously does not help very much.

There were also scoundrels, scalawags, and rapscallions. You can discern who they are easily enough. Something about zoning disputes brings out the beast in people. It is the procedure of zoning that encourages this fierceness. Zoning by law involves a public hearing, an invitation to what Babcock called "trial by neighborism." Undoubtedly, the cause of the hysteria is an irrational fear of change on the part of the neighbors and arrogance or greed on the part of the developer. Yet it is a reality—the hysteria, that is.

The Courts

What do we conclude about the role of the courts in these conflicts? If we look only at *Hernandez* and *Gautreaux*, the score is not very good: six years of litigation in the former, and thirteen in the latter—and it is not over yet. But those cases differ from each other. One cannot quarrel with Judge Austin's initial opinion; the Chicago practices offended not only our sense of justice but the U.S. Constitution as well. It is the remedy that created the problems. The formula was so unpopular that the politicians made hay for decades. *Hernandez*, on the other hand, was at heart a rather simple zoning case, a neighborhood dispute of which there have been hundreds of the same ilk and for which the courts offer little solution. The characters on both sides often put on unattractive displays of temper, which is not unusual in such cases.

In *Grand Central*, preservation reached its apogee. But will the case stand up? Justices Rehnquist, Burger, and Stevens—three of the youngest justices on the bench—dissented. Justice Stewart, who joined in the majority opinion, has retired. If, as some prophets predict, President Reagan has an opportunity to appoint as many as four justices, may the Court modify, qualify, or limit that opinion? It is probable that it will.

Sea Ranch? What *can* one say about the California courts other than that one has to be a madman to challenge a government regulation in that bizarre jurisdiction? And then there is *Mount Laurel II*. Surely the Court was acting as a seven-man legislature; it acknowledged as much. The municipalities and their attorneys were mad as hell. Both houses of the legislature squabbled for months over the proper legislative remedy. Finally, they passed a bill but Governor Kean conditionally vetoed it. The revised bill passed, presumably taking the issue out of the 1986 campaign but leaving everyone confused about the status of current lawsuits. If the New Jersey Court can be faulted, it is not for lack of courage. In Justice Louis Brandeis's words in *New York State Ice Company* v. *Liebmann*, 285 U.S. 262 (1932): "Denial of the right to experiment may be fraught with serious consequences to the Nation. It is one of the happy incidents of the federal system that a single courageous state may, if its citizens choose, serve as a laboratory."

The *Mount Laurel* decision is particularly interesting because it is, as far as we know, the only *state* court opinion that goes so far in the direction of legislating. Yet in the federal courts, the judiciary often has felt obliged to act in a manner that disturbs many people. We think of the cases involving prisons, mental institutions, schools, and voting rights. Those decisions are very tough and far-reaching. They seem more akin to the decisions of an administrative agency.

Yet, as the Honorable Frank M. Johnson, Jr., Judge of the U.S. Court of Appeals for the Fifth Circuit, pointed out in 1980:

> Although this increasing attention given by the courts to the functioning of government and its agencies has not gone unnoticed, it has been widely misunderstood. Judicial "activism" is not new. From the beginning of the

republic, judges have been actively involved in the determination of the pressing problems of their day. Despite the recurrent waves of criticism, typically from those who have been the losers in these determinations, the simple truth is that the role of the judge in our constitutional system permits no other course.[1]

The examples are legion and have continued ever since *Marbury* v. *Madison*. The battle over one man, one vote, finally resolved in *Baker* v. *Carr* (369 U.S. 186 [1962]), in what had to be the most convoluted and repetitive explanation of why *Colegrove* v. *Green* (328 U.S. 549 [1946]) and "subsequent *per curiam* cases" were no longer valid. The Court became just plain fed up with the intractable state legislatures that refused to alter their rotten boroughs. Or read the U.S. Supreme Court opinion in *National League of Cities* v. *Usery*, 426 U.S. 833 (1976), where Justice Rehnquist went on for three pages about how much it would cost the states if the 1938 Fair Labor Standards Act were extended to include public bodies. And *Brown* v. *Board of Education*, 347, U.S. 483 (1954), where, relying on social science data, the Court reversed *Plessy* v. *Ferguson*, 163 U.S. 537 (1896). And on and on. Policy is the soul of the Constitution. Every high school civics teacher knows this. When the federal courts sense that the time has come, they have never hesitated to propel themselves into troublesome social issues such as abortion, capital punishment, and school prayer.

We predict that when lawyers become more sensitive to the importance of state constitutions, we will see more of the *Mount Laurel II* litigation spilling over into other jurisdictions.

Yet one senses that the courts are not always a happy solution to the tensions aroused by land use problems. Professor Phillip Kurland may be right: the courts venture into treacherous waters when they upset long-held prejudices (see Chapter 9 on *Gautreaux*). This concept is reminiscent of Winston Churchill's observation about democracy: "It's not very good but it's the best damn thing so far."

The remedy is the rub. Should one man, such as Judge Austin in *Gautreaux* (or two if Alex Polikoff, the plaintiff's counsel, is counted) or a group of men, such as the seven in *Mount Laurel II*, try to fashion the remedy? There can be no dispute. There was liability in both cases, under the Fourteenth Amendment in one, under the New Jersey Constitution in the other. Would it be possible for the Court to find a violation and then warn that it would fashion a remedy itself unless a named panel of selected persons submits an acceptable proposal in two to four months? Former Judge Harold Levanthal, of the District of Columbia Court of

---

[1]Johnson, "The Role of Courts in Institutional Litigation," 32 *Alabama Law Review* 271 (1981).

Appeals, has suggested a similar course in complex environmental litigation, in "Environmental Decisionmaking and the Role of the Courts."[2] And, of course, much the same procedure is performed by professional planners as masters in trials of cases after *Mount Laurel II*.

The Honorable Frank M. Coffin, Chief Judge of the United States Court of Appeals for the First Circuit, has expressed his concern over the role of the judge in these public law cases:

> For example, an independent, self-reliant judge, drawing on the professional disciplines he has perfected over a lifetime, can approach a conventional trial, confident of his capacity to judge credibility, winnow wheat from chaff, find facts, reason logically, and arrive at conclusions of law. As a generalist, he brings a broad perspective to even technical issues. But it is quite a different enterprise to send a solitary trial judge to hear a choir of experts, review voluminous data, step into the shoes of a social planner and public executive, and devise a long-range multifaceted public impact program without any guidance or support from an organization.[3]

Political Pressure

Often, zoning is put down as being political. So, what else is new? Of course, it is highly political; perhaps that is why it is so exciting a game. Some planners seem not to understand this or, if they do, they are appalled as though it were a cockroach in the cola bottle. But that is a circumstance one must anticipate before the game begins. The lawyer for the developer or landowner must almost expect to lose in the trial court. The preparation for the trial really should be preparation for the appellate court. The record is crucial. Even the dullest testimony must go in, even at the risk, as happened in *Hernandez*, of causing the judge to fall asleep and tumble off the bench. That case was eventually won on appeal through the testimony of Tony Wiles and Richard Gern. (We had correctly expected that the Cajun country trial judge in the Cajun area would be put off by it.)

A trial judge, after all, is part of the home scene and may not be able to avoid the infection of "neighborism" that permeates the community. As one observer of the trial court's decision in *Hernandez* notes: "Bumpy [the Judge's nickname] wasn't going to let the Mayor get away with it." Certainly Judge Downey in the *Palm Beach* case, to begin with, was influenced by the general resentment of West Palm Beach residents to

---

[2]122 *University of Pennsylvania Law Review* 509 (1974).
[3]Coffin, "The Frontier of Remedies: A Call for Exploration," 67 *California Law Review* 983 (1979).

the smugness and ostentatious wealth of its municipal neighbor to the east, although he would, we are sure, deny it. Sioux City lost its fight, not in the courts but at the polling place. Simple revenge was a large part of the long battle between Mayor Kenneth Bowen and the Hernandezes, and the courts were not unaware of it. It is difficult to believe that at least some of the appellate courts in the *Grand Central* case were not moved by the noise generated by the Committee to Save Grand Central. The San Antonio imbroglio started because of a dramatic switch in the political loyalties of the City Council that could not possibly have escaped the attention of the trial court judge—the same judge who had heard the original NEPA litigation where the City supported development in the recharge area. *Gautreaux* dripped with politics, from the frustrated judge, disappointed in his close defeat in a gubernatorial election, to the prolonged diversionary tactics of Mayor Daley.

Is all this good or evil? Should we turn into cynics or be wide-eyed with disbelief? We believe these are the wrong questions. Rather, we should be asking whether the judiciary is qualified to deal effectively with these issues. In some cases, they clearly are qualified. In others, such as in *Gautreaux* and *Mount Laurel II*, you will share with us some doubts. Yet our uniquely American system has for better than 200 years had its share of "activist" judges. The opportunity to "make law" has been a prevalent characteristic although this propensity often has not been applauded until decades have passed.

We must still acknowledge that the process of land use control remains unfair. Not in the venal sense—we never were faced in any of these stories with so much as a hint that a little "lubrication" would further our cause. (We never encountered "the zoning man" as one witness in a federal zoning bribery case described him.[4]) Corruption is not the fundamental problem in land use, although it does exist. Rather benign manipulation continues to affect the system. The problem lies with the parochialism, the NIMBY complex (Not In My Back Yard), with which the process is festooned. It was most dramatically evidenced in Tuxedo, where the "teenagers" were triumphant over costly and meticulous planning—and in Palm Beach, where the planning consultants fashioned their reports to meet the wishes of the Town.

It is this intellectual corruption that has saturated land use regulation for fifty years and shows little sign of abating. It is apparent when we compare the local antics of the howling crowd in Tuxedo with the professionalism and detachment of Terry Moore in the Pinelands. The locals are too selfish or bloody close to the actions to bring any objectivity to

---

[4]See *City of Eastlake* v. *Forest City Enterprises,* 426 U.S. 668, Stevens J., dissent, footnote 7 at 685 (1976).

their judgment. Recall the old gentlemen in Palm Beach who testified against any further adjacent high-rises because the high-rise buildings they lived in were enough.

The Importance of Planning

Planning has been scorned, mocked, disparaged, and disdained since the earliest days of land use regulation. Worse yet, it has been ignored. Oh, there have been millions and millions spent on planning (most of it lavished on local government by various agencies of the federal government), but the officially adopted, actually used planning instrument is a rare beast indeed. It was, for starters, a stepchild of land use regulation, sitting by the hearth while its more robust sisters, zoning and subdivision controls, went cavorting across the American landscape. Siemon and his partner, Wendy Larsen, noted in 1979 (more than fifty years after the Standard State Zoning Enabling Act apparently mandated planning):

> The Standard State Zoning Enabling Act (SZEA), first published in 1924 and ultimately adopted in whole or in part by forty-four states, provided that zoning shall be made "in accordance with a comprehensive plan." Nevertheless, comprehensive plans were rarely adopted, and when they were, they were ignored in the preparation and implementation of land use regulations. After years of academic debate, the role of planning began to re-emerge in the late 1960's in the form of increased judicial awareness of planning and a variety of new mandatory planning statutes. However, adopted comprehensive plans continue to be few and far between, and comprehensive relationship to implementing land use controls are even less common.[5]

Even the illustrious American Law Institute (ALI) Model Land Development Code, drafted with glacial speed over a decade in the 1970s, did not require a plan; it simply offered more regulatory goodies to the municipality that did plan. (That result was occasioned by considerable infighting among the ALI Advisory Committee.)

Only recently have a few courts, notably in Maryland, Oregon, and New Jersey, insisted that a zoning ordinance be consistent with a comprehensive plan and a few states, particularly California, Florida and Kentucky, have mandated by statute that regulatory ordinances conform to a prescribed plan.

But what is "consistency?" Joseph DiMento, in his book, *The Consistency*

---

[5]"Comprehensive Planning Revisited," *Planning, Zoning, and Eminent Domain.* (Dallas: Institute of Planning, Zoning, and Eminent Domain, 1979), pp. 105, 106. Footnotes omitted.

Doctrine and the Limits of Planning, discusses the arguments against a requirement for consistency. He notes that planning is not done well and although it could be improved, it presently does not merit "greater influence":

> The planning process is "costly," "conservative," "noninnovative," and "highly subjective." In addition, the actors who plan — not only the professional planners but those who are involved in even the most advanced of participatory schemes — are incompetent to plan. Citizens are ignorant of means-ends relationships and are unwilling to make long-range decisions; when they do take action, results tend to be poor.
>
> Design with nature, planning within a technically optimum area, mid-range plans, and well-developed policy plans are among the innovations that someday may improve the local plan. But present approaches to planning, especially evident at the local level, should not become the basis for regulation under the state's police power. Reports of actual planning practice in local government describe it as pedestrian. Even planners themselves conclude that implementation of comprehensive plans is an activity that the planning profession has performed poorly.

Yet DiMento concludes by defending the following requirement:

> Plans that reflect responsible and knowledgeable participation, that are assembled by those who are committed to increasing the predictability and fairness of decisions, that are technically informed, and that balance the interests of all those groups who would be involved deserve to be translated into regulations — official development controls.[6]

It should be obvious that in the volatile arena of zoning where changes are constantly requested, where 500 people show up to scream, and bone-tired members of Plan Commissions try to make decisions at 2 A.M., that some guidelines should have been set out in advance so that the decision be based on more than impulse, prejudice, or just plain fatigue. The existence of a plan provides the Court with a yardstick by which to measure the reasonableness and fairness of the particular action taken by the local authority. We acknowledge that this is not the only reason to insist upon some evidence of planning as a prerequisite to regulatory ordinances. There are many, as any comparative study of good corporate and military strategies indicate. But in the land use field, the role of the judiciary is paramount, and as the courts become more willing to question the tactics of local governmental agencies, we may expect more frequent challenges to the evidence of parochialism and a denial of procedural due process.

---

[6] *The Consistency Doctrine and the Limits of Planning* (Cambridge, Mass.: Oelgeschlager, Gunn & Hain, 1980).

The plan in Sanibel was costly to prepare, and yet it gave Town officials a leg up when they had to litigate. The plan in the Pinelands was based on careful analysis not only by planners but also by limnologists, archaeologists, economists, sociologists, demographers, and others. The absence of much serious litigation over the regulations is attributed to the thorough planning behind them. On the other hand, in *Hernandez* there was no plan and the resulting confusion and bitterness is the result largely of that dismal omission. There was, until too late, little or no planning in Sioux City and the results were apparent. The Palm Beach "plan" was a sham designed simply to satisfy the client. We look with some skepticism at Justice Brennan's suggestion that the description of more than 300 landmarks was a "plan." Yet even careful planning, as prepared by the developer in Tuxedo, may go down the drain when it is faced with determined amateurs.

The State of Zoning

The country is becoming crowded with professionals, mostly academics, who claim that zoning is dead. Professor John Reps of Cornell University years ago wrote a piece entitled, "Requiem for Zoning." More recently, similar pieces have been written: Professor Jan Krasnowiecki, of the University of Pennsylvania Law School—"Abolish Zoning"; Orlando E. Delogu, of the University of Maine Law School—"Local Land Use Controls: An Idea Whose Time Has Passed"; M.S. Pulliam, "Brandies Brief for Decontrol of Land Use: A Plea for Constitutional Reform"; and Professor Edward H. Zeigler, Jr., of Dayton School of Law—"The Twilight of Single-Family Zoning."[7]

We are reminded of Mark Twain's retort about his premature demise. Don't believe a word of it; zoning is alive and well! True enough, some of the familiar labels have disappeared and new techniques emerge, but the principles have stable vital signs.

Such conclusions emerge from a reading of the reported decisions, not just from practicing in the market place and working in the pit. In truth, zoning is indeed alive and healthy. Even Houston, that aberration with no "zoning ordinance," has adopted a half-dozen ordinances, dealing with signs, setbacks, pornography, and other baggage that typi-

---

[7]Reps, "Requiem for Zoning," *Planning* (American Planning Association, 1964), p. 56; J. Z. Krasnowiecki, "Abolish Zoning," 31 *Syracuse Law Review* 719 (1980); Delogue, "Local Land Use Controls: An Idea Whose Time Has Passed," 36 *Maine Law Review* 261 (1984); Pulliam, "Brandeis Brief for Decontrol of Land Use," 13 *Southwestern Law Review* 435 (1983); Zeigler, "The Twilight of Single Family Zoning," 3 *UCLA Journal of Environmental Law and Policy* 161 (1983).

cally appear in a zoning ordinance. New York and San Francisco never seem to cease proposing new concepts such as "quantitative zoning" in the latter and special districts each bearing the name of the area or use in the former (e.g., Fifth Avenue District, Theater District, Little Italy District). It appears that they believe that zoning is still a cure-all for every municipal ill. In Chicago the City Council clings with tenacity to its absolute control over all amendments and both factions, black and white, would devour anyone who suggested that the Plan Commission, not the Zoning Committee of the City Council, should hold hearings on amendments. It is a vibrant issue because the elected and the electorate in those and other cities understand the system and by law their voices are heard. Cliff Weaver and Richard Babcock have observed that the people who don't believe in urban zoning also don't live in urban neighborhoods. The urban residents who once fled these areas are now rezoning them. Weaver and Babcock have noted:

> In cities, as everywhere else, the importance of zoning is most clearly recognized by those citizens who view it as an understandable, workable, and controllable device for protecting their homes and neighborhoods from whatever they define as a deteriorating influence . . . and who believe that zoning and land use issues are, in fact, among the most important of current urban issues.[8]

Nor is there any evidence that enthusiasm for the exercise has diminished or abated in the suburban communities. Each year new experiments are all tested under the name of zoning.

Zoning ordinances are bizarre animals. The same ordinance will be a stew of the old and the new; the ordinance that carries over from its 1922 predecessor a dubious definition of "family" and a hoary provision for "home occupation" will have a provision for transfer of development rights and a demand for impact fees. The crowds still boo at the hearings; the courts still spew out hundreds of opinions each year from the most mundane involving a denial of a variance to the more sophisticated as illustrated by *Mount Laurel II.*

The system is patently in need of reform. If the surgery is much the same as we have suggested for decades, it is because the illness is chronic and is not much different than it was thirty years ago: the incredible discretion left to the public decision makers; the administrative procedures which permit, if they do not deliberately encourage, delay; the intolerable recordkeeping; the ex parte dealings; the arrogance of ad hoc demands for public gifts—exactions—in return for permission to

---

[8]*City Zoning: The Once and Future Frontier* (Chicago: Planners Press, 1979), p. 22.

develop. All these and more remain or are incorporated into current land use regulations.

There is some slight evidence that the courts are becoming wiser and less tolerant of these practices. Perhap we are, as Norman Williams, Jr. has suggested, in the fifth period of zoning where the courts are beginning to look with greater suspicion and with a jaundiced eye on land use procedures. A trial court in a Georgia case was appalled by the record in a zoning case, *Pendley* v. *Lake Harbin Ass'n.*, 198 S.E.2d 503, 505 (1973):

> The evidence in this complaint for injunctive relief shows 36 zoning petitions were scheduled to be heard before the Commissioners of Clayton County on October 11, 1972, at 7:30 o'clock p.m.; that the hearings continued until 3:30 o'clock a.m., October 12, 1979; that from 1,200 to 1,500 people were present to attend the public meeting; that the hearings were held in the commissioners' hearing room, which accommodates approximately fifty people; that there were three other larger rooms in the courthouse where the hearings could have been legally held; that people were packed so closely in the entire corridor outside the hearing room that those interested in various petitions could not get close to the door, much less inside the hearing room. Zoning is a matter of highest governmental business.

Or, the Michigan Supreme Court which exclaimed: "What in truth, was the warrant for the Board's action? We are not told. The Board says we do not have to be told."[9]

Perhaps there is hope!

---

[9] *Tireman-Joy-Chicago Improvement Ass'n.* v. *Chernick,* 105 N.W.2d 57, 58 (1960).

Comments

Chapter 2
Tuxedo, New York

1. We say the neighbors are "generally victorious." A warning note: this is intended to refer to the local administrative sparring, and it is in that context that the statement is intended. Norman Williams is quite correct in pointing out that in court in what he calls "neighbor suits," the complainants are less successful (Williams, *American Land Planning Law,* §2.01). Presumably this is because of the continued position of most state courts that the decision of the local town council is "legislative" and hence is valid if it is fairly debatable. See *City of Miami Beach* v. *Lachman,* 71 So.2d 148 (Fla. 1953). Under the so-called *Fasano* doctrine (*Fasano* v. *Washington County,* 507 P.2d 23 [Ore. 1973]), the decisions at the local level, even when made by the legislative body, are "quasi-judicial," not legislative, and the courts will scrutinize them with a different standard of review. The courts will inquire whether the local decision is arbitrary because the evidence heard by the local decision makers does not support the decision. Thus, in that context much depends on the skill and thoroughness of the parties to the dispute, including the local government, at the public hearing stage. Would neighbors be better or worse off under such a rule?

2. Moratoriums such as the one established by Tuxedo are not uncommon and have generally been upheld if they have a reasonable time limit. See *Deal Gardens, Inc.* v. *Loch Arbour,* 226 A.2d 607 (N.J. 1967). There the court stated:

> Although the municipality may adopt a "stopgap" zoning ordinance, which if not temporary might be considered unconstitutional, such power is strictly limited and must be exercised with great caution. One of the more dangerous aspects of this type of legislation, arises from the damage which may result if there is no restriction of the period of time during which a restraint against some land uses is permitted to continue. Plainly there must be some terminal point. It is impossible to establish an inflexible rule applicable to every case. The situation must be assayed in its own

particular factual setting to ascertain whether the elapsed time during which the ordinance has been in effect is reasonable.

See also *City of New Berlin* v. *Stein,* 206 N.W.2d 207 (Wis. 1973), and *Matter of Rubin* v. *McAlevey,* 282 N.Y.S.2d (1967); but see Chapter 5 on San Antonio. However, if a moratorium forbids issuance of building permits for, say, eighteen months, is that a temporary "taking" under Justice Brennan's dissent in *San Diego Gas & Electric Co.* v. *City of San Diego,* 450 U.S. 621 (1981)?

3. Why did Sterling Forest Corporation build those single-family houses in the late 1960s? Should its officers not have been aware of the hostility of single-family residents to different building styles and clustering? See Babcock and Bosselman, "Suburban Zoning and the Apartment Boom," 111 *U. Pa. L. Rev.* 1040 (1963).

4. Sterling One was a planned unit development. Even had the joint venturers been successful in obtaining the preliminary permit, they would have had to return to the Town for final approval. Of what value is a preliminary approval in a long-range project (ten years was the estimate for Sterling One)? How can a developer protect himself from a new and hostile Town Board that still holds some discretionary power over subsequent reviews? When, if at all, does the developer acquire a vested right? A few states provide a period of time during which the developer is protected from changes in the local law; see N.J.S.A. 40:55D-52. The widespread discretion vested in the city or town under most PUD ordinances is their most serious flaw.

> The final objection to the PUD approach is simply that the basic principle is wrong. Along with the obvious possibilities for favoritism and/or corruption, the establishment of such a system is a step away from government by rule of law, and back to the system of government by deal. From this viewpoint, planned unit development regulations are not a new idea; they are an invitation to regress, under rather stylish auspices, to the worst abuses of the past. (Williams, *American Land Planning Law,* §48.05).

5. Should the lawyers for Sterling One have alleged a conspiracy in violation of the Sherman Act? Who would be the alleged conspirators? Or should Sterling One have brought an action for damages under Section 1983 of the Act of 1871? (See Chapter 10.) Would either of these approaches have been successful in 1971? On reflection, in our opinion, Sterling One should have pursued its zoning lawsuit with vigor. Only in that way could the joint venturers have been able to demonstrate the dubious quality of the new zoning ordinance, and by depositions under oath have challenged the purposes of the opponents and shown the need for additional housing in Tuxedo. The exhaustive preparation for a lawsuit with excellent witnesses may be the only way to deal with a determined group of amateurs who generally can defeat the developer in the local administrative process. Not all our colleagues agree with this belief. Marlin Smith points out that there is no "builder's remedy" in New York; the only

relief is a declaration of invalidity. See, for the frustration of a developer who repeatedly won in court, *Davlee Construction Corp.* v. *Brooks,* 188 N.Y.S.2d 847 (N.Y. Sup. Ct., 1959); *Davlee Contrustion Corp.* v. *Town of Huntington,* 223 N.Y.S.2d 376 (Sup. Ct. Nassau County, 1961). But the New York Court of Appeals had already spoken on the matter of attempts to exclude, in *Berenson* v. *Town of New Castle,* 341 N.E.2d 236 (1975).

6. The overwhelming desire to try negotiation as a less costly alternative to litigation is somewhat reminiscent of the dispute in Ramapo, New York — only a few miles from Tuxedo — where the opponents of the Town's "phased growth" plan decided not to have a full-scale trial but to go to summary judgment. See *Golden* v. *Planning Board of Ramapo,* 285 N.E.2d 291 (1972), appl. dis. 409 U.S. 1003 (1972). Summary judgment was far less costly, but the opportunity to examine all the facts was lost. As might be expected, Ramapo's elaborate plan did not work out in succeeding years. Manuel Emanuel, Tuxedo's planning advisor, was also the planner for Ramapo. In 1974, five years after the phased growth plan was adopted and only two years after the decision by the New York Court of Appeals, Emanuel wrote, in *Management and Control of Growth,* Vol. 3 (Washington, D.C.: Urban Land Institute, 1975):

> On a project basis, there have been, and will continue to be, fluctuations [in the capital budget program] as a result of several factors, most notably:
> 1) unanticipated emergencies (Hurricane Doria in 1971);
> 2) changing circumstances dictating revised local priorities;
> 3) inflation and unpredictable construction costs;
> 4) delays in related state or county projects; and
> 5) delays or moratoria on state and federal aid affecting critical projects.
>
> A classic example of the later situation occurs with respect to sewer service in Ramapo. Although sewer construction is not included in the capital budgeting process, the provision of sewers is a major factor in the managed growth program in determining the eligibility of any tract of land for development or subdivision activity. At the time the managed growth program became operational, local sewer planning and construction was quite advanced. As a result, the proposed benefited area and the date by which service would become available was defined. (p. 313)

7. On December 6, 1981, the *Middletown Sunday Record* published an article by Ruth Boice that was headlined "Is Tuxedo Too Small for M&M?" (Maute and Martineau). In the long article, Ms. Boice summarized the conflict:

> Both leave the Town Board carrying the baggage of personal and political battles that ranged from absurd and childish to vituperative and personally damaging. Their feud left each a victim, and a creator, of a climate of conflict in Tuxedo that finally hurt them both.
>
> The feud has taken several forms, including:
> — Disagreement about the appointment of a Town Attorney, which precluded the town from having counsel for months;
> — Refusal to recognize each other at an organizational meeting that resulted in

both of them speaking in unison on different topics;
— Bitterness so deep that Martineau refused to run on the same ticket with Maute, although they are both Republicans;
— A town Ethics Board investigation of Martineau instigated by Maute;
— Adoption of a rule aimed at the councilman's "longwinded" speeches that limited comments from board members on an issue to five minutes; and
— Charges by Martineau that Maute submitted false vouchers for repayment from town funds.

* * *

It all started when officials were debating putting all of the town's development marbles into one basket in the form of one proposal or adopting a cautious wait-and-see philosophy through small developments.

With the two men pushing strongly for opposite view points, the town became divided, much as it still is today. "Tuxedo wasn't big enough for both of them," says a town official. Another observer suggests the two men select arms and end their intense and tiresome battle with a duel.

While the story is one of a town's conflict, the feud also is an example of a friendship gone awry. The men began their life in Tuxedo politics by campaigning on the same platform. Some town residents called them the "[Bobbsey] twins" and the "M and M pair." They were personal as well as political friends.

Now they rarely speak to each other. When they do, there are no clues about their amicable past. Martineau publicly calls Maute a "Vicious little man" and is less restrained in private. Maute says he ignores Martineau. "To do anything about him would be to use a 16 mm rifle to blow a fly off a wall," he says.

The deterioration of the friendship can be traced to the issue that divided Tuxedo — Sterling I. Maute led the opponents of the proposed 3,900-unit development project that would have been one of the biggest on the Eastern seaboard if it had reached fruition. Martineau lead the proponents.

Those favoring the project said the town needed growth badly and Sterling, as a single developer, would be easier for a town board to control.

8. To what extent may the environmental—review process be used as a subterfuge to hassle the developer and practice exclusion? See Bernard Frieden, *The Environmental Protection Hustle* (Cambridge, Mass.: MIT Press, 1979), and Smith, "Does Petaluma Lie at the End of the Road from Ramapo?," 19 *Villanova L. Rev.* 739 (1974). How do you protect the landowner or developer from politicization of the EIS process? The story of the proposed power facility at Storm King on the Hudson River is a classic: see "Environmentalism and the Leisure Class," *Harpers Magazine,* February 1978, pp. 7-8.

Chapter 3
Palm Beach, Florida

1. The principal reported decision in this case is *Town of Palm Beach* v. *First Bank & Trust Co. of Boca Raton, as Trustee,* 279 So.2d 353 (1973); *Town of Palm Beach* v. *Gradison,* 296 So.2d 473 (1974).

2. The most difficult problem the plaintiff had to overcome was the "fairly debatable" doctrine, pervasive throughout most jurisdictions in the United States. This rule has two principles: (1) that the decision of the city council in a zoning case is a legislative act, and (2) that such a decision carries a presumption of validity, or, if it is fairly debatable, the courts will not upset it.

3. Comprehensive "down zonings" have become very common throughout the United States in the past ten to fifteen years. In part this was undoubtedly due to the early enthusiasm that zoning generated, leading many communities to overzone for commercial and apartment uses. Later as communities became interested in slowing or controlling growth they moved to change this condition. Some were successful when challenged; others were not. *Golden* v. *Planning Board of Ramapo,* 30 N.Y.2d 359, 334 N.Y.2d 138, 285 N.E.2d 391 (1972); *Beck* v. *Town of Raymond,* 118 N.H. 793 A.2d 847 (1978); *City of Boca Raton* v. *Boca Villas, Inc.* 371 So.2d 154 (1979).

4. The planning for the Town became a source of real embarrassment . . . and it should have. The plan was replete with statements such as the following:

> The system is critically overloaded, both in the older section as well as the expanding area south of Sloan's Curve.

* * *

> The capability to serve continued high-density development [south of Sloan's Curve] is highly questionable.

On water:

> The [West Palm Beach] Department's established distribution system and water source has a limited capability and cannot serve unrestricted development in the Town.

And on pollution:

> Continued development of the Town, which has accelerated within recent years, had increased the level of pollutants in the water table as well as adversely affecting both Lake Worth and the ocean to more limited degrees.

Of course, the plaintiff had to demonstrate that each of these allegations was not true. Where would you turn to obtain evidence to dispute these assertions?

5. In spite of the plaintiff's arguments, Palm Beach is indeed unique, world-renowned for its glamour and glitz. Is there anything "wrong," as a policy matter, with such a community trying to protect its image in a state whose population is exploding?

6. The Town's plan states, "The major growth will occur south of Sloan's Curve where the winter population will increase from about 9,000 to between 40,000 and 65,000 persons." The plaintiff's planner had to demonstrate that this unsubstantiated projection was grossly in error (by about 100 percent). How would you determine the maximum population under the 1970 ordinance? There are two steps.

7. The plaintiff had three witnesses to show the damage to the landowner: the former local tax appraiser, a nationally known appraiser from Miami, and a land economist from Washington, D.C. For parcels, I, II, and III their appraisals on the impact of the 1970 ordinance were as follows:

Edgar Maxwell

	Before 1970 Ordinance	After March 1970 Ordinance	Loss in Fair Market Value
Parcel I	$5,900,000	$1,375,000	$3,525.00
Parcel II	4,350,000	2,400,000	1,950,000
Parcel III	800,000	500,000	300,000
		Aggregate Loss in Fair Market Value:	$5,775,000

Marion McCune

	Before March 1970 Ordinance	After March 1970 Ordinance	Loss in Fair Market Value
Parcel I	$5,425,000	$1,130,000	$4,275,000
Parcel II	3,775,000	2,250,000	1,525,000
Parcel III	815,000	510,000	305,000
		Aggregate Loss in Fair Market Value:	$6,105,000

Philip Hammer

	Economic Value before 1970 Ordinance	Economic Value after 1970 Ordinance	Loss in Economic Worth
Parcel I	$5,822,000	$1,302,000	$4,520,000
Parcel II	4,020,000	2,231,000	1,789,000
Parcel III	815,000	512,000	303,000
		Aggregate Loss in Economic Worth:	$6,612,000

Many ingredients go into an appraisal. What are the tests and what factors must be discounted?

8. The Town claimed that more high-rises south of Sloan's Curve would cause irreparable damage to the mansions north of the Curve. There were many high-rises already south of Sloan's Curve, all of which were made nonconforming by the 1970 ordinance. What evidence would you look for to dispute this claim by the Town?

Chapter 4
Grand Central Station

1. The New York state court decisions are *Penn Central Transportation Company* v. *City of New York,* 50 A.D.2d 265, 377 N.Y.S.2d 20 (1975), and *Penn Central Transportation Company* v. *City of New York,* 42, N.Y.2d 324, 366 N.E.2d 1271 (1977). The earlier cases involving the landmark ordinance of New York City had not been so sympathetic. See *Lutheran Church* v. *City of New York,* 316 N.E.2d 305 (1974). See also *Fred F. French Investing Co.* v. *City of New York,* 350 N.E.2d 381 (1976). For a detailed discussion of these cases and the Grand Central case, see Williams, *American Land Planning Law,* §71A.11, 1984, Supp. Vol. 3.

2. In *Fred F. French Investing Co.* v. *City of New York,* 350 N.E.2d 381 (1976), the plaintiffs pressed for damages. Justice Breitel, who also wrote the court of appeals opinion in *Penn Central,* refused to grant damages. Referring to Justice Holmes's statement in *Pennsylvania Coal Co.* v. *Mahon,* 260 U.S. 393 (1922), that "the general rule at least is that while property may be regulated to a certain extent, if regulation goes too far it will be recognized as a taking" (p. 415), Breitel responded: "The metaphor should not be confused with the reality" (p. 385). Do you believe Breitel was right? See comments on Chapter 10.

3. Many years ago, Professor Ernst Freund stated in *The Police Power,* "It may be said that the state takes property by eminent domain because it is useful to the public, and under the police power because it is harmful. . . . From

this results the difference between the power of eminent domain and the police power, that the former recognizes a right to compensation, while the latter on principle does not" (sec. 511, pp. 446–547). Other, more recent writers have joined in this distinction, for example, Dunham, "A Legal and Economic Basis for City Planning," 58 *Colo. L. Rev.* 650 (1958). Do the facts in *Penn Central* and Justice Brennan's opinion support this view? What "harm" would the construction of an office tower at 42nd Street and Park Avenue cause to the public, or, as the scholars ask, what "harmful externalities" would have occurred if the tower had been built? Or were the courts affirming a "public benefit"?

4. The attorneys for the railroad in all the appeals of the case appeared to concede that the Terminal complex could earn a reasonable return. Did this give away the entire case? The New York Landmarks Law states that if a property designated a landmark does not earn 6 percent it may be deemed to have a hardship. Professor John Costonis, in an article in *Land Use and Planning Digest* (No. 9, Vol. 30, 1978), said:

> It is a non-case because, by conceding that the Grand Central terminal complex could earn a reasonable return even in its landmark status, Penn Central conceded the central issue that had been litigated in the three New York court decisions below. Given this concession and the U.S. Supreme Court's wholly predictable conclusion that landmark preservation advances a valid police power goal, a result favorable to New York City was absolutely preordained. (p.6)

5. In his opinion, Justice Breitel of the New York Court of Appeals observed: "A fair return is to be accorded the owner, but society is to receive its due for its share in the making of a once great railroad. The historical, cultural, and architectural resource that remains was neither created solely by the private owner nor solely by the society in which it was permitted to evolve." The briefs in the New York Court of Appeals did not raise this issue. See Henry George, *Progress and Poverty* (1879). Is this equally true of any major development? How would you distinguish the *Penn Central* case from a major shopping center that, after its construction, benefits from development of a subdivision of 1,000 units in the vicinity? Or of a 200-acre public recreation park? How would you separate the publicly and privately contributed ingredients of property value? What about the construction of a high-speed intraurban rail line and the expenditure of public funds for stations that dramatically increase the value of private lands adjacent to the stations? Should there be a recapture of those increments of value? See Callies and Siemon, "Value Capture Hypotheses: A Second Analysis," 8 *Transp. L. J.* 9 (1976).

6. What did the Committee to Save Grand Central hope to accomplish? The case was moving through the courts. If the Committee expected to influence the courts, was such an effort proper? Or did the Committee simply hope to move the Court's clerks? There were numerous telephone calls from clerks to the New York Corporation Counsel's Office inquiring about how the Transfer of Devel-

opment Rights worked. (Interview with Kent Barwick, September 15, 1983.)

7. Suppose the developer had come in with a proposal to build a tower similar to the tower in the *original* design but not constructed in 1913, and the New York Landmarks Commission refused him permission. Would it have had a justiciable claim?

8. Are we correct to suggest a conflict between Justice Brennan's opinions in *Penn Central* and *San Diego Gas?* After all, in the former Justice Brennan found there was no taking and in the latter he was discussing the appropriate remedy.

9. If it is correct, as Justice Brennan states in *Grand Central,* that the Court has not been able to provide a clear line for when a regulation "goes too far" and constitutes a taking, how can a city planner or a city attorney provide an adequate opinion on whether a City Council's decision will result in a financial liability? Try writing the form of advice a city attorney should give his city council when he is asked whether they should resist in court a damage suit by a developer. The typical card carried by a policeman since the *Miranda* decision reads in part as follows:

Miranda Warning

1. You have the right to remain silent.
2. Anything you say can and will be used against you in a court of law.
3. You have the right to talk to a lawyer and have him present with you while you are being questioned.
4. If you cannot afford to hire a lawyer, one will be appointed to represent you before any questioning, if you wish.
5. You can decide at any time to exercise these rights and not answer any questions or make any statements.

10. All the appellate courts noted that the property was still being used for its original purpose. If Grand Central had been abandoned as a railroad terminal fifteen years ago—say, in 1970—and converted to some other use (e.g., a shopping mall) which in turn was failing, would the decision have been the same?

11. What steps might be taken to improve the terminal as a healthy shopping mall in one of the busiest areas in Manhattan? Many buildings older than Grand Central have been refurbished into vibrant shopping areas, such as Faneuil Hall and Quincy Market in Boston, Ghirardelli Square and the Cannery in San Francisco, and Brightleaf Square in Durham, North Carolina. Are there differences?

12. Was the presence of over 400 landmarks in New York City evidence, as Justice Brennan suggests, of a plan? Or was Justice Rehnquist correct when he observed:

> Although the Court refers to the New York ordinance as a *comprehensive* program to preserve *historic* landmarks, the ordinance is not limited to historic buildings and

gives little guidance to the Landmarks Preservation Commission in its selection of landmark sites. Section 207-1.0(n) of the Landmarks Preservation Law, as set forth in N.Y.C. Admin. Code, ch. 8-A (1976), requires only that the selective landmark be at least 30 years old and possess 'a special character or special historical or aesthetic interest or value as part of the development, heritage or cultural characteristics of the city, state or nation.'

13. Landmarks are not designated by the New York City Planning Commission. That is the function of the Landmarks Commission. Is the divergence of planning and landmark designation a flaw? Should the plan commission and landmarks commission be separated as they are in New York City?

14. A landmark, by definition, is a single building or cluster of buildings in an area of nonlandmark buildings that are subject only to the usual zoning regulations. By contrast, in a historic district an entire area (such as the Vieux Carre in New Orleans or Beacon Hill in Boston) is subject to special rules and benefits. This latter condition is what Justice Holmes in *Pennsylvania Coal* v. *Mahon*, 260 U.S. 393, 415 (1922), referred to as "an average reciprocity of advantage." What did Holmes mean? Would this theory lead one to require that all landmarks be publicly purchased but allow that buildings in a historic district be restrained by regulation?

Chapter 5
San Antonio

1. The authors were retained by the City of San Antonio after the initial moratorium ordinance was challenged in Court. Subsequently the authors, together with their partners Wendy U. Larsen and David L. Callies, prepared a replacement ordinance and assisted the City in its implementation.

2. There are no reported decisions in this dispute, but the new town development to be subsidized by the Department of Housing and Urban Development weathered protracted litigation over the environmental impact statement requirements of the National Environmental Policy Act. *Sierra Club* v. *Lynn*, 502 F.2d 43(5th Cir. 1974), cert. denied 421 U.S. 994 (1975).

3. Reasonable moratoria are not uncommon even in Texas and often have been upheld. See e.g., *Miller et al.* v. *Board of Public Works of the City of Los Angeles*, 234 P.381 (Calif. 1925), *Deal Gardens, Inc.* v. *Board of Trustees of Lock Arbour*, 226 A.2d 607 (N.J. 1967), *Collura* v. *Town of Arlington*, 329 N.E.2d 733 (Mass. Sup. J. Ct. 1975) and *City of Dallas* v. *Crownwich*, 506 S.W.2d 654 (Tex. Ct. App. 1974).

4. There were two basic problems with the ordinance as originally drafted. The most glaring error was the absence of procedural due process because the ordinance made no provision for relief from its terms, even if all that was required to complete a structure was to turn on the electricity. The plaintiffs, of course, used this example in court to characterize the unreasonableness of the ordinance.

The replacement ordinance responded to this situation with an express provision for relief if a landowner or developer had a claim of vested rights:

> Notwithstanding any other provision of this ordinance, developers who claim vested rights to develop may, in the manner set forth in section 302 hereof, submit an application for development approval during the effective period of this ordinance. In determining whether the applicant has vested rights, the City Council shall consider whether the applicant has demonstrated:
> a. an act of an agency of the City of San Antonio,
> b. upon which the developer has in good faith relied to his detriment,
> c. such that it would be inequitable to require the applicant to delay development during the time this ordinance is in effect.

The fact that property has been and is in a particular classification in the zoning ordinance shall not, in itself, establish a claim to vested rights.

See generally Siemon, Larsen, and Porter, *Vested Rights: Balancing Public and Private Development Expectations* (Washington, D.C.: U.L.I., 1982).

5. In some jurisdictions referenda on zoning issues are not available or have been declared invalid by the state courts. In fact, the referendum involving the super mall was eventually invalidated as adding a procedural step not contemplated in the zoning enabling act. See *San Pedro North, Ltd.* v. *City of San Antonio,* 526 S.W.2d 260 (Tex. Civ. App. 1978). Other states that have disapproved of zoning referenda include Idaho, Missouri, New York, Pennsylvania, and Utah. These states generally reason that a zoning decision is not a legislative act and cannot, therefore, be subject to referenda. Other states, including California, have no problem with this procedure. See *Arnel Dev. Co.* v. *City of Costa Mesa,* 620 P.2d 565 (Calif. 1980), and also *City of East Lake* v. *Forest City Enterprises, Inc.* 426 U.S. 668 (1976). Do you see any problems with permitting the people to vote to approve or reject a zoning amendment? Is it, as Justice Burger suggested in *Forest City,* the equivalent of a New England town meeting? Is there any problem with procedural due process?

6. Compare the San Antonio experience with the Pinelands program. If the aquifer is a regional resource, why not a regional management approach? What aspects of the San Antonio experience would have been changed if there was a regional approach. Beware, however, of the seductiveness of the regionalism given the experience of Tahoe and the California Coastal Commission, which Governor Deukmajian is threatening to abolish.

7. Consider that the aquifer suit preceded *Monell* v. *Dept. of Social Services of the City of New York.* 436 U.S. 658 (1978). What effect would *Monell* have had on the proceedings? Is it possible to attribute the relatively amicable outcome of the Encino Park Venture matter, as compared to the *Hernandez* litigation, to the fact that money damages as a remedy were far more remote prior to *Monell* and *Owen* v. *City of Independence,* 445 U.S. 622 (1981), and therefore less of a motivation for litigation?

Chapter 6
Sanibel Island

1. Fred P. Bosselman and Charles Siemon were subcontractors to the City of Sanibel's planning consultants responsible for legal elements of the planning program. As the plan began to unfold, Siemon and Bosselman were called on to defend the City in land use litigation, and they served as special counsel through the resolution of the Wulfert Point matter.

2. There is only one reported opinion resulting from the Sanibel Land Use Plan: *Goode* v. *City of Sanibel*, 372 So.2d 181 (Fla. 2 DCA 1979).

3. As a planning exercise based on carrying capacity, the City of Sanibel was an ideal setting—an island with clearly defined capacities and strong consensus on community character. J. N. "Ding" Darling's cartoon, "The Outline of History," which charts the colonization of an offshore island from "Utopia" to ruin, was constant reminder of the threat of uncontrolled growth and development to the Island.

4. How important to the success of the Sanibel story was the fact that it was a new city? What difference, if any, should it make that a comprehensive plan is a particular area's first plan?

5. One sure lesson from the Sanibel experience is that the City used legal experts in an proactive rather than reactive mode. Too many communities wait until they are in trouble to seek legal counsel.

6. One problem the Sanibel Land Use Plan did not solve was the housing needs of the island's employment force. If a landowner were to challenge the plan as being exclusionary, what standard of review would apply? What could Sanibel do to alleviate the inflationary effects of a limitation on the number of dwelling units?

7. The Wulfert Point litigation illustrates the difficulty a landowner faces when he challenges a land use control on substantive grounds under the "fairly debatable rule." Was the landowner's decision to pursue procedural defects a good one? What would have been the landowner's remedy if he had prevailed on the procedural challenges? See footnote 22 of Justice Brennan's dissent in *San Diego Gas & Electric* v. *City of San Diego*.

8. How does a city protect itself from the *Goode* situation? If the planning effort is carried out in the open as it should be, then a legislative body's decision to ignore its staff or consultant's advice will inevitably be used against the City in subsequent litigation.

Chapter 7
Sioux City, Iowa

1. There is a short but winding trail from the *Lafayette* case to the federal

statute exempting municipalities from damages in antitrust cases. Only one of them involved Sioux City. This case was not directly involved in our dispute, but Scott did own land zoned ML close to the parcel originally owned by General Growth before it traded for Lincolnshire. Scott alleged that the new comprehensive zoning ordinance that prohibited commercial uses in industrial districts violated the federal antitrust laws. The district court first refused to dismiss the case but subsequently, after the opinion of the Eighth Circuit Court of Appeals in *Gold Cross Ambulance* v. *City of Kansas City,* 705 F.2d 1005 (1983), the court granted summary judgment for Sioux City and on appeal the Eighth Circuit affirmed. *Scott* v. *Sioux City,* 736 F.2d 1207 (1984).

Gold Cross was a monopoly licensing case. Alleged violations of the Sherman Act embrace many different types of municipal activities. Concessionaires at stadiums, contracts with ambulance companies, and cable television licensing — all have been challenged. These are considerably different from the issues in land use cases. Does or should this affect judicial (or legislative) attitudes? How do you fashion a rule that fits all cases?

2. One of the cases involved Mason City, Iowa. The plaintiffs, Mason City Center Associates, alleged that Mason City had entered into a conspiracy with downtown developers. The complaint stated that the CBD developers had received an express agreement from the City that it would not allow any regional shopping center that would be competitive with the CBD redevelopment. Of course the defendants alleged that they were immune under *Parker* v. *Brown,* 317 U.S. 341 (1943), and filed a motion to dismiss. The trial court denied the motion, *Mason City Center Associates* v. *City of Mason City,* 468 F. Supp. 737 (N.D. Iowa, 1979). The City argued that the zoning statutes of Iowa granted them immunity under the theories expressed in the plurality opinion in *Lafayette,* namely a "clearly articulated, affirmatively expressed policy to authorize anticompetitive practices." The trial court held that the Iowa zoning statutes, Iowa Code ch. 414 (1978), did not even mandate that municipalities adopt zoning ordinances, much less expressly authorize anticompetitive zoning practices, and the case went back for trial. Ironically, at the trial the jury awarded the City $250,000 on a counterclaim that Center Associates had tortiously interfered with a business relationship. On appeal, the Eighth Circuit affirmed that the City was not guilty of an antitrust violation but struck the $250,000 award as too speculative (*Mason City Center Associates* v. *City of Mason City,* 671 F.2d 1146 [8th Cir. 1982]). In the same year the U.S. Supreme Court, in *Community Communications Co.* v. *City of Boulder,* 455 U.S. 40 (1982), held in a cable television dispute that the legislative grant of broad home-rule powers to Colorado cities did not make them immune from the Sherman Act.

In the meantime, there was increasing confusion among the federal courts over whether there must be not only a clearly expressed state policy but also active state participation, as was the case in *Parker* v. *Brown.* Compare *California Liquor Dealers Ass'n.* v. *Midcal Aluminum, Inc.,* 400 U.S. 937 (1980); *Westborough*

Mall v. *City of Cape Girardeau,* 693 F.2d 733 (8th Cir. 1982); *Miracle Mile* v. *City of Rochester,* 617 F.2d 18 (2d Cir. 1980); *Jonnet Development* v. *City of Pittsburgh,* 558 F. Supp. 962 (W.D. Pa. 1983); *Parks* v. *Watson,* 716 F.2d 646 (9th Cir. 1983). Finally, in *Town of Hallie* v. *City of Eau Claire,* 53 U.S.L.W. 4418 (1985), the U.S. Supreme Court held that when the defendant was a city, there need be no active state participation. For additional discussion of recent developments, see Deutsch, "Antitrust Challenges to Local Land Use Controls," 6 *Zoning and Planning Law Report* (December 1983); Areeda, "Antitrust Immunity for State Action" after Lafayette," 95 *Harv. L. Rev.* 435 (1981); M. S. Levin, "The Antitrust Challenge to Local Government Protection of the Central Business District," 55 *Univ. Colo. L. Rev.* 21 (1983).

3. The federal statute (Local Government Antitrust Act of 1984, PL 98-544) immunizes cities from damages but presumably permits injunctions. Is it true, therefore, that there is no financial risk to a city in an antitrust suit? To date, no local government or its local officials have paid any damages resulting from an antitrust judgment. Would attorneys' fees be awarded in a Sherman Act suit for an injunction?

The first paragraph of a story in the *Washington Post* on September 18, 1984, read as follows:

> In Richmond [Va.], city officials recently shelled out $3 million in attorneys' fees and settlement costs to avoid a trial in a hotel zoning case that could have cost the city its entire $280 million annual budget.

4. In *Unity Ventures* v. *County of Lake,* No. 81 C 2475 (N.D. Ill. 1984), an agreement between Lake County and the Village of Grayslake, Illinois, permitted the Village veto power over sewer connections in the unincorporated area adjacent to the Village Boundaries. The landowners sued under the Sherman Act and section 1983 and were awarded $9.5 million in damages trebled to $28.5 million. Subsequently, federal legislation was passed and signed by President Reagan on October 25, 1984, prohibiting damages. The compromise between the House and Senate provided that the legislation should not be retroactive and damages would be *prima facie* valid when there had been a jury verdict. Of the more than 300 suits filed involving allegations of antitrust violations, *Unity Ventures* is the only one to which the exception against money damages would apply. William Freivogel, one of the attorneys for the County of Lake, wrote in an article in *The Florida Bar Journal,* February 1985:

> In the *Unity Ventures* case, there was no showing that the individual defendants were anything but competent, honest public servants. However, there was disputed testimony that during one meeting one of them, who happened to be a lawyer, "pounded the table" and shouted at the plaintiff that he was a lawyer, knew the law, and knew that he could deny plaintiff sewer service. Much was made of this throughout the trial. The verdict was $9.5 million (trebled to $28.5 million). The court directed the lawyers not to talk to the jurors, so it is impossible to assess just how harmful

this testimony and the argument were. (p. 54, note 8)

5. How would this legislation affect the many state antitrust laws? See, e.g., Fla. Stat. §542.15. Could such actions be brought only in state courts? A few states have tried to grant a similar exception. Ill. Rev. Stat. c85 §2901 (1985 supp.).

6. Even before the antitrust issue was raised, the attitudes of courts in zoning cases were opposed to using zoning to interfere with business competition. Edward Bassett, the drafter of New York City's first zoning ordinance, laid down the accepted dogma: "Neither can distribution of business be forced by zoning. . . . [I]t is not a proper field for zoning" (See E. Bassett, *Zoning*, p. 53 [1936]). For a collection of the pre-antitrust cases, see Weaver and Duerksen, "Central Business District Planning and the Control of Outlying Shopping Centers," 14 *Urban Law Annual* 57 (1977). Is this general disapproval of using zoning to restrain business competition any different—economically and socially—from keeping apartments out of single-family districts? For a debate on this issue among a trial judge, a planner, and the author, see Richard F. Babcock, *The Zoning Game* (Madison: University of Wisconsin Press, 1966), pp. 76–79.

7. Are the CBDs of towns ranging in population from 50,000 to 250,000 inevitably going to succumb to the outlying shopping centers? Will they become the repositories of banks, lawyers, and accountants? Why do these professionals remain? Presumably, most of them live out near the shopping centers.

8. Weaver and Duerksen, in their article "Central Business District Planning" (see comment 6), quote Maurice Alpert, a former shopping center developer turned CBD redeveloper, as follows:

> I know how major regional shopping centers are developed and I know something about the planning and zoning processes that screen such centers. Among the things I know is that rather than fitting into a logical community master plan, these centers often dictate the community plans. . . . Planted haphazardly as they are in America's suburbs, these centers affect every aspect of American life. (p. 62)

9. Why do there seem to be more shoestores in shopping malls than any other single type of business? Weary feet?

10. Was the creation of the legal nonconforming use a form of monopoly? If so, why was it not condemned? What would be the alternative? Or is there no such thing as a "neighborhood" monopoly?

11. Note that generally the Plan Commission of Sioux City remained more loyal to the CBD than did the City Council (e.g., finally issuing a strong support of the CBD; refusing to approve the Lincolnshire rezoning). Why would this be so? What more might the Plan Commission have done to bring its convictions to the attention of the voters? . . . Yes, but would that have made any difference? Was Babcock right in 1966: "It is my view that the plan commission, except, perhaps, in the smallest communities, is a dodo" (*The Zoning Game*, p. 40)?

12. What other techniques might the City Council (when a majority favored fighting General Growth) have chosen to block the shopping center? To remove shopping centers as a permitted use in the ML District would have created innumerable nonconforming uses probably to the point of invalidity. The so-called Interim Zoning Ordinance was not very subtle. A moratorium on building permits for a limited time? Or was there some other way? There is no evidence that, with respect to the Lincolnshire site, any of the more usual objections were voiced before the Council: such as traffic impact, consequences to the residential area around Lincolnshire, aesthetic imbalance, or availability of public transportation.

13. Why will residents fight without compromise to keep a different type of residential development out of their town (see Chapter 2, on Tuxedo, New York), but apparently welcome a shopping center that clearly will threaten their downtown? Is it because few residents (except CBD property owners) think about the CBD as they do about their neighborhood? Is the CBD simply a convenience and if a more convenient source of commercial supplies comes along, so much the better?

14. Was Justice Stewart correct in his dissent in *Lafayette* when he said the following?

> First, the very vagueness and uncertainty of the new test for antitrust immunity is bound to discourage state agencies and subdivisions in their experimentation with innovative social and economic programs. In the exercise of their powers local governmental entities often take actions that might violate the antitrust laws if taken by private persons, such as granting exclusive franchises, enacting restrictive zoning ordinances, and providing public services on a monopoly basis. But a city contemplating such action in the interest of its citizens will be able to do so after today only at the risk of discovering too late that a federal court believes that insufficient statutory "direction" existed, or that the activity is "proprietary" in nature. [Footnote omitted.]

Is there basically something different between the duties of a municipal corporation and those of a private corporation that justifies the distinction that appears to have emerged in the Local Government Antitrust Act of 1984? But suppose the municipality decides to be an entrepreneur by acquiring investment opportunities? Boston, Indianapolis, and Hartford, Connecticut, have engaged in "private" ventures. See Weaver and Babcock, *City Zoning* (Chicago, 1979), pp. 224–228.

15. Was Justice Burger correct in *Lafayette* when, in his concurring opinion, he drew the ancient distinction between "governmental" function (e.g., operating a fire department) and a "proprietary" function (e.g., owning and operating a public utility)?

Chapter 8
The Pinelands

1. The authors served as "Land Management Consultants" to the New Jersey Pinelands Commission and were responsible for a comprehensive survey of management techniques used around the world, the design of the Commission's management strategy, and the preparation of the implementing regulations.

2. The Pinelands experience stands four-square for the proposition that careful and open study is the strongest foundation for stringent land use controls. Consider whether the ordinary litigiousness of developers was deterred by the extensive array of background data that was compiled.

3. Although it may be difficult to pin down, it is nevertheless undoubtedly true that federal involvement in policy making, funding, and implementation has lent credibility to the Pinelands program. What are the advantages and disadvantages of a federal role in a regional land management system?

4. One of the most confusing aspects of transferable development rights is their relationship to "just compensation." See *Fred F. French Investing, Inc.* v. *City of New York,* 39 N.Y.2d 587, 350 N.E.2d 381, 385 N.Y.S.2d 5. The Pinelands Commission's position was that PDCs were a use right and should be considered as preserving a beneficial use to the landowner, thereby avoiding the need for compensation. Is there a real distinction or is this perspective a distinction without a difference? If a PDC has reasonably beneficial value on the open market, how could the regulations effect a "taking"? See *Hollywood Inc.* v. *Hollywood, Inc.* 432 So.2d 1332 (1983).

5. Is the Pinelands story a model for comprehensive management programs, or is it limited by the extraordinary resource that was involved? Some observers, including the authors, suggest that the Pinelands is a good model and a classic illustration that planning is a wise investment. In many comprehensive revisions legal fees to defend the new plan far exceed the budget made available to prepare the plan.

6. What standard of review should be applied to a challenge to the "piney exemption"? Is there a fundamental right or suspect classification involved? If the standard of review is what Judge Goldberg of the Fifth Circuit Court of Appeals calls "the anything goes test" (See *City of New Orleans* v. *Dukes,* 427 U.S. 297 [1976] and 501 F.2d (5th Cir. [1974]), what limits are there on regulatory actions?

7. A critical factor in the initial defense of the plan was its procedural posture before the courts. As an appeal from an administrative agency's action, there was no trial *de novo* and the developers were stuck with the compendious record established by the Commission. How different would the litigation have been if it could have been challenged in a *de novo* proceeding?

8. One interesting aspect of the Pinelands situation was the obvious and direct

economic value of an environmentally sensitive area. Would wetlands protection be as legally challenging if wetlands had the sort of direct and immediate value for a cranberry bog rather than the values generally attributed to other wetlands? See Cowdery, Scheuerman, and Lombardo, "The Valuation of Wetlands," 1 *J. Land Use & Env. L.* 1-24 (1985).

Chapter 9
Gautreaux

1. The judicial proceedings reported from 1966 on include the following: *Gautreaux* v. *Romney*, 448 F.2d 731 (7th Cir. 1971); *Gautreaux* v. *Chicago Housing Authority*, 436 F.2d 306 (7th Cir. 1970), *cert. denied,* 402 U.S. 922, 91 S.Ct. 1378, 28 L.Ed.2d 661 (1971); *Gautreaux* v. *Pierce*, 538 F. Supp. 1009 (N.D. Ill. 1982); *Gautreaux* v. *Chicago Housing Authority*, 524 F. Supp. 56 (N.D. Ill. 1982); *Guatreaux* v. *Chicago Housing Authority*, 523 F. Supp. 684 (N.D. Ill. 1981), *aff'd,* 690 F.2d 601 (7th Cir. 1982); *Gautreaux* v. *Landrieu*, 498 F. Supp. 1072 (N.D. Ill. 1980); *Gautreaux* v. *Chicago Housing Authority*, 384 F. Supp. 37 (N.D. Ill. 1974), *petition for writ of mandamus denied sub nom. Chicago Housing Authority* v. *Austin*, 511 F.2d 82 (7th Cir. 1975); *Gautreaux* v. *Romney*, 363 F. Supp. 690 (N.D. Ill. 1973), *rev'd sub nom. Gautreaux* v. *Chicago Housing Authority*, 503 F.2d 930 (7th Cir. 1974), *aff'd in part sub nom. Hills* v. *Gautreaux*, 425 U.S. 284, 96 S.Ct. 1538, 47 L.Ed.2d 792 (1976); *Gautreaux* v. *Chicago Housing Authority*, 342 F. Supp. 827 (N.D. Ill. 1972), *aff'd sub nom. Guatreaux* v. *City of Chicago,* 480 F.2d 210 (7th Cir. 1973), *cert. denied,* 414 U.S. 1144, 94 S.Ct. 895, 39 L.Ed.2d 98 (1974); *Gautreaux* v. *Romney*, 332 F. Supp. 366 (N.D. Ill. 1971), *rev'd,* 457 F.2d 124 (7th Cir. 1972); *Gautreaux* v. Chicago Housing Authority, 304 F. Supp. 736 (N.D. Ill. 1969); *Gautreaux* v. *Chicago Housing Authority,* 265 F. Supp. 582 (N.D. Ill. 1967); *Gautreaux* v. *Pierce,* 690 F.2d 616 (7th Cir. 1982); *Gautreaux* v. *Pierce,* 707 F.2d 265 (7th Cir. 1983).

2. Why do most critics of cases such as *Gautreaux* and *Mount Laurel II* applaud the decision and bemoan the remedy? See Costonis remarks (on *Mount Laurel II*) and J. F. Feurst on *Gautreaux*. Such commentators, were they on the court, presumably would vote against the decision. Or would they? If they supported the decision, what alternative remedy could they propose?

3. Chicago, today, is split between a black Mayor and his administration and a white majority in the City Council (who do not have enough votes to override Mayor Washington's veto). Why is Chicago so polarized between the races? Contrast the bitterness in that city with Philadelphia, Atlanta, and Los Angeles. Chicago probably has more black millionaires than any other major city.

4. In spite of Alexander Polikoff's optimism, he recently went back into fed-

eral court to protest that HUD is unnecessarily delaying the financing of units they had approved for the CHA.

5. Which is better (or worse)? To have all black neighborhoods with more new housing, or to have segregation *and* inadequate housing in black neighborhoods? Is that the only choice?

6. If Mayor Daley had been, say, a Mayor John Lindsay of New York City, would things have been any different? Daley grew up in a lower-income Irish, all white neighborhood. He lived and died in the same bungalow area. Lindsay was an East Side liberal, from a well-to-do background.

7. This is probably the most vicious political story in all these chapters. Should Polikoff have kept up the fight for twenty-some years? What did he gain? If a white is elected mayor in 1987 — Jane Byrne, who has announced her candidacy, or Edward Vrdolyak, or Roman Pucinski — will the conditions revert?

8. Is there merit in regarding the entire Chicago metropolitan area as one entity for solving the problem of segregation? As Devrise points out, by far the large majority of blacks who live in the suburbs are concentrated in a very few of the hundreds of communities. Presumably a very wealthy black person can live any place he chooses (with the possible exceptions of Cicero and Berwyn). This probably was not true as recently as twenty years ago.

9. If, as the U.S. Supreme Court said in *Hills* v. *Gautreaux,* suburban communities still have the right "to require that zoning and other land use restrictions be adhered to by builders," how can any significant racial change be achieved in suburban communities? Does it require that freedom from economic discrimination be read into the U.S. Constitution? If so, what ramifications flow from that principle? All the trappings of exclusionary zoning exist throughout the metropolitan area and no successful effort has been made to break them down. See *Hope, Inc.* v. *County of DuPage,* 738 F.2d 127 (7th Cir. 1984). And the suburbs know better than to use some of the blatant tactics previously struck down by the federal courts. See *Parkview Heights Corp.* v. *City of Blackjack,* 335 F. Supp. 899 (E.D. Mo. 1971), rev'd. 467 F.2d 1208 (CA 8th, 1972); *Kennedy Park Homes Assn. Inc.* v. *City of Lackawanna,* 318 F. Supp. 669, (W.D.N.Y. 1970) 36 F.2d 108, cert. denied, 91 S.Ct. 1256 (CA 2d, 1971); *Anderson* v. *Town of Forest Park,* 239 F. Supp. 576 (W.D. Okla. 1965); *Dailey* v. *City of Lawton,* 196 F. Supp. 266 (W.D. Okla. 1969), *aff'd.* 425 F.2d 1037 (CA 10th, 1970).

10. Polikoff vigorously defends the scattered site housing that had begun to make some progress under the present city administration. In response to an intemperate and highly personal attack in the "Letters" column in the June 1984 *North Shore Magazine* (a guide to gracious living for the affluent), he replied in part:

> The supposed "sell-out" to former Mayor Byrne and former Chicago Housing Authority (C.H.A.) Chairman Swibel is presumably a reference to a court-approved agree-

ment in 1979 that changed the ground rules for scattered site public housing. But the change was in a direction that Keck would presumably favor: it eliminated the former requirement that the first 700 scattered site apartments had to be in white neighborhoods, and it changed the ratio of white neighborhood apartments to black neighborhood apartments from 3 to 1 to 1 to 1. The effect was to permit the scattered site program to go forward on a "50-50" basis, half the units in white neighborhoods and half in black.

[He] speaks of emotional and financial loss in neighborhoods such as Cragin, Marquette Park and Avondale. To provide perspective, here are some figures on these three communities:

	Scattered Site Buildings	Apartments	Population (1980)
Cragin	2	4	53,371
Marquette Park	2	15	46,568
Avondale	3	15	33,527

The figures make it clear that these neighborhoods have but tiny amounts of scattered site housing.

Chapter 10
Hernandez v. City of Lafayette

1. The reported opinions in the *Hernandez* cases are *Hernandez v. City of Lafayette*, 643 F.2d 1188 (5th Cir. 1981); Hernandez v. *City of Lafayette*, 399 So. 2d 1179 (La. Ct. Appl. 1981), 401 So.2d 1192 (La. S. Ct. 1981), *appeal dismissed*, 455 U.S. 901 (1982).

2. The federal litigation was focused on a single issue — money damages as a remedy for the City's wrongdoing. The availability of money damages as a remedy in land use cases had long been an interesting academic issue. See generally Bosselman et al., *The Taking Issue* (CEQ, 1972). However, the decision in *Monell* v. *New York City Dept. of Social Services*, 436 U.S. 658 (1978), made the threat an evident reality to the City. In *Monell* the Court ruled that a municipality was a "person" for the purposes of 42 U.S.C. §1983; however, it reserved ruling on whether a municipality would continue to be entitled to traditional immunities from money damages. *Owen* v. *City of Independence, Missouri*, 445 U.S. 622 (1980), decided amid the *Hernandez* litigation, made it clear, as did the Fifth Circuit's opinion in *Hernandez*, that municipalities are not entitled to immunity.

The so-called taking issue was a central issue in *Hernandez* and at one point in the litigation it appeared that the Supreme Court might consider the issue in these cases. After the Fifth Circuit ruled that the City was not entitled to immunity and reversed the District Court's ruling in favor of the City, the City filed a petition for a writ of certiorari with the Supreme Court. Mr. Hernandez did not file a memorandum in opposition until directed to do so by the Court, a practice the Court follows before it grants an unopposed petition for certiorari. Nevertheless, the Supreme Court denied the writ while at the same time dismissing the *Hernandez* appeal in the state court matter. On three other occasions the Court has approached the "taking issue" (*Agins* v. *City of Tiburon*, 447 U.S. 255 [1980]; *San Diego Gas & Electric* v. *City of San Diego*, 450 U.S. 621 [1981]; and *Williamson County Regional Planning Commission* v. *Hamilton Bank*, 53 USLW 4769 [1985]. However, on each occasion the Court has disposed of the matter on procedural grounds without reaching the merits of the issue. Consider the extent to which litigation like the *Hernandez* matter is encouraged by the jury, due to the unresolved state of the taking issue. See generally Siemon, "Of Regulatory Takings and Other Myths," 1 *FSU J. Env. & Land Use Law* (1985) and Williams et al., "The White River Junction Manifesto," 9 *Vermont L. Rev.* 193 (1984).

3. Consider the following questions implicit in the taking issue:

   a. Is a moratorium in order to prepare a new ordinance a temporary taking? All permit issuing halted. If so, why have most state courts upheld moratoria for a reasonable period — say, six months or a year?

   b. If the court upholds the damage award, must it thereby explicitly or implicitly overrule *Hadacheck* v. *Sebastian, Chief of Police of the City of Los Angeles*, 239 U.S. 394 (1915), and *Goldblatt et al.* v. *Town of Hempstead, New York*, 369 U.S. 590 (1962)? Do you agree that not all of those were nuisance cases? (Even if they were, the U.S. Supreme Court in *Village of Euclid, Ohio, et al.* v. *Ambler Realty Company*, 272 U.S. 365 [1926], analogized zoning to nuisance law.)

   c. If damages are to be paid, how does a city attorney advise his municipal client when a proposed zoning ordinance goes too far? The U.S. Supreme Court — notably Brennan in *Penn Central Transportation Company, et al.* v. *City of New York et al.*, 438 U.S. 104 (1978) — admitted there was no easy rule (as in *Miranda*); it is an ad hoc, case-by-case process. You are the attorney for a city. If a councilman asks, "If we do this and the landowner sues us, will he get a damages award?" What is your answer? Assume a downzoning will lower property values by 51 percent. (Brennan said "most.") Is that a taking?

   d. Policy is a vital element in U.S. Supreme Court decisions. We have seen policy in scores of such opinions — the court in *Baker* v. *Carr*, 369 U.S. 186 (1962), and *Brown* v. *Board of Education*, 347 U.S. 483, to mention a few. Yet Brennan in *San Diego Gas and Electric Co.* v. *City of San Diego*, 450 U.S. 621 (1981), said policy is not to be considered "when an express constitutional right is involved." We do not know why he added that adjective. May "policy" be considered when an express constitutional provision is involved? Do we have a hierarchy of constitutional rights? Brennan in *Penn Central* starts out in his first substantive paragraph by noting, "Over the past 50 years, all 50 states and over 500 municipalities have enacted laws to encourage or require the preservation of buildings and areas with historic or aesthetic importance."

Later in the opinion, in responding to Penn Central's argument, Brennan observed that "agreement with this argument would, of course, invalidate not just New York City's law but all comparable legislation in the nation." This is very real to a municipality. Millions of dollars can be involved. The budget may be irreparably damaged. And no one can in most instances advise with certainty whether a particular decision in a zoning case will result in money damages.

e. Suppose a utility commission sets a confiscatory rate on an electric utility. It takes two years for the utility to have the commission's order overturned by the court. But it has lost the additional rate for two years. Has the utility's property been "taken" during the interval? Should damages be awarded? If not, why not? Or assume a rent control law sets a confiscatory rate, or a price control statute. Damages of both are eventually overturned. Condemnation lawyers would be ecstatic, but is that sound law?

4. There can be no denying many municipalities have replicated Mayor Bowen's record against the Hernandezes. One common practice, if the municipality lost the decision, was to rezone the property as the plaintiff wanted and in effect invite him to bring another lawsuit. If, for example, the plaintiff wanted C-commercial for property zoned single-family (R-1), the municipality would reclassify the land to duplex (R-2). See *San Diego Gas and Electric Company* v. *City of San Diego,* 450 U.S. 621, 656 n. 22.

5. What type of relief would be appropriate to resolve the apparent dilemma between an award of damages and the understandable frustration, delay, and costs brought to landowners or developers? A stay of proceedings to give the city an opportunity to reclassify the property? See the ALI Model Land Development code, §9-112. *City of Richmond* v. *Randall,* 211 S.E.2d 56 (Va. 1975). For cases of zoning with compensation, see *City of Kansas City* v. *Kindle,* 446 S.W. 807 (Mo. 1969). Annot., 41 ALR 3d 637 (1972).

6. Was the Hernandez attorney wise when he elected to go into both state and federal courts? Why? Would the decision in the *Williamson* case have led him to make a different choice?

7. How do you believe the Hernandez property should have been zoned? Consider traffic and neighboring uses. How important, in your opinion, was the sewage treatment plant?

8. The Hernandezes' attorney made the most of "Chicago lawyers," "Washing-

ton, D.C., experts," and the Mayor's acrimonious remarks to and about Mrs. Hernandez. We tried to keep the focus on zoning issues, which is probably why we won in the Louisiana Appellate Court.

9. The Hernandezes' attorney claimed that the Mayor was not immune because the use of the veto is not legislative, but executive, in nature. The federal courts disagreed. Compare *Buckley* v. *Valeo,* 424 U.S. 1, 121 (1976), and *Edwards* v. *United States,* 286 U.S. 482 (1932), for the President's veto, with *Smiley* v. *Holm,* 285 U.S. 355 (1932), for the Governor's veto. Note that in Louisiana, the Mayor frequently does not sit as part of the legislative body. Should that make a difference?

Chapter 11
Mount Laurel II

1. The principal cases are *Southern Burlington County NAACP* v. *Mt. Laurel,* 336 A.2d 713 (1975) and *Southern Burlington County NAACP* v. *Mt. Laurel,* 456 A.2d 390 (1983). See also *Vickers* v. *Gloucester Township Committee,* 181 A.2d 129 (1962). For cases following *Mount Laurel I* that suggest a retreat from that decision, in addition to the *Madison* case, see *Pascack Ass'n. Ltd.* v. *Washington,* 379 A.2d 6 (1977); *Fobe Associates* v. *Demarest,* 379 A.2d 31 (1977); *Swiss Village Assoc.* v. *Municipal Council of Tp. of Wayne,* 392 A.2d 596 (App. Div. 1978); and *Township of Washington* v. *Central Bergen Community Mental Health Center, Inc.,* 383 A.2d 1194 (1978).

2. What other remedy might the court have devised? Would a ban on *all* building permits have led the New Jersey Legislature to act more readily?

3. A "builder's remedy" is not unheard of in other jurisdictions. See *Sinclair Pipeline Co.* v. *Village of Richton Park,* 167 N.E.2d 406 (Ill., 1960). By statute in Pennsylvania there is what is known as a "curative amendment." The Pennsylvania zoning legislation gives the courts power to order site-specific relief when a landowner demonstrates that the zoning restrictions are invalid in their application to his property. Pa. Stat. Anno., Title 53, §11011(2) (Purdon's Supp., 1980) provides

> If the court . . . finds that an ordinance or map or a decision or order thereunder which has been brought up for review unlawfully prevents or restricts a development or use which has been described by the landowner through plans and other materials submitted to the governing body, agency or officer of the municipality whose action or failure to act is in question on the appeal, it may order the described development or use approved as to all elements or it may order it approved as to some elements and refer other elements to the governing body, agency or officer having jurisdiction thereof for further proceedings, including the adoption of alternative restrictions, in accordance with the court's opinion and order.

290 · *Comments*

4. Exclusionary zoning has become a popular epithet in recent years. See Sager, "Tight Little Islands: Exclusionary Zoning, Equal Protection and the Indigent," 21 *Stan. L. Rev.* 767 (1969); Babcock, *The Zoning Game* (Madison: University of Wisconsin Press, 1966); Symposium, Exclusionary Zoning, 22 *Syracuse L. Rev.* 465 (1971). Apart from New Jersey, only two or three other states have even so much as discussed the issue. See *National Land Investment Co. v. Kohn*, 215 A.2d 597 (Pa. 1965); *Associated Home Builders of Greater Eastbay, Inc. v. City of Livermore*, 557 P.2d 473 (Calif. 1976), and *Berenson v. Town of New Castle*, 341 N.E.2d 236 (N.Y. 1975). Is this a peculiarly suburban issue? Would the same reasoning apply in a small, rural, resort town in New Hampshire? See *Steel Hill Development Co. v. Town of Sanbornton*, 469 F.2d 956 (N.H. 1st Cir. 1972); *Burrows v. City of Keene*, 431 A.2d 15 (N.H. 1984). What reasons can you think of that this occurred in New Jersey and not in Connecticut, Ohio, Illinois, or any of half a dozen other states?

5. Can the *Mount Laurel II* remedy work unless the below-market housing is rented rather than offered for sale? How narrow is the gap between an income at or below 50 percent of the median income of the region and the amount that can be borrowed under a mortgage with that income? Who will take advantage of the below-market housing in suburban developments? Is Jerry Rose right that this decision can only hurt the urban areas? In its conclusion, the Court states: "We intend here only to make sure that if the poor remain locked into urban slums, it will not be because we failed to enforce the constitution."

6. Would courts do better to abstain from such political thickets? One of the affidavits filed with the New Jersey Supreme Court on behalf of the municipalities in the *Cranbury* case was by the well-known and highly respected land use lawyer and law professor (now Dean of Vanderbilt Law School) John J. Costonis. He said, in part:

> 16. Like virtually every other court system, state or federal, in the nation, I believe that the issues posed by a finding of the invalidity of a challenged zoning measure are distinct from those posed by the establishment of a remedy for this invalidity. It does not follow, that is, that a court that declares the measure unconstitutional ought to take it upon itself to declare what the substitute measure should be.
>
> 17. Most courts, in fact, do no more than invalidate the offending measure, remitting to the political branches that establishment of an appropriate substitute. A minority take the further, but still modest, step of directing that the challenger's desired use of a particular parcel be permitted. None takes the position that the sole judicial response to unconstitutional zoning is the threatened or actual imposition of what, in effect, is a judicial receivership on the land use powers of entire classes of municipalities throughout an entire state, and the concomitant prerogative to fix the policies to which these powers will be exercised.

Is this decision "anti-democratic"? Or are the practices of New Jersey municipalities "anti-democratic"? Or both? Or worse, do such cases so embroil the judiciary in the resolution of difficult social issues as to impair the primary function of the judicial system?

7. If Justice Hall had not chosen to base his decision in *Mount Laurel I* on the New Jersey Constitution but instead had placed his reliance on both the state and federal constitutions, and the U.S. Supreme Court had granted certiorari, what position, in your opinion, would the Court have taken? See *Warth v. Seldin*, 422 U.S. 490 (1975), and *Village of Belle Terre v. Boraas*, 416 U.S. 1 (1974). Lawrence Sager, cited *supra,* summed up:

> No man should be denied the capacity to defend himself against criminal charges or the right to vote because of his poverty; no man should be unable to live where he pleases by reason of his color. This certainly is not the case with indigency and residential access: 'No man should be unable to live in the neighborhood of his choosing because of his poverty' is simply not a proposition for which one could expect to find firm nationwide support in 1969. Exclusive neighborhoods, indeed, an entire range of neighborhoods of graduated exclusivity, are commonplace and, unlike racial ghettos. are not even the objects of widespread verbal lamentation. [Footnotes omitted.]

Is housing any greater a "fundamental right" requiring "strict scrutiny" than education? See *San Antonio School District v. Rodriguez*, 411 U.S. 1 (1973). Consider Sager's remark that his hypothetical proposition would not be accepted in 1969; would it be accepted in 1985?

8. Do the *Mount Laurel* opinions suggest the emergence of the state constitutions as a new source of protection for civil rights? Professor Norman Williams, Jr., in Section 66.13b to the 1984 Supplement to Volume 3 of *American Land Planning Law,* notes:

> Another and a secondary theme of this treatise has been that some of the leading state courts, secure in the experience of half a century of intensive litigation in the field of law, have quite consciously been handling the current transition as a matter of state constitutional law—i.e., in such a way as to preclude review by the United States Supreme Court. This policy has clearly been justified by that Court's forty-year abstention from this field (see Appendix, Vol 5, p 557), and by the fact that its recent rulings on related matters, and finally in Belle Terre (see §66.34), have been quite out of key with recent developments in the state courts (that is to say, with the transition). This state court policy was implicit in the New York Court's circumvention of Belle Terre [*City of White Plains v. Ferraioli*, 313 N.E.2d 756 (1974)], and was explicit in the school financing cases. As a result, an elaborate analysis of Supreme Court doctrine on due process (and "taking") is rather beside the point, if what is desired is an understanding of current developments in the state courts, where the action is.

See also W. J. Brennan, "State Constitutions and the Protection of Individual Rights, 90 *Harv. L. Rev.* 489 (1977).

The Supreme Court of Vermont is clearly swinging in this direction. See Williams, Smith, Siemon, Mandelker, and Babcock, "The White River Junction Manifesto," 9 *Verm. L. Rev.* 193 at 229, n. 110 (1985). The paragraph of the New Jersey Constitution (Art. 1, par. 1) that Justice Hall in *Mount Laurel I* inferred embraced equal protection reads as follows:

> All persons are by nature free and independent, and have certain natural and unalienable rights, among which are those of enjoying and defending life and liberty, of acquiring, possessing, and protecting property, and of pursuing and obtaining safety and happiness.

Does this sound more like a clause out of the Declaration of Independence? Some state constitutions have expressly included equal protection provisions. See Illinois Constitution, Art. 1, §2 (1970).

9. If the New York firm apparently concluded that there was no hope in a federal court (in spite of all the talk by Mayor Gagliano and others of going into the federal courts), what theories, in your opinion, might induce a federal court to hear the case? Equal protection? Might some buyers of market housing units have to pay a larger subsidy in some areas of the state than in others because of significant variances in the median incomes? Or is the requirement that the buyers of market housing subsidize the below-market housing a form of taxation that should be borne by the public at large? See Ellikson, "The Irony of Inclusionary Zoning," 70 *S. Cal. L. Rev.* 1167 (1981).

Chapter 12
Sea Ranch, California

1. The principal cases are *Sea Ranch Assoc. v. California Coastal Zone Conservation Commission*, 396 F. Supp. 533 (D.C.N.D. Cal. 1975); *Natural Resources Defense Council, Inc. v. California Coastal Zone Conservation Commission*, 129 Cal. Rptr. 57 (Cal. App. 1976); *Sea Ranch Assoc. v. California Coastal Zone Conservation Commission*, 537 F.2d 1058 (9th Cir. 1976); *Oceanic California Inc. v. North Central Coast Regional Commission*, 133 Cal. Rptr. 664 (Cal. App. 1976); *Sea Ranch Association v. California Coastal Commission*, 527 F. Supp. 390 (D.C.N.D. Cal. 1981); but see 102 S. Ct. 622 (1981); *Sea Ranch Assoc. v. California Coastal Commission*, 552 F. Supp. 241 (U.S.D.C. N.D. Cal. 1982). Oceanic or the Association lost them all.

2. For an excellent account of the California saga from 1850 through the progressive era, see Kevin Starr's two books, *Americans and the California Dream 1850–1915* and *Inventing the Dream* (New York: Oxford University Press, 1973, 1985).

3. Article 10, Section 4, of the California Constitution reads as follows:

> §4. Access to navigable waters.
>
> Sec. 4 No individual, partnership, or corporation, claiming or possessing the frontage or tidal lands of a harbor, bay, inlet, estuary, or other navigable water in

this State, shall be permitted to exclude the right of way to such water whenever it is required for any public purpose, nor to destroy or obstruct the free navigation of such water; and the Legislature shall enact such laws as will give the most liberal construction to this provision, so that access to the navigable waters of this State shall be always attainable for the people thereof.

(Added June 8, 1976.)

4. California has always been notorious for being the first jurisdiction to sustain extreme municipal regulations. Practitioners in other states have joked about why a developer would sue a California community when it would cost a lot less and save much time if he simply slit his throat. The City of Manhattan Beach zoned a private beach as "beach recreational district" with no building permitted. It was upheld in *McCarthy* v. *City of Manhattan Beach,* 264 P.2d 932 (1953), cert. den. 348 U.S. 817 (1954). The court suggested that if houses were built on stilts there was the risk of immoral activity underneath them. California has the key case on "exactions"—demanding off-site gifts from developers before they were given a permit to build. See *Ayres* v. *City of Los Angeles,* 207 P.2d 1 (1949), and also *Assoc. Home Builders* v. *City of Walnut Creek,* 484 P.2d 606 (1971). The practice is now endemic across the country. A developer who believes he may have a vested right because of some permits had better read *Avco Community Developers, Inc.* v. *South Coast Regional Commission,* 553 P.2d 546 (1976). California has resisted all efforts by developers to get payment for alleged "taking" by a regulatory ordinance. See *Agins* v. *City of Tiburon,* 598 P.2d 25 (1975), 447 U.S. 255 (1980), but also see *San Diego Coast Regional Comm'n.* v. *See the Sea Ltd.,* 513 P.2d 129 (1973). Prior to November 8, 1972, Oceanic spent $26.9 million in direct project expenditures.

5. The commissions' demand for further exactions of access after Oceanic already had faced one exaction—that is, of Gualala Point Park—was the most important and difficult issue the Sea Ranch homeowners faced in the years of dispute with the commissions. Should a second government agency be permitted to double up on exactions after the developer has been hit once, on the theory that the second government thinks the first government did not go far enough? If so, when does the police power end?

6. Inevitably, Bill Kortum saw the "people's own interest" as his own, that is, in more access. Is there another public interest that might be involved here, such as the right to be free from repeated governmental exactions of property? If so, how do we measure and reconcile these conflicting formulations of the public interest? Must it be done in theory, or should the parties have used good will and common sense to negotiate a compromise ten years earlier than they did?

7. The alleged effort by the Commission staff to "defeat the best" echoes Malcolm Misuraca's belief that the commissioners were revolutionaries bent on a complete discontinuity with past development law. Is it appropriate, to insure that a radical new departure in the law takes hold, to repudiate all past govern-

ment regulation seen as too weak or too soft? If so, what are the limits to the police power, and where does the right to just compensation begin?

8. How can a government that may commit a "taking" of private property, that is, by inverse condemnation, claim that it has no power of eminent domain? Isn't this the equivalent of saying that "we may regulate you out of existence, but we hereby declare that since we don't have the power of eminent domain, we don't have to pay you"? Is this denial of the power of eminent domain itself unconstitutional? Or does it simply mean that any act of the Commission that would otherwise be compensable is unconstitutional? Who do you suppose drafted and supported this provision — the commissions or the developers?

9. The homeowners did not really object to monitoring septic systems. They did this anyway. But the Commission imposed draconian and further controls over septic systems, such as very long leach fields and the requirement that there be a second, stand-by leach field. This meant that many lots that were fit for use of septic systems under prior regulations might now be unbuildable, and the homeowners saw this as just one more attempt to regulate the Sea Ranch out of existence without payment of just compensation.

10. Picchi demonstrated that any house he built would block views from the highway, but the Commission imposed restrictions anyway.

11. To what extent may a single lotowner be lumped with other lowowners and forced to incorporate their difficulties into his own design? This problem came up again in the Commission's exaction of $1,500 from each home builder, which would be released only if the homeowners' association performed certain Sea Ranch–wide conditions. See *Washington ex rel. Seattle Trust Co.* v. *Roberge*, 278 U.S. 116 (1928).

Brief List of Books Cited

Babcock Richard F. *Billboards, Glass Houses and the Law.* Colorado Springs: Shepards, 1977.
Babcock, Richard F. *The Zoning Game.* Madison: University of Wisconsin Press, 1966.
Bosselman, Fred. *The Taking Issue.* Washington, D.C.: Council on Environmental Quality, 1973.
DiMento, Joseph F. *The Consistency Doctrine and the Limits of Planning.* Cambridge Mass.: Oelgeschlager, Gunn & Hain, 1980.
Forman, Richard R., ed. *Pine Barrens: Ecosystem and Landscape.* New York: Academic Press, 1979.
Gailey, Ben, ed. *Zoning and Planning Law Handbook.* New York: Clark Boardman, 1983.
George, Henry. *Progress and Poverty.* New York: The Schalkenbach Foundation, 1979. (Originally published in 1879.)
McPhee, John. *The Pine Barrens.* New York: Farrar, Straus & Giroux, 1968.
Morgan, Judith and Neal. *Island in the Coast.* Oceanic California, Inc., 1974.
Nevins, Deborah, ed. *Grand Central Terminal: City within the City.* New York: Municipal Art Society, 1982.
Newman, Oscar. *Defensible Space: Crime Prevention through Urban Design.* New York: Macmillan, 1973.
Sabatier, Paul A., and Daniel A. Mazmanian. *Can Regulation Work?* New York: Plenum Press, 1983.
Schmidt, John. *Historical Profile of Sioux City.* Sioux City, Iowa: Sioux City Stationery Company, 1969.
Weaver, Clifford L., and Richard F. Babcock. *City Zoning: The Once and Future Frontier.* Chicago: American Planning Association, 1979.

Index

Abshier, James, 130
Albertson, Jan, 124
Alinsky, Saul, 82
Allen, Mary, 254
American Civil Liberties Union, 159, 162
  See also Gautreaux v. Chicago Housing Authority
American Law Institute Model Land Development Code, 261
Andrus, Cecil, 155
Aquifer Protection Association (San Antonio, Texas), 82-83
Arrighetti, Peter, 22
Asbury Park Press, 136
Ashman, Candace, 143
Askew, Reuben, 116
Aspen, Marvin, 178
Atlantic City Press, 215
Audino, Frank, 122
Auger, Caroline S., 224
Austin, Richard, 159-160, 162-169 passim, 172
Azevedo, Margaret, 244, 252

Babcock, Richard, 256
  as consultant, 172-177
  as counsel, 45, 47, 85, 196
  Billboards, Glass Houses and the Law, 171-172
  City Zoning: The Once and Future Frontier, 8, 264
  The Zoning Game, 1-2, 6, 56, 208
Bailey, Francis, 100
Baker v. *Carr*, 258
Bane, Tom, 248
Bartley, Ernst, 45-46
Barwick, Kent, 66, 69, 74

Batory, Joan, 143
Beame, Abraham, 65
Bergen Record, 215
Bilandic, Michael, 177
Billboards, Glass Houses and the Law (Babcock), 171-172
Blucher, Walter, 46, 47
Bosselman, Fred: as counsel, 102, 103, 105, 115
  The Taking Issue, 103
Bowen, Kenneth A., 188-189, 190, 192, 194, 195-196, 199-200, 260
Brandeis Department Store, 122, 127, 129, 130, 131
Brandeis, Louis, 257
Brennan, William, 59-61, 66, 70, 201-202, 263
Brietel, Judge, 66-67
Brown, Jerry, 250
Brown v. *Board of Education*, 181, 258
Burchell, Robert, 218, 219
Burger, Warren, 75, 257
Busher, Carl, 220
Butler, Cecil, 163
Butler, Zee, 100
Byrne, Brendan T., 139, 140-141, 149, 153-154, 155, 215
Byrne, Jane, 177, 179

Calendar, Loren, 127
California Coastal Commission, 3, 241-252 passim
  See also Sea Ranch, California
Californians Organized to Acquire Access to State Tidelands (COAAST), 239-242, 250
Can Regulation Work? (Sabatier and Mazmanian), 240

Cantrelle, Billy, 193-194
Captiva. *See* Sanibel Island, Florida
Case, Clifford P., 139
Castle and Cook, 236, 251
Center for Urban Policy Research of Rutgers, 219
Central business districts. *See* Sioux City, Iowa
Central Intelligence Agency, 99-100
Chavooshian, Budd, 143
Chicago, Illinois, 264
  See also Gautreaux v. Chicago Housing Authority
Chicago Defender, 167
Chicago Magazine, 178
Chicago Tribune, 166
Churchill, Winston, 258
Cisneros, Henry, 84, 85
City Investing Company, 11-12, 14-35 passim
  early development of Sterling Forest, 14-15
  experts hired by, 18-19
  and Martineau, 30-31
  Sterling One development planning, 17-19
  See also Tuxedo, New York
City of Lafayette v. *Louisiana Power and Light*, 126
City Zoning: The Once and Future Frontier (Weaver and Babcock), 8, 264
Clarke, William, 20, 21
Clausen, Larry, 130
Coffin, Frank M., 259
Cole, George, 130
Collins, Cardiss, 171-172
Communities Organized for Public Service (San Antonio, Texas), 82-83
Condon, Walter, 100-102
Connolly, Mr., 125
Consistency Doctrine and the Limits of Planning (DiMento), 261-262
Corruption, 260
Courts, role of, 256-259, 265
Cranston, Alan, 240
Crosby, Sazz, 24
Crowley, John, 173, 177
Curfman, John, 124, 132-133

Daily News (Chicago), 164

Daley, Richard, 160, 163, 164-166, 169, 256, 260
Damages claims, 84, 86-87, 196, 201-202
Darling, J. N., 96
Darlington, Tom, 148, 149
Defensible Space (Newman), 160-162
Delogu, Orlando E., 263
Demarest v. *Mayor and Council of Borough of Hillsdale*, 210
Design with Nature (McHarg), 102
Des Moines Register, 122, 129
de Vise, Pierre, 165
DiMento, Joseph: *The Consistency Doctrine and the Limits of Planning*, 261-262
Dobbs, Leonard, 221-223
Dorsey, John, 216, 229
Dowling, Robert, 14, 17
Downey, Judge, 259
Due process, 251-252
Duffy, Ryan, 166

Eastwood, Roland, 118
Edwards Underground Aquifer. *See* San Antonio, Texas
Ellman, Howard, 247, 251, 253, 254
Emanuel, Manny, 22, 33
Emanuel and Associates, 19, 22
Encino Park Venture case, 84-85, 90
English, Michael, 216
Environmental Impact Statement: federal, 81-82, 155
  New York state, 26, 27, 28
Environmental Land and Water Management Act (Florida), 114
Estuaries case, 113-116
"Exactions," 227-229
Exclusionary zoning practices, 208-209, 221
  See also Mount Laurel II
Experts: disagreement among, 219-220
  for Lafayette, 197, 199
  out-of-town and local, 6, 197
  for Palm Beach, 47-48
  for Pinelands, 141, 143, 144-145
  for Sea Ranch, 237
  for Tuxedo, 18-19

Faust, David, 40, 42, 43, 47, 53-55, 57

Feurst, J. F., 172
Field, Mervin, 240
Fisher, Michael, 241-243, 245, 246, 248, 250
Fix, Jerry, 15, 19-21, 32
Florida Supreme Court, 116-117
Florio, James, 139
Forsyth, Edwin, 155
Forte v. *Borough of Tenafly*, 126
Fox, William, 216
Furman, David, 207

Gagliano, Thomas, 229, 231
Gangplank syndrome (residents' opposition), 15, 33, 44, 55-57, 260-261
Garibaldi, Peter, 215-216
Garrity, Paul G., 176
Gautreaux, Dorothy, 162, 169
Gautreaux v. *Chicago Housing Authority*, 3, 159-181, 256-257, 260
  Babcock Report, 172-177
  black response, 164, 167, 171-172
  CHA actions, 163-165, 173-177, 178
  City strategy, 162, 163, 165-167, 172
  community opposition, 166-167, 179
  conclusions, 180-181
  court decisions, 162, 165-166, 167-169, 177-178
  demographics, 160, 162, 165
  exisiting public housing, 160-162
  historical background, 160-162
  Leadership Council activities, 164, 169-170
  Model Cities areas, 164, 166, 167
  Newman Report, 178-180
  receivership, 174-178
  suburban public housing, 164, 165-166, 168-171
Gavin, Paul, 224
General Growth Corporation, 122-131 passim
George, Henry, 66-67
Gern, Richard, 197
Gill, Brendan, 64, 66, 68, 71, 75
Gladstone Associates, 18
Goode, John, 108
Goss, Porter J., 97-98, 99-102, 112, 117-118, 256

Gourlay, John, 19-21
Grace, Bob, 40, 42
Graham, Bob, 118
Grand Central Station, 4-5, 59-75, 257, 260
  Committee to Save Grand Central campaign, 65-70
  conclusions, 70-75
  current state of terminal, 71-75
  historical background, 62-64
  New York Supreme Court decision, 64
  supporters of preservation, 65, 66, 68-69
  United States Supreme Court proceedings, 59-61, 63, 66-67, 70-71
Grand Central Terminal (Hardy), 71-74
Grand Central Terminal: City Within the City (Nevins), 62-63, 74
Gribbon, Daniel, 63, 66-67, 70

Haar, Charles, 256
Hackensack Meadowlands Commission, 218-219
Hagie, Ruth and Frank, 249
Hall, Frederick, 207, 208-210, 232, 256
Hardy, Hugh: *Grand Central Terminal*, 71-74
Harriman, Averell, 14
Hauser, Philip, 162
Hendricks, Carol, 170
Herbold, Arlo, 131-132, 133
Hernandez, Mr. and Mrs. James, 185-189, 190, 198-199, 203-204
Hernandez v. *City of Lafayette*, 5-7, 183-205, 256-257, 259, 260, 263
  attempted settlement, 190-194
  conclusions, 204-205
  court decisions, 197, 200, 202-203
  historical background, 183-185
  litigation, 190-192, 194-195, 199-200, 201-203
  rezoning petitions, 185-190, 195, 203-204
  RUDAT Report, 195
  traffic problem, 188, 197-199
  West Bayou/Girard Park realignment, 188-189, 190, 192, 197-199
Hill, Henry, 221, 225-226

300 · *The Zoning Game Revisited*

Hills Development Company, 221-226
Hills v. Gautreaux, 168-169
Hines, Donald, 242
Hluchan, Rich, 156
Hoffman, Ted, 21, 22, 23, 26-27
Horan, Matt, 34
Houston, Texas, 263-264
HUD. *See* United States Department of Housing and Urban Development
Hudson Dispatch, 215
Hughes, William J., 155
Hutt, Stewart, 216-217, 229

Independent Coast Observer, 239, 249
Institute for Community Design Analysis, 178
Island Reporter, The, 100, 117
Islands in the Coast (Morgan), 236

Jackson, Jesse, 163
Johnson, Frank M., Jr., 176, 257-258
Johnson, Reverdy, 243, 245-246
Jurco, Olga, 168

Kean, Thomas H., 215, 229-231, 233, 257
Kerwin, John H., 224-225, 226
Koerner, Leonard J., 70
Kortum, Bill, 237-239, 240, 241
Krasnowiecki, Jan, 263
Kurland, Phillip, 180-181, 258

Lafayette, Louisiana. *See Hernandez v. City of Lafayette*
Lafayette Daily Advertiser, 193-194
Landmark preservation. *See* Grand Central Station
Lane, Melvin, 237, 239, 253, 254
Larsen, Wendy, 261
Laurent, Mr., 171
Lawrenson, Donald, 127
Leach case, 39-40, 42
LeBuff, Charles, 100
Lee County. *See* Sanibel Island, Florida
Lerman, Carla, 218
Levanthal, Harold: "Environmental Decisionmaking and the Role of the Courts," 258-259

Lipman, Wynona, 229
Listokin, David, 219
Lundborg, Bradford, 244, 247, 250

McCarthy, John, 26, 27, 28, 29
McClure, Dean, 17
McHarg, Ian: *Design with Nature*, 102
McIntosh, Robert, 122
MacKenzie, Vernon, 99, 100, 104
McLaughlin, Joanna, 239, 250-251
Macon, Jane, 91-92
McPhee, John, 136, 138-139
   The Pine Barrens, 138, 218
Mallach, Alan, 213n, 226
Mandel, Myron, 22, 23, 29, 30-31
Marchant, John, 249
Marshall, Thurgood, 60
Martineau, Neal, 14, 15, 20-34 passim
   conflict of interest, 30-31
Martino, Felix, 207
Master, Charles, 176-177
Matthews, George, 42
Maute, Fred, 15, 21-29, 33, 34
Mazmanian, Daniel A.: *Can Regulation Work?*, 240
Merriam, Bob, 29, 32
Metropolitan Transit Authority (New York), 73-74
Miami Beach, Florida, 98
Michigan Supreme Court, 265
Middletown Record, 23, 25, 26, 28
Milliken case, 167-169
Miner, Dorothy, 64
Misuraca, Malcolm, 246-248, 251-252, 254
Model Cities, 164, 166, 167
Monell v. New York City Dept. of Social Services, 194
Moore, Terrence D., 141, 256, 260
Morgan, Judith and Neal: *Islands in the Coast*, 236
Mount Laurel I, 209-211
Mount Laurel II, 4, 207-233, 257-258, 260
   Bedminster, 221-226
   Branchburg, 229
   builders' and developers' response, 220-221
   conclusions, 231-233
   consensus formula, 217-218, 219

Mount Laurel II (cont.)
  Cranbury, 227
  demographics, 216-217, 226
  historical background, 207-211
  house prices, 213-214, 223, 225-226, 227-229, 232
  Lipman bill, 229-231, 232
  litigation, 220-21, 231, 232
  Monroe Township, 215-216
  Mount Laurel I, 209-211
  Mount Laurel II decision, 211-215
  Mount Laurel II policies, 212-214
  reaction to ruling, 214-217, 220-221, 229-231, 233
  Rutgers formula, 218, 219-220
  state legislation, 218-219, 229-231, 233
  Vickers decision, 207, 208-209, 232
  Warren Township, 217-218, 227
Mulligan, William, 166-167
Municipal Art Society (New York), 64, 65-70, 74
Municipal immunity, 126-127, 184, 196-197, 201-202
Murphy, Martin, 174

National Association for the Advancement of Colored People (NAACP), 172, 209
National Environmental Policy Act, 81
National Geographic, 138-139
National Parks and Recreation Act of 1978, 139-140, 155
National Reserves, 139
Nevins, Deborah: *Grand Central Terminal: City Within the City*, 62-63, 74
New Brunswick Home News, 233
Newhouse, Richard, 163
New Jersey Builders Association, 219, 220
New Jersey Supreme Court, 207, 208-214, 231n, 232, 233
Newman, Oscar, 178
  Defensible Space, 160-162
New York, New York, 264
  See also Grand Central Station
New York Daily News, 66
New Yorker, The, 64
New York Supreme Court, 64
New York Times, 24, 68-69, 215
Nixon, Richard, 167

Oakland Tribune, 243
Oakwood v. *Madison*, 211, 221
O'Brien, Patrick, 163, 168
Oceanic, Inc., 236-237, 241-251 passim
O'Conner, Peter J., 226
Owen, Mel, 247
Owen v. *City of Independence*, 201

Palm Beach, Florida (Sloan's Curve), 7-8, 37-57, 259-260, 263
  Comprehensive Plan, 42-51
  conclusions and recommendations, 55-57
  court decisions, 46-47, 49-52
  expert testimony, 47-48
  historical background, 38-39
  inadequacy of Plan, 45-49
  Leach case, 39-40, 42
  outcome, 53-55
  previous development, 40-42
  property values, 43, 47-48
  residents of early development, 44, 55-57
  residents' opposition, 40, 42-45
  traffic problem, 49, 56
  zoning ordinances, 42-45, 51-52
Palm Beach Daily News, 50
Parker, Frank, 143, 149
Parker v. *Brown*, 126
Pascack Ass'n. Ltd. v. *Washington*, 210
Patterson, Gary, 143, 148
Pendley v. *Lake Harbin Ass'n*, 265
Penn Central Transportation Co. v. *New York City*, 59-61, 63, 66-67, 70-71
Pennsylvania Supreme Court, 208
Pereira, William L., Associates, 18
Perez v. *Boston Housing Authority*, 176
Philadelphia Enquirer, 226
Picchi, Joseph, 242-243
Pillsbury, Madison and Sutro, 248
Pine Barrens, The (McPhee), 138, 218
Pinelands, New Jersey, 2-3, 135-157, 263
  agriculture and logging interests, 138, 145, 147-148, 152, 155-156
  background and description, 135-139
  Coalition for Sensible Protection, 147, 150, 155

Pinelands, New Jersey (cont.)
  Comprehensive Management Plan, 140-153
  conclusions, 156-157
  designated growth areas, 145, 146, 147, 150
  development moratorium, 140
  Galloway Township, 150
  grandfather rights, 152, 154
  land value, 145, 146, 147-148, 150, 151-152, 155-156
  local government activities, 143, 145, 146-147, 148, 150, 154, 156
  main elements of Plan, 146-147
  military facility, 156
  National Parks and Recreation Act of 1978, 139-140, 155
  opposition to Plan, 145, 147-149, 150, 152-154, 155-156
  Pinelands Commission, 140-145, 149-150, 152-153, 156-157, 218-219
  Pinelands Development Credit and transferable development rights, 144, 146-147, 150-152
  Pinelands Protection Act, 140, 154
  residential development, 146-147
  vested rights, 146, 154
  water quality, 138, 146
Pizzo, Kenneth, 229
Planning, importance of, 261-263
Polikoff, Alex, 159, 162-172 passim, 178, 179-180, 181, 256
Political pressure, 259-261
  and court decisions, 61, 69-70, 260
Powell, Lewis, 60
Prahl, Margaret, 125, 128-129
Property values: Palm Beach, 43, 47-48
  Pinelands, 145, 146, 147-148, 150, 151-152, 155-156
  Sanibel Island, 106-107, 113
  Sea Ranch, 243, 250
Public access. *See* Sea Ranch, California
Public Advocate, 221, 223
Public housing. *See Gautreaux* v. *Chicago Housing Authority*
Public Records Act (Florida), 111
Pucinski, Roman, 163
Pulliam, M. S., 263

PUSH (People United to Serve Humanity), 163, 171

Ralph, Leon, 248
Rand, Bill, 243
Rathkopf, Arden, 11, 28, 30-31
Reagan, Ronald, 127, 257
Receivership, 174-178
Red flags doctrine, 103
Rehnquist, William, 60, 66, 75, 201, 257, 258
Reps, John, 263
Restraint of competition, 126-127
  See also Sioux City, Iowa
Richards, Stanley, 124, 127
Roberts, William, 102
Romney, George W., 166
Rose, Jerome, 216, 217
Rossetti, Nick, 15, 26-27, 33

Sabatier, Paul A.: *Can Regulation Work?*, 240
Sager, Larry: "Tight Little Islands," 208
St. George, Katherine, 21
San Antonio, Texas, 7, 77-93, 260
  aquifer pollution, 80-81, 87-88, 90-93
  Aquifer Protection Association, 82-83
  City Council, 79, 80, 82-83
  Communities Organized for Public Service, 82-83
  court decisions, 81-82, 84-85, 86-87, 90
  damages claims, 84, 86-87
  first moratorium ordinance, 83-86, 91-92
  historical background, 77-79
  Natural Resources Disclosure Statement, 89
  Northside Independent School District, 86-87, 90
  previous development, 79
  San Antonio Ranch, 81-82, 83, 84-85, 89-90
  second moratorium ordinance, 88-90
  super-mall development, 82-83
  Texas Water Quality Board, 80, 82, 91, 92-93
  vested rights, 89-90

San Antonio Light, 86
San Diego Gas & Electric Co. v. *City of San Diego*, 59-61, 201-202
San Francisco, California, 264
San Francisco Sunday Examiner and Chronicle, 252
Sanibel Island, Florida, 9, 95-118, 263
  commercial zoning, 107-108
  Comprehensive Land Use Plan, 102-104
  court decisions, 103, 105-106, 116-117
  Estuaries development, 113-116
  historical background, 95-97
  hurricane protection, 96, 103
  Lee County Board of Commissioners, 97-98, 99, 115-116, 117
  Lee County planning, 97, 115, 117
  municipal incorporation, 98-100
  previous development, 96-97
  property values, 106-107, 113
  rate of growth, 108
  Sanibel-Captiva Planning Board, 97
  Sundial case, 103, 105
  traffic, 107
  vested rights, 102-103, 105-107
  Wulfert Woods, 110-113, 116-117
Saypol, Irving, 64
Schnadelbach, R. T., 18
Sea Ranch, California, 3, 235-254, 257
  background and description, 235-236
  Bane bill, 248-250, 254
  California Coastal Commission, 241, 246, 257, 249-250
  Californians Organized to Acquire Access to State Tidelands (COAAST), 239-242, 250
  conclusions, 252-254
  court decisions, 247-248, 250, 257
  design of development, 237, 242, 251
  due process, 251-252
  land value and building costs, 243, 248, 250-251
  North Central (Regional) Commission, 241-248, 251-252
  Picchi case, 242-243
  Proposition 20, 239-242

public access, 237-239, 240, 242, 244, 246, 248-251
  residents of early development, 241, 245-246, 248-249
  vested rights, 245-246, 251
Serpentelli, Eugene, 218, 221, 227
Shanahan, Miles, 18, 23, 34
Sherman Antitrust Act, 126
Shettino, Thomas, 209
Shinn, Robert, 143
Shopping centers, 122, 132, 133
  See also Sioux City, Iowa
Siemon, Charles, 261
  as counsel, 85, 88, 102, 103, 105, 115
Sierra Club v. *Lynn*, 81-82
Simpson, Robert H., 103
Sioux City, Iowa, 8, 119-133, 260, 263
  central business district development, 120-122, 123, 132-133
  City Council elections, 127, 129-130
  city zoning strategies, 123-124, 127-129, 130, 132
  conclusions, 132-133
  court decisions, 126, 129
  General Growth Corporation, 122-123, 124-131
  historical background, 119-121
  Interim Development Ordinance, 124
  Lincolnshire parcel, 128-129, 130-132
  litigation, 125-127, 129
  Metro Center, Inc., 121-122, 130-133
Sioux City Journal, 124, 128, 129, 131
Skinner, William, 130
Sloan's Curve. *See* Palm Beach, Florida
Smith, R. Marlin, 47
Spears, Adrian, 81, 84-85, 87
Sports Illustrated, 117
Standard State Zoning Enabling Act, 261
State-enabling acts, 1-2
State Environmental Quality Review Act (New York), 26, 30
  Environmental Impact Statement, 26, 27, 28

Stegmann, Edgar P., 28
Sterling Forest. *See* Tuxedo, New York
Sterling Forest Corporation. *See* City Investing Company
Stevens, John Paul, 75, 257
Stewart, Potter, 60, 63, 66-67, 257
Stockman, Gerald, 230, 232
Sturgeon, Richard, 127
Sundial case, 103, 105
Sunshine Act (Florida), 46-47, 50-51, 111
Sun-Times, 179
Swibel, Charles R., 159, 163, 174-175, 177, 178-179, 256

"Taking" issue, 59-61, 71, 103, 116, 201-202
Texas Water Quality Board, 80, 82, 91, 92-93
Thompson, J. Walter, 65, 67, 68
Times Journal, The (New Jersey), 215
Traffic: Lafayette, 188, 197-199
  Palm Beach, 49, 56
  Sanibel, 107
Travis, Dempsey, 164, 167
Trenton Times, 144
Tunney, John, 240
Tuxedo, New York (Sterling Forest), 5, 11-35, 260, 263
  community relations, 31-32, 33
  conclusions and recommendations, 31-35
  emotional intensity of debate, 21, 24-25, 26, 28, 34, 35
  historical background, 12-14
  housing development, 15, 33
  industrial development, 14-15
  Planning Board, 20, 22, 26, 27, 28
  residents of early development, 15, 33
  residents' opposition, 22, 24, 28
  state involvement, 26, 28
  support for development, 22, 23, 32, 33
  Town Board, 19-29
  town-developer negotiations, 23-26
  zoning ordinance, 19-20, 23-26
Tuxedo Conservation and Taxpayers Association (TCTA), 24, 28, 29

United States Department of the Army, 156

United States Department of Housing and Urban Development, 81
  and Chicago Housing Authority, 160, 164, 166-170, 174, 176, 178-179
United States Supreme Court, 82, 209, 210
  antitrust immunity, 126, 184, 201-202
  Hills v. *Gautreaux*, 168-169
  Milliken case, 167-169
  Monell v. *New York City Dept. of Social Services*, 194
  Owen v. *City of Independence*, 201
  Penn Central Transportation Co. v. *New York City*, 59-61, 63, 66-67, 70-71
  San Diego Gas & Electric Co. v. *City of San Diego*, 59-61, 201-202
Urban Investment and Development Company, 18, 29

Vavoulis, George, 166
Venezia, Sam, 21, 22, 27, 29
Vested rights, 89-90, 102-103, 105-107, 146, 154, 245-246, 251
Vickers v. *Gloucester Township Committee*, 207, 208-209, 232

Washington, Harold, 179-180
Water quality, 114-115, 138, 146
  See also San Antonio, Texas
Weaver, Cliff: *City Zoning: The Once and Future Frontier*, 8, 264
Weiderer, Thomas, 227
Weiner, Howard, 122, 125, 130-131
Wellington, Margot, 67-68, 69-70, 74
Whitaker and Baxter, 240
White, Duane, 104-105
Wilentz, Robert, 211, 220, 229
Wiles, Tony, 48
Williams, Harrison A., Jr., 139
Williams, Norman, Jr., 208, 209, 265
Winslow, Albert, 21
Wood, Elizabeth, 160
Wyatt v. *Stickney*, 176

Zeigler, Edward H., Jr., 263
Zoning, current state of, 263-265
Zoning Game, The (Babcock), 1-2, 6, 56, 208